MINOAN CRETE

Along with Mesopotamia, Egypt, and the Levant, Minoan Crete was one of the primary cultures of the prehistoric Mediterranean world. In this book, L. Vance Watrous offers an up-to-date overview of this important ancient society. Using archaeological evidence from palaces, houses, surveys, caves, and mountain shrines, he describes and traces the development of Minoan Crete from the Neolithic era through the Late Bronze Age. Watrous also presents and interprets Minoan artworks in a range of media, including fresco paintings, pottery, and seals, and explains how Minoan Crete affected the culture of classical Greece.

Aimed at undergraduate and graduate students, this book can be used in courses on the ancient Mediterranean world and classical archaeology.

L. Vance Watrous is the Director of Excavations at the Minoan town of Gournia. He has worked on Crete for over forty-five years, on archaeological projects – surface surveys (Lasithi, Mesara, Galatas, Gournia) and excavations (Knossos, Kommos, Chania, Gournia).

MINOAN CRETE

AN INTRODUCTION

L. VANCE WATROUS

State University of New York, Buffalo

CAMBRIDGE
UNIVERSITY PRESS

CAMBRIDGE
UNIVERSITY PRESS

University Printing House, Cambridge CB2 8BS, United Kingdom

One Liberty Plaza, 20th Floor, New York, NY 10006, USA

477 Williamstown Road, Port Melbourne, VIC 3207, Australia

314–321, 3rd Floor, Plot 3, Splendor Forum, Jasola District Centre, New Delhi – 110025, India

103 Penang Road, #05–06/07, Visioncrest Commercial, Singapore 238467

Cambridge University Press is part of the University of Cambridge.

It furthers the University's mission by disseminating knowledge in the pursuit of education, learning, and research at the highest international levels of excellence.

www.cambridge.org
Information on this title: www.cambridge.org/9781108424509
DOI: 10.1017/9781108339292

© Cambridge University Press 2021

First published 2021
3rd printing 2022

Printed in Great Britain by Ashford Colour Press Ltd.

A catalogue record for this publication is available from the British Library.

Library of Congress Cataloging-in-Publication Data
NAMES: Watrous, Livingston Vance, 1943– author.
TITLE: Minoan Crete : an introduction / L. Vance Watrous, State University of New York, Buffalo
DESCRIPTION: Cambridge, United Kingdom ; New York : Cambridge University Press, [2021] |
   Includes bibliographical references and index.
IDENTIFIERS: LCCN 2020018683 (print) | LCCN 2020018684 (ebook) | ISBN 9781108424509
   (hardback) | ISBN 9781108440493 (paperback) | ISBN 9781108339292 (epub)
SUBJECTS: LCSH: Minoans–Greece–Crete. | Crete (Greece)–Antiquities. | Art, Minoan. |
   Bronze age–Greece–Crete. | Crete (Greece)–Civilization.
CLASSIFICATION: LCC DF221.C8 W375 2021 (print) | LCC DF221.C8 (ebook) |
   DDC 939/.1801–dc23
LC record available at https://lccn.loc.gov/2020018683
LC ebook record available at https://lccn.loc.gov/2020018684

ISBN 978-1-108-42450-9 Hardback
ISBN 978-1-108-44049-3 Paperback

Dedicated to the people of Crete
Προς τον λαον Κρητης

CONTENTS

ACKNOWLEDGMENTS

In writing this general book on Minoan civilization I have been helped in one way or another by many people. As a student, I learned about Crete at the knees of Machteld Mellink (who suggested I write this book), Sinclair Hood, Gerald Cadogan, and Joseph and Maria Shaw, and later from my contemporaries Erik Hallager, Christof Nowicki, Harriet Blitzer, and John McEnroe. I owe special thanks to Margaret Curran who edited portions of the book and to Angela Drakakis-Smith who managed the tedious task of copyright permissions.

I must thank the following for their support and advice: Malcolm Weiner, Judith Weingarten, Maria Andreadaki-Vlaski, Philip Betancourt, Vili Apostalakou, Anne Chapin, Nanno Marinatos, Sabine Beckmann, Eleni Banou, Costis Davaras, Georgos Rethemiotakis, Sandy MacGillivray, Metaxia Tsitsipoulou, Katerina Kopaka, Brian Kunkel, Evi Margaritis, Harvey Weiss, Todd Whitelaw, Hugh Sackett, Donald Haggis, Jenny Moody, Barbara Hayden, Antonis Vasilakis, Vincenzo La Rosa, Vronway Hankey, Dimitri Tsoungarakis, Jennifer Shay, and Mervyn Popham. Many thanks go to my colleagues who allowed me to reproduce their published illustrations: Ingo Pini, J.-C. Poursat, Nanno Marinatos, John McEnroe, Phil Betancourt, Antonis Vasilakis, Keith Branigan, Peter Warren, Metaxia Tsipoulou, Jeffery Soles, Sanine Beckmann, Matthew Buell, Georgos Rethymiotakis, Ian Swindale, Manfred Biatak, Claire Palyvou, Elpida Hadjidaki, Tom Palaima, Robert Laffineur, Joseph Shaw, Sandy MacGillivray, Robert Koehl, and Christof Nowicki. I must also mention the Institute for Aegean Prehistory (INSTAP) East Cretan Center whose facilities and staff, Eleanor Huffman, have been helpful, and the American School of Classical Studies at Athens for its help with administrative matters. The Heraklion and Agios Nikolaos museums have kindly provided me with permission to publish photographs of their holdings.

ABBREVIATIONS

AAA	*Athens Annals of Archaeology*
AJA	*American Journal of Archaeology*
Asatene	*Annuario della Scuola archaeologica di Atene e delle Missioni italiane in Orient*
BAR	*British Archaeological Reports*
BCH	*Bulletin de Correspondance Hellenique*
BSA	*Annual of the British School at Athens*
CMS	*Corpus der minoischen und mykenischen Siegel*
INSTAP	Institute for the Study of Aegean Prehistory
SAA	Scuola Archaeologica di Atene
SIMA	*Studies in Mediterranean Archaeology*

CHRONOLOGY

The chronology below is based on P. Warren and V. Hankey, *Aegean Bronze Chronology*, Bristol: Bristol Classical Press, 1985.

Neolithic	7000–3500 BC
Early Minoan I	3500–2900 BC
Early Minoan II	2900–2200 BC
Early Minoan III	2200–2100 BC
Middle Minoan IA	2100–1950 BC
Middle Minoan IB	1950–1850 BC
Middle Minoan II	1850–1700 BC
Middle Minoan III	1700–1600 BC
Late Minoan IA	1600–1500 BC
Late Minoan IB	1500–1425 BC
Late Minoan II	1425–1390 BC
Late Minoan IIIA	1390–1330 BC
Late Minoan IIIB	1330–1200 BC
Late Minoan IIIC	1200–1050 BC

INTRODUCTION

Minoan Crete

T HIS BOOK IS AN INTRODUCTION TO THE CULTURE OF MINOAN CRETE through its archaeology and art. It explores the island's stark natural beauty, its mythical past, and its artistic and archaeological remains. Most books on Minoan Crete over the years have either been popularizing accounts or specialized treatments aimed at scholars. *Minoan Crete: An Introduction* was written to transcend this divide. It presents a broad cultural history of Minoan Crete and an up-to-date discussion of Minoan art and archaeology for the general reader and enough detail to interest the student/scholar. Crete is unique in the Aegean for its close connections with the civilizations of the Near East. For this reason, the text often discusses Minoan Crete in the light of Egypt and the Levant with the goal of making clear the unique features of Minoan civilization.

The format of the book is an outgrowth of the present state of our knowledge about Minoan Crete. The book draws on the immense amount of new information that has accumulated over the past two generations on the Minoan economy, settlements, society, foreign relations, sanctuaries, architecture, seals, pottery, and fresco painting. New technological studies have helped us to date and locate the origin of objects, and identify the interaction of people with their environment. Theoretical studies have become popular in Aegean archaeology. Many recent studies of the Aegean are thematically organized and more interested in adhering to a particular theory than in examining the archaeological evidence from a broad cultural perspective.

As a result of these developments, much recent Minoan scholarship has become quite complex and specialized, written largely for other scholars. In contrast, this book is a cultural history – its goal is a broad understanding of the cultural identity of Minoan Crete.

This book examines Minoan Crete in its eastern Mediterranean context. It documents types of foreign evidence on Crete, and attempts to explain how many of the innovative political and ideological decisions made by Minoans were stimulated in response to foreign ideas they had learned from abroad. This is the approach adopted by recent Aegean studies following the anthropological publication by Mary Helms, *Ulysses' Sail: An Ethnographic Odyssey of Power, Knowledge, and Geographic Distance* (Princeton, 1988). Far from showing that Minoan Crete developed in a derivative fashion – *ex oriente lux* – from older, more developed Eastern cultures, this approach will demonstrate the cultural distinctiveness of Minoan culture. The evidence consistently suggests that the Minoans drew upon their knowledge of the Near East which they creatively adapted to their own local needs. Most often, we can see that a foreign idea was adopted but significantly changed in the process. Footnotes cite recent publications where earlier bibliographies can be found. The people of Bronze Age Crete are referred to as "Minoans" for sake of simplicity, rather than as any claim of an ethnic or linguistic unity. Additionally, the basic term "palace" is used here for the same reason, without intending the term to be understood in its conventional sense, that is, as the monumental residence of a powerful ruler. The nature of a Minoan "palace" is discussed in Chapter 4.

The Minoans have left us no historical written documents. Therefore, in order to understand their society, it is necessary to examine the archaeological remains. Each class of artifact has its own distinct story to tell and is particularly sensitive to certain aspects of ancient life. Architecture, for instance, reflects the social organization of society and displays its identity. Pottery is essential for chronology and the activities of daily life. Its distribution reveals cultural and commercial patterns, such as trade. Art and iconography, the study of the symbolic meaning of images, play a particularly important role in this book, since it is a window into the intellectual life of a culture. Visual imagery, its choice of subject and style, in wall painting, seal scenes, vase painting, jewelry, and sculpture expresses the attitudes and religious beliefs of the Minoans. Metal and ivory objects, stone vases, and clay loomweights offer evidence of Minoan craft production, including textiles. Since the interpretation of artifacts is often complex, the text will attempt to explain why archaeological finds are understood in the way they are.

This book is also a narrative, in that it traces and interprets the development of Minoan civilization over time. Egyptian and the Near Eastern societies were dominated by powerful kings and priests, a pervasive religious system, and a concern for an elaborate afterlife. These social aspects are, for the most part, absent in Minoan Crete. The island's nobility and middle class seem to have played the most important social role.

In *Minoan Crete: An Introduction*, Chapters 1 and 2 are introductory. Chapter 1 provides a sketch of the natural environment of Crete and the ways it has deeply shaped the traditional life of its inhabitants who depend on this environment. Chapter 2 presents the ancient myths of Minoan Crete – of Minos, the Minotaur, and Daedalus, and the subsequent development of archaeological research since 1878, undertaken by Arthur Evans, Spyridon Marinatos, and others on Crete. Chapters 3–5 focus diachronically on the archaeology of Crete during the Paleolithic – the Early Minoan, early Middle Minoan periods, and the Neopalatial period. Chapter 3 describes the earliest archaeological evidence for architecture, diet and agriculture, crafts, tombs and burial practices, and trade at this time. Chapter 4 traces and explains the radical transformations of Minoan society just before and after 2000 BC, changes recognizable in the establishment of the first palaces and mountain peak sanctuaries on the island. Chapter 5 describes Minoan Neopalatial society and its organization into states, classes, and professions, focusing on the palace at Knossos as well as life in outlying towns and villages. Chapter 6 presents the evidence for Minoan overseas relations during the Neopalatial period. Chapter 7 discusses Minoan religion and cult practices at peak sanctuaries, caves, urban shrines, tombs, festivals, and the Minoan pantheon of gods. In Chapter 8, the various types of Minoan art are presented and interpreted. Chapter 9 focuses on the Mycenaean kingdoms of Crete and the evidence from the Linear B tablets during the Late Minoan III period 1450–1200 BC.

ONE

CRETE

The Island and Traditional Life

Mountains come first.
F. Braudel, *The Mediterranean and the Mediterranean World in the Age of Philip II*

THE ISLAND AND THE ENVIRONMENT

A visitor arriving on Crete first notices the majestic mountains that form the backbone of the island. They create an intense three-dimensional landscape that surrounds those living there. I can remember the first time I arrived on Crete – as the ferry neared Heraklion, I came out on the deck. The sun had just begun to rise, and I could see the peak of Mount Jouktas on the horizon where Zeus was worshiped. I felt as if I were entering a new world of myth and legend.

The Cretan landscape is dry, rugged, and primal – mountains, sky, and sea. Caves are part of this landscape, several of which were famous shrines in antiquity, such as the Dictaean Cave where Zeus was said to have been born, and the Amnissos Cave, with its shrine to Eileithyia, goddess of childbirth, mentioned by Odysseus (*Odyssey*, XIX 188). In size, Crete dwarfs all other Aegean islands (Figs. 1.1 and 1.2). It is some 260 km long east–west and 8,261 sq. km in area. In width the island is relatively narrow, ranging from 12 to 57 km north to south. Peaks rise to great heights: from east to west, Thryphti (1,476 m), Mount Dicte (2,148 m), Mount Ida (2,456 m) and the White Mountains (2,453 m). This mountainous landscape has created today a patchwork of small, separate valleys and plains, each with its main town or city.

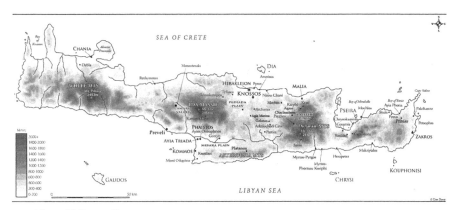

1.1 Map of Minoan Crete.
Shelmerdine (2008), xxxxiii, map 4.

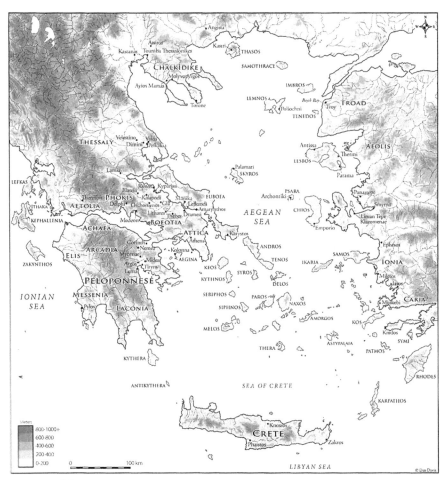

1.2 Map of the Aegean.
Shelmerdine (2008), xxxi, map 2. Redrawn by Amanda Killian.

During the Minoan era, Crete was similarly occupied by a large number of small independent states located in these inland and coastal valleys, a situation comparable to the rival city-states of early Renaissance Italy. In the Classical period we know the island was divided into at least fourteen major city-states and an additional thirty towns.[1]

The island's environment has had two important consequences for Cretan culture. First, these areas created small, peer communities where everyone knew each other. This is the antithesis of the large kingdoms of the Near East whose society was headed by a distant ruler, elite officials, and a huge peasant class. Second, all of these local regions on Crete were and are natural rivals and competitors with one another. During the Minoan and Classical periods, settlements on the island repeatedly suffered destructions at the hands of their neighbors. Today local village jokes about other parts of Crete abound.

Crete's location in the Mediterranean is also significant for its history. Situated at the southern edge of the Aegean (Fig. 1.2), the island has always had close connections with the Aegean islands and the Greek mainland. Odysseus, for example, posed as a Cretan during his far-flung travels (*Odyssey*, XIII, 256–86; XIV, 199–359). From Karphi in the Dictaean mountains one can actually see the Cycladic island of Santorini (ancient Thera). The Greek mainland is also visible from the White Mountains in western Crete. Most importantly, Crete has always been a stepping-stone between the Aegean and the Near East. Several of the most important sea routes in the Mediterranean pass along the north and south coasts of the island. According to the ancient Greek geographer Strabo (*Geographia*, 10.475), Crete was only a two-day sail from Cyrene in Libya. This location has been both a blessing and a curse. Crete was open to ideas traveling between the Near East and the Aegean and far enough away to reinterpret these ideas to form its own distinctive culture. Crete produced the first literate high civilization in Europe, but has been repeatedly invaded during its history.

We will begin with a short description of the physical environment of the island. We can recognize four major areas on the island: west Crete (with Chania/ancient Kydonia as its capital) and the plain of Rethymnon, north central Crete dominated by Knossos, the Mesara Plain in the south with Phaistos its Minoan capital, and eastern Crete with many smaller plains and valleys, each with their own town (Malia, Herapetra, Siteia). Like most present-day travelers to Crete, we will begin at Heraklion, the current capital, in the center of the island. Just south of Heraklion is the famous archaeological site of Knossos, which attracts over a million visitors a year. Rising south of the palace at Knossos is Mount Jouktas, the Minoan peak sanctuary for Knossos. Standing on Mount Jouktas, one can see the north center of the island, the territory of ancient Knossos. To the south, the landscape rises to the spine of the island that runs east–west between Mount Ida and the Dictaean mountains. This central elevated plain (400 m), called the Pediada today, had its own Minoan palace, at Galatas (Chapter 5) that was uncovered in 1987 by Georgios Rethemiotakis.

South of the Pediada, the land drops off sharply, down to the largest (362 sq. km) arable area in Crete, the Mesara Plain. This broad plain runs westward between Mount Ida on the north and the Asterousia mountain range (elev. 1,231 m) along the south coast, and opens out onto the Libyan Sea to the west. Southbound travelers today come to the summit of the Pediada and catch their first glimpse of the Mesara Plain. In the nineteenth century, travelers made the journey with pack animals between the Mesara and Candia (the Venetian name for Heraklion) in two days. These distances, however, can be deceptive to modern eyes. Some forty years ago, I sat with an elderly gentleman at a *kapheneion* in the tiny mountain village of Miamou on the south slope of the Asterousia Mountains. He told me, as a youth, he used to take his mule in the morning darkness from the village 5 km down to the south coast, arriving there at dawn when the fishermen were returning from the sea. He bought their fish, loaded his mule, and ascended the Asterousia Mountains. By midday he had walked (24 km) to the market town of Moires in the center of the Mesara Plain and was selling fresh fish. Today, the visitor from the busy north coast coming into the Mesara can feel as if they have entered a different world. Europe is left behind. In the African climatic zone, the region is bathed in a warm and mellow light and enjoys a quiet, slower pace of life. Phaistos, the Minoan center of the western Mesara, sits on a ridge top (Fig. 1.3) near the coast overlooking the surrounding plain. The Minoan harbor of Phaistos is visible on the shore, at Kommos. Large Minoan *tholos* tombs dot the Mesara Plain. To the north of the Mesara, the Idaean massif separates the Mesara from the northern coast of Crete.

Moving eastward from Heraklion along the north coast of Crete, one passes the palatial settlement at Malia on the coast, and then on to the town of Agios Nikolaos. To the south, the Isthmus of Herapetra, a north–south corridor 12 km long, runs between the Aegean and Libyan seas. The palace town of Gournia on the north coast of the Isthmus was an administrative center for this area during the Minoan period. The eastern end of the island beyond the Isthmus is formed by many valleys running down to the coast, separated by low mountains. The present-day towns and villages of Siteia, Palaikastro (Fig. 1.4), and Zakros, are each situated in their own coastal valley. During the Minoan period they were independent palace states with their own urban settlement. They have been excavated and are visible to visitors today.

West of Heraklion lies the coastal valley of Rethymnon, another independent state in Minoan and Classical times. Chania (Classical Kydonia) was the

1.3 Eastward view of Phaistos Palace.
Photo by the author

1.4 View of Palaikastro Bay.
Photo by the author

center of the westernmost region of the island. In this area the pine- and cypress-covered slopes of the White Mountains run down to a tree-filled, lush coastal plain. Coming from the east, the modern visitor will notice the unusually fertile nature of western Crete, an effect of the western rain-bearing winds. Under less economic and social pressure than central and eastern Crete, this area developed relatively slowly during the Early and Middle Bronze Ages.

Crete straddles the Mediterranean and African climatic zones, a cross-fertilization that has produced an intense profusion of wildlife on the island. Crete has some 140 species of flora, among the highest in Europe. Wild animals are numerous: wolves, foxes, rabbits, deer, boars, goats, badgers, weasels, bees, and birds (e.g., hoopoe, pigeons, quail, pheasants, and par-tridges). Swallows remain on the island all year, rather than migrate to North Africa. In the winter, when a south wind blows, the snow-capped mountains turn red, dyed by Libyan sand. Winters are moderately cool and wet and summers are warm and dry. Rainfall is concentrated between the months of November and February. During the summer the prevailing northwest winds (called *meltemia* in modern Greek) bring dry, sunny days. Temperatures differ with elevation. Higher elevations are cooler and receive more rainfall. In the spring one can swelter in the Mesara Plain and look up to the snow-covered peaks of Mount Ida. The western portions of Crete receive significantly more rainfall than the rest of the island. Chania in the west has an average of 70 cm, while Herapetra in the east gets on average 52 cm a year.[2]

Much of Crete's landscape, even before the introduction of mechanically drilled deep wells in the 1960s, was well watered by springs and good for agriculture. The mountains of Crete, formed of limestone, absorb the winter rainfall, which reappears, gushing out along their base in the form of natural springs. Many villages today are situated at these springs. This water also dissolves the mountains, creating hundreds of caves. These caverns, with their eerie stalagmitic formations, became sacred spots venerated by the Minoans. Crete sits astride a north–south geological faultline that divides the two tectonic plates in the Aegean. The grinding of these two plates causes frequent, mostly minor, earthquakes on the island. North of Crete these plates have caused volcanic eruptions, most famously on the Cycladic island of Santorini, ancient Thera (Chapter 8). During the Bronze Age, quakes damaged or destroyed Minoan towns on several occasions. In terms of valuable metals – copper, tin, silver, and gold – Crete is poorly provided, a fact that motivated Minoan seafaring abroad (Chapter 6).

Crete's mountainous landscape has created a vertical ladder of environmental zones – sea, low and high plains, and finally mountains. The diversity of wildlife existing between these different zones is immediately noticeable. Cretans have lived by exploiting these different environments, primarily through a combination of fishing, farming, and shepherding. In its most extreme form, villagers practice a transhumant way of life, maintaining separate summer and winter residences, growing crops at both locations, and driving their herds between them. The lowest of these zones is the sea itself. Encircling the island, the sea provides the Cretan people with many edible species. During the summer months, the sea is a source of small fish, mullet, tunny, crab, octopus, and squid (*kalamari*), the last two delicious when grilled and nibbled and accompanied by *raki* (the Cretan equivalent of tequila, or grappa). Along the north coast grow tamarisk, sea-juniper, mastic (*Pistacia lentiscus*), myrtle, yellow horned poppies, lilies, and many other species. The south coast is dotted by date palms and banana trees. The Minoans also depicted local marine life, such as flying fish, dolphins, octopus, the sea squill and triton on their *seals* and frescoes (Chapter 8).

Ascending from the sea, we come to the coastal plains, the best agricultural land on the island. They are relatively narrow and are mostly found along the north coast, or in the southern Mesara Plain. The Mediterranean quartet of crops – cereals, grapes, legumes, and olives – flourish in this environment. Low valleys and plains teem with life. At night, owls call back and forth to each other, "beep ... boop." Dry, rugged shrubby grasslands are particularly rich in crocus, broom/crop, cyclamen, the Cretan iris, and many types of orchids and hyacinth. Pungent herbs, such as thyme, sage, oregano, and fennel, used as spices and scents, are common. The spectacular and menacing-looking purple snake lily (*Dracunculus vulgaris*) omits the smell of rotting flesh; it is depicted on Minoan sarcophagi. Many of these wild plants are, and probably were in Minoan times, used for a variety of purposes, including food or fodder, seasoning, incense, medicine, and fuel. The island has a total of more than 1,700 plant species, and more endemic plants (some 180 species) than any island in Europe. Grassy plains are dotted with trees – the dark green olive, lighter colored almond and pear. Cicadas in trees fill the air with their noise. Hares, hedgehogs, and many birds, such as swallows, harriers, falcons, hawks, doves, bee-eaters, and other species make their home here. Several were inspirations for Minoan art (Chapter 8). Streambeds, lined with pink oleanders, watercress, rushes, fig, willow, and poplars, provide hiding spots for herons, egrets, and cranes.

Above the plains are the foothills and elevated plains (elevation 300–800 m), such as the Lasithi Plain (Fig. 1.5). Cereals, grapes, and cherries are grown there. Climbing into the foothills and higher plains, one can see many flowers and trees, such as asphodel, the pink-flowered rock rose (*Cistus creticus*), and maple. Olives are conspicuous by their absence; they are unable to survive the winter cold at this elevation. *Ebenus creticus*, a heather-like shrub, covers hillsides with bright purple in the spring. White cyclamen carpet the hills during the month of May. Like the coastal plains, this environmental zone was thickly settled in antiquity.

1.5 View of upland Lasithi Plain.
Photo by the author

Finally, reaching the high mountains (elev. 800–2,400 m), one enters forests of oak, cypress, and pine. Downy-leaved dittany, known as an aphrodisiac (called *erontas*, "love" in Cretan dialect) and for its flavor and healing properties, grows in mountain ravines and gorges. In traditional Crete, young men would scale the mountains in search of dittany as a gift for their would-be lovers. In Book XII of the *Aeneid*, Venus cures the wounded Aeneas with dittany from Mount Ida. Its pink flowers bloom in the summer months. Grazing land supports shepherds and their flocks during the summer months. This zone is the home of the wild mountain goat, the Cretan *agrimi*, famous for its agility (Fig. 8.9). Equally impressive, the Lammergeyer and the griffin vulture with wing spans of 1.8–2.7 m, sweep through the air high in the mountains. Shepherds say the griffin vulture can swoop down and carry off a lamb. One day many years ago I was climbing with my six-year-old son to the mountaintop site of Karphi. High above us I saw a large griffin vulture soaring in the sky. As we ascended, the slope became rougher and rougher and my son was beginning to struggle. Just then I looked up and the immense bird had suddenly descended and was circling my son! Remnants of a primary forest of giant oak exist in the Selakano valley high in the Dictaean mountain range. Oak, cypress, and pine from the mountains were used to build the palace at Knossos.

The Cretan landscape is the focus of much Minoan art. Frescoes, vase painting, engraved seals, and jewelry depict local sea creatures, birds, the wild goat, flowers, and trees. Minoan artists painted the olive, wheat, barley, lilies, crocus, iris, ivy and grape vines, pomegranate, palms, tulip, and reeds (Chapter 8). Minoan art's intimacy with nature verges at times on a pantheistic spirit, which reemerges in the Byzantine period in spiritual icons and later in the famous paintings of the Cretan painter, Dominikos Theotokopoulos, known in the West as El Greco. Filled with energetic life, Crete's environment continues to produce strong religious responses from villagers. I remember a day in 1972 when I was walking high on the slopes of Mount Dicte above the Lasithi Plain. Far below me the Lasithi Plain spread out in all its natural beauty (Fig. 1.5). I stopped at a small spring to refill my canteen. As I sat at the base of a tree to drink my water, suddenly a wild-looking shepherd appeared out of nowhere and approached me. His clothes were in tatters, the soles of his boots flapping as he walked. He sat down next to me. His first words were, "Do you believe in God?"

In recent history, the island's people have been a mixture of different origins and religions – Greeks, Byzantines, Arabs, Venetians, Christian Anatolians, Muslims, Jews, and Armenians – an ethnic palimpsest of the island's history. In 832 Spanish Arabs conquered and ruled Crete until 960 when the Byzantine Emperor Nicephorus Phocus recaptured the island. In 1204 Crete was captured by the Crusaders and sold to Venice. In 1645 the Ottoman Turks began their conquest and occupation of Crete, which lasted until 1898. This has not changed entirely – along the harbor quays in Heraklion or Herapetra one can hear Arabic spoken by sailors. Fifty years ago, the elder generation of every village spoke Turkish. As we shall see, Minoan archaeology hints that the island's population also consisted of diverse groups. The eighth-century BC poet Homer says that in Crete, "There are ninety cities. They have a mixture of languages, for there are Achaeans, stout-hearted Eteocretans, Kydonians, Dorians with their three tribes and god-like Pelasgians" (*Odyssey* XIX, 175–9). In the modern period (2011), Crete has a population of about 623,000 inhabitants. Until recently, the island possessed one of the highest densities of agricultural population – people living out in the farmland – per square mile in Europe. During the Bronze Age the island's population was one of the highest in the Aegean, a basis of Minoan political strength. Traditionally, most of Crete's population lived in the interior of the island, close to natural springs. Mountainous areas were thickly settled, and villages there today can be large. The village of Zaros, on the south slope of Mount Ida, for example, has over 2,000 inhabitants.

Crete's landscape has molded a distinct Cretan character – hardy, proud, exuberant, and competitive. The island has a challenging environment that has created passionate people who interact vigorously with the landscape. This intense relationship with the land can be seen in Minoan fresco scenes of the natural world. A generation ago, Crete had the highest life longevity in Europe. Cretans are known for their pride (or arrogance, depending on one's point of view), love of freedom, guns, and hospitality. The Cretan Nobel Prize nominee Nikos Kazantzakis writes in his memoir, *Report to Greco*: "I look down into myself and shudder. On my father's side my ancestors were bloodthirsty pirates on water, warrior chieftains on land, fearing neither God nor man."[3] Years ago when doing my thesis in a small mountain village in Crete, one of my friends was an old shepherd. When we went for a hike he would *run* up the mountainsides! One day, he finally decided I had won his trust, so he took me, without a word, to his house in the village. Once inside he brought me to his bedroom. We went up to his marriage bed, and with a slight smile he lifted up the bed cover so I could see under the bed the German machine gun he had captured in the Second World War.

Crete has its own expressive and distinctive literary forms. Poetry, called *mantinadas*, rhyming fifteen syllabic couplets played on the lyra and lute, expresses all aspects of life, especially love. A young man sings to his beloved,

> A yearning in my breast has bloomed, an ever-roaring fire.
> And every beating of my heart increases my desire.

Cretan folk music accompanied by the lyra, lute, or mandolin has become famous (e.g., songs by Nikos Xylouris). The island's literature (e.g., Nikos Kazantzakis' *Zorba the Greek*) and art (Minoan and Renaissance, as El Greco) seizes the heart. All of this has made Crete a visitor's paradise.

TRADITIONAL LIFE ON CRETE

Traditional life on Crete two generations ago, before the modernizations beginning in the 1960s, provides a view of life that can help us to understand aspects of Minoan culture. We cannot expect that traditional village life is a simple, unbroken continuity of the practices in the ancient past.[4] Nevertheless, the realities of life – human nature, its basic needs, and the Cretan environment (landscape, animals, plants) – of Crete have changed little since the Bronze Age. Traditional rural life on Crete illustrates certain patterns that we will recognize in subsequent chapters (e.g., see Chapter 7).

Life on Crete before the 1960s depended closely on crops, domestic animals, hunting, and gathering wild plants. During the 1940s, Crete's main agricultural exports included olive oil, grapes, raisins and wine, and citrus fruit.[5] Domesticated animals were a mainstay, especially sheep and goats. Herds were driven up into the mountains in April/May, marked by the festival on April 23 of St. Georgos, the patron saint of shepherds. There, shepherds made and stored cheese in their stone huts (*mitatos*). Village families below kept a goat at home for milk. Pigs were valued as a source of tasty meat. Beehives were a common sight in the mountains surrounded by purple thyme and other sweet-scented herbs. A family might have a cow or ox as a plow animal. Donkeys and mules were common, used for riding and as pack animals. Horses were rare, a status symbol owned by the wealthy. Most families owned a working dog, useful for guarding their animals and for hunting. These curly-tailed hounds are depicted on Minoan art (Chapter 8).

Wild plants also played an important role in village life. Crete has been known for its aromatic plants, such as sage, dittany, thyme, bay, myrtle, mint, and oregano. In the southern Mesara Plain, over a hundred species and types of plants had a wide variety of uses: kindling, food and salads, fodder, making furniture, tools, brooms, cloth, matting, roofs, enclosures, stuffing mattresses, glue, binding, spices and condiments, brushes, baskets, dyeing, mosquito repellent, preservatives, medicines for stomach ailments, disinfectants and for stopping bleeding wounds, apotropaic (good luck), tea, pollen to attract bees, as beautiful and fragrant bouquets in and around the house, and for specific holy days at church.[6] Strong drink (*raki*) serves as a panacea for ills – a scorpion sting or deep wounds from thorns.

While plants had many practical functions, they also possessed a spiritual aspect.[7] This is an old tradition. In Classical Greek myth, certain plants and flowers were linked to specific deities, for example wheat with golden-haired Demeter, pomegranates and lilies with Persephone, grape vines with Dionysus, and asphodels with the Underworld (*Odyssey*, xxiv). Today in the Greek Orthodox religion, certain flowers are also linked with sacred figures, for example the white lily with the Virgin. Holy days in the Orthodox calendar are defined by their colorful flowers: only white flowers may be brought to church on the Annunciation and Epiphany; red, orange, and yellow for Easter service; palms and willow for Palm Sunday. As we shall see, Minoan culture provides parallel practices.

Traditional life on Crete was closely linked to the annual cycle of the seasons. In June and July the sun bakes the landscape and the cicadas shrill in the olive trees. As one walks through the countryside, the dry brush under foot is redolent with aromatic thyme, oregano, and sage. The land is a mosaic of dry, tan fields, dark green olive groves, and clumps of bright purple thyme. Pomegranates are still in bloom. Shepherds are up in the mountains with their flocks – alone with God, as they say. If the wind is not blowing, fishermen go out to sea. Fresh fish, octopus, squid, and shellfish become available in the taverns. All these appear as motifs in Minoan art. Caiques come from North Africa and ply the south coast. Harvesting of the grain crops begins in June and continues through the summer. Barley and wheat are threshed and winnowed, and the grains are carefully gathered to be taken home. The Cretan farmer lived a vulnerable existence. He must keep two years' produce in his store-room, as a hedge against bad harvests. Periodic droughts are a life-threatening disaster. On these occasions, Cretan villagers are known to take their cattle out of the fields and stake them out on a barren crossroads, so that God will hear their sorrowful lowing and bring rain.

During the summer, village women can be seen grinding grain on stone handmills in the courtyard of their house. Aromatic herbs, such as sage, oregano, and marjoram, are gathered. In August, bee hives are scooped out for their honey. By the middle of August, the smell of autumn is in the air. Cranes, storks, and egrets visit the island, resting in the watercourses, on their way south to Africa. As time passes, pears, figs, and grapes become ripe and are ready to eat. The largest task ahead is the fall plowing and sowing of the fields, work that must be started before the onset of the heavy winter rains in the late fall.

Work was broken during the year by the celebration of local weddings and festivals. These often involved making a pilgrimage to a rural chapel. July 1 is the festival day of the healing saints, Cosmas and Damian. Those suffering ailments go the saints' chapel for the evening liturgy. After the service, the pilgrims wrap themselves up with a blanket and spend the night in prayer sleeping on the courtyard outside the chapel. It is established practice today to bring the saints at Orthodox chapels, often located on mountaintops, a metal plaque, available only at church stores, that illustrates the nature of the illness the pilgrim needs help with, or a wish that s/he prays for. These plaques, called *anathemata*, depict legs, torsos, and children (Figs. 7.20–7.22). Similar objects in clay were dedicated at Minoan and later Greek peak sanctuaries (Fig. 7.20a). In this particular case, the continuity of religious practice between prehistory and today seems fairly certain.

On July 17, people in central Crete still make a pilgrimage to the Monastery of Agia Marina near Galatas on her festival day. Leaving at night, women from Heraklion walk a day and half to the festival that draws thousands of people. In the summer, Cretan villagers celebrate a holy day dedicated to the Prophet Elias (Elijah) on July 20. The Cretan writer Pendelis Prevelakis describes this festival:

> The prophet Elijah is the saint who marshals the clouds. It is he who musters their battalions and controls where they are to let fly their waters. The rain that will soften the earth for the plowshare, swell the seed in its furrow and turn the field green is at his command ... The Christians gaze up towards the hilltops looking for the chapels dedicated to the saint ... Early in the morning of this day (July 20) the farmer stations himself on a high point, from where he surveys the heavens and studies the weather to see what the winter will be like ... The feast day of the cloud saint is celebrated in the villages of the valley with sacrifices of bulls, which are slaughtered in front of his little church ... and are consumed on the spot by the menfolk at a common table.[8]

On August 6, groups of men and women climb to the nearest peak-top chapel of Efendi Christos (Christ the Lord) to celebrate the ascension and metamorphosis of Christ. This is also an ancient custom, taken over by the Church, originally dedicated to Zeus and accompanied with great bonfires to pray for plentiful winter rains.[9] Such a festival certainly existed in the Minoan era (Chapter 7). When I was a graduate student I lived with a Greek family in a mountain village in the Lasithi mountains in Crete. My family decided we would make the journey to the peak (elev. 2,141 m) for the morning liturgy at the chapel of Efendi Christos there. We woke at 4.00 a.m. We were fasting according to custom so we ate nothing. We packed food on the mule and set forth by moonlight up the mountain. The path up to a higher plain, Limnarcharos, occupied by shepherds' huts was gradual. After stopping at a spring next to a chapel of the Holy Spirit we began the slow steep ascent up the mountain side. An hour later we had reached the ridge top and as we walked, dawn slowly appeared before us. By early morning we came to the chapel. About a dozen families were sitting in small circles on the ground around the chapel where, inside, the priest was conducting the liturgy. All around us a bare, majestic world of mountains was spread out below as far as one could see. We could hear the chanting and hymns from inside. I was ravenous. The service over, the priest came out and pronounced a blessing. We all fell on our food. In a state of exhilaration, we pilgrims walked easily back down to our village.

On August 15 *all* work comes to a stop, and the great festival of the Assumption of the Virgin is celebrated. Today, many still celebrate this holy day by making a pilgrimage, walking what seem to us today great distances to a church of the Virgin. In eastern Crete, Cretans from miles around leave the night before, walking all night to reach the monastery of Agia Phaneromi (Lady of Sacred Revelation) located high in the mountains. The liturgy takes place in a chapel, inside a cave, lit by candles and filled with incense and chanting. As one approaches the chapel, one is surrounded by pilgrims making their way, walking by the side of the road, some on their hands and knees, a sign of their humility. Similar celebrations existed in the Bronze Age (Chapter 7). By August, shearwater birds, called *ximonies* ("wintery ones" in modern Greek), appear skimming over the sea, signifying the coming of fall.

In September the fierce summer winds cease. Days are spent in the vineyards gathering grapes that are brought back to the village and piled in stamping basins and trod barefoot by men. The new wine is prepared and stored away to ferment. Some two months later the wine barrels are opened on the festival day of Agios Demetrios, October 26. Picked fruits, currants, and figs are laid out to dry. After the first rains, the saffron crocus appears, signaling the time for plowing and sowing. Hunters venture out looking for game – hare, quail, partridge, and doves. Soon, men and women come into the village, their donkeys loaded with firewood for the winter. Before the onset of winter cold, November rains and the birth of new lambs, shepherds drive the flocks down mountain paths to the warmer coasts and plains where they will spend the winter, a pattern of seasonal movement thousands of years old. Rains begin by December. The temperature drops. Winter winds roil the sea. Villagers huddle at home and women do their weaving.

At the beginning of the new calendar year, on January 6, the festival of the Epiphany is celebrated. In the service the village priest blesses water in the church, which is shared by the congregation. The purifying power of this holy water is taken home to bless the house and the fields and drive away the underworld spirits of the old year. After the service, the priest leads a procession to the harbor where he sanctifies the water of the sea by throwing a wooden cross into the water. Rain transforms the countryside that was, three months ago, hot and bare into green carpets of grass. Down from the mountains, the sheep graze in the fields. The peaks of Mount Ida, Dicte, and the White Mountains. are covered with snow. On days when there is no rain, the fields are alive with villagers collecting olives from the trees. In traditional thought, the olive tree is female, that is, unpredictable. Some are well taken care of, but they produce nothing; others are neglected and are still fruitful. Olives are taken back to the village for storage, or to be pressed to make oil. Toward the end of the winter, the family vineyards are pruned. Amid this wintry landscape, one tree, the almond, flowers with white blossoms.

Cretans sense God's hand at work in the reawakening of the world. A passage by the Cretan writer, Nikos Kazantzakis, expresses the relation of God to the natural world. One spring day, sitting in his courtyard, he remembers a poem he had heard at Mount Athos. The poet sings:

> Sister almond tree,
> "speak to me of God."
> And the almond tree blossomed.[10]

This reverence for nature is an ancient one in the Mediterranean, already recognizable in Minoan fresco painting (Chapter 7).

By March, the rain has come to an end and the landscape is covered with flowers. Soon, Easter, the most joyful festival of the year, is celebrated. Olive trees have burst into a bloom of pink flowers. Friday is a fast day, and the village cemetery is visited where small offerings are placed before the family graves. Flowers, such as poppies, pomegranates, and hyacinth, come into bloom. Spring flowers, violets, roses, and lemon blossoms appear, and are taken to the church. Known as "Christ-flowers," they were thought to have magic power against illness. On Sunday, new bread is made and the yeast is covered with these flowers. On the evening of Holy Saturday families carry flickering lamps down the dark lanes of the village to congregate inside the candle-lit chapel where, in their liturgy, they reenact the mystical resurrection of Christ at the arrival of the new year. By this time, spring has transformed the countryside. Fields are filled with herbal scent and color – yellow broom, red poppies and tulips, sweet-smelling cyclamen, blue and white irises, and deep blue lupins. Cranes and hoopoes, harbingers of spring, return from Africa to the coasts. Swallows wheel overhead, mating. The earth has reawakened!

NOTES

1   These sites are identified in map 60 in R. Talbert, ed., *The Barrington Atlas of the Greek and Roman World*, Princeton: Princeton University Press, 2000.

2   O. Rackham and J. Moody, *The Making of the Cretan Landscape*, Manchester: University of Manchester Press, 1996. A. Legakis and Z. Kypriotakis, "A Biogeographical Analysis of the Island of Crete," *Journal of Biogeography* 21 (1994) 441–5.

3   N. Kazantzakis, *Report to Greco*, New York: Simon and Schuster, 1965, 19.

4   The relation of present-day (nineteenth century to the present) Greek culture and to the ancient past is a much discussed subject. See J. Lawson, *Modern Greek Folklore and Ancient Greek Religion: A Study in Survivals*, Cambridge: Cambridge University Press, 1910, and M. Herzfeld, *Ours Once More. Folklore, Ideology, and the Making of Modern Greece*, Austin: University of Texas, 1982.

5   L. Allbaugh, *Crete: A Case Study of an Underdeveloped Area*, Princeton: Princeton University Press, 1953.

6   H. Blitzer, "Agriculture and Subsistence in the Late Ottoman and Post-Ottoman Mesara," in V. Watrous, D. Hadzi-Vallianou, H. Blitzer, *The Plain of Phaistos*, Monumenta Archaeologica 23, Los Angeles: Cotsen Insititute of Archaeology, University of California, 2004, 111–217.

7   S. Beckmann, "An 'Agricultural Calendar' from the Bronze Age?" in A. van Gijn, J. Whitttaker, and P. Anderson, eds., *Exploring and Explaining Agricultural Diversity*, Oxford: Oxbow, 2014, 319–37.

8   P. Prevelakis, *The Cretan*, Athens: Nostots, 1991, 151.

9   G. Megas, *Greek Calendar Customs*, Athens: Rhodis, 1963, 142.

10 Kazantzakis, *Report to Greco*, 451.

TWO

CRETE

Land of Myth and Archaeology

> *In the midst of the wine-dark sea there is a land called Crete,*
> *a fair land and fertile, seagirt, and there are many people in it,*
> *innumerable, and ninety cities ... and there is Knossos, the great city*
> *where Minos was king and conversed with great Zeus every nine years.*
> Homer, *Odyssey* xix, 172–4

MYTHIC BEGINNINGS

The famed singer of tales, Homer, is our earliest (eighth century BC) written source that describes prehistoric Crete.[1] Homer knew of Minos, son of Zeus and Europa, with his brothers Sarpedon, king of the Lycians, and Radymanthos, king of the Elysian Fields, the underworld for heroes. On his death, Minos was appointed by Zeus as the golden-sceptered ruler of Hades, who passed judgments over the dead (*Odyssey* xi, 568–70). On Crete, King Minos was succeeded by his son Deukalion, and after him, his grandson, Idomeneus, who led a large contingent of Cretan ships to Troy. Idomeneus is said to have ruled over Knossos, Phaistos, Gortyn, Lyktos, and many other cities in Crete (Chapter 9). Homer also knew of Daedalus, the architect of the Cretan Labyrinth, who also built a dancing floor at Knossos for Ariadne, the beautiful daughter of King Minos.

Later Greek poets continued to sing of Minoan Crete. The Greek poet, Hesiod (*Theogony*, 477–84) records that Zeus, father of gods and men, was born on Crete, in a cave on Mount Aigaion near Lyktos at the eastern edge of the Mesara Plain. Tradition has identified the nearby Dictaean Cave above the Lasithi Plain as Zeus' birthplace. Hesiod (*Minos*, 320d) called Minos the strongest of mortal kings who ruled over many cities, by virtue of the scepter given to him by his father Zeus. Every nine years Minos met with Zeus in a cave. Classical writers record other details. Plato and Aristotle (*Laws* I, 624; *Politics* II, 1271b) claim that Minos introduced a divinely inspired system of laws from his father Zeus that were famous in antiquity for their wisdom and justice. The Athenian historian Thucydides (1. 4) wrote that Minos was the first king known to build a navy. With it, he conquered the Cyclades, expelled their inhabitants, colonized many of them with his own sons, and cleared the Aegean sea of pirates. As we shall see, archaeology provides information confirming Thucydides' report of the spread of Minoan influence in the Aegean (Chapter 8). Bacchylides, the fifth-century poet from the island of Keos, records the myth that Minos conquered his island and established his son as ruler there. The empire of Minos was remembered by the ancient Egyptians, in another, very different story, as the Kingdom of Atlantis (Plato, *Timaeus*, 24d–25d. See Chapter 6).

Cretan myths begin with Europa and the Bull. One day, Europa, the daughter of a Phoenician king, went to the shore to play with her friends. Zeus saw her and was attracted to her, so he changed himself into a beautiful bull. Seeing the bull, Europa was so taken by its beauty that she climbed on his back. Whereupon Zeus took her to Crete where she bore him three sons, the oldest of which was Minos. When Minos became king of Crete, he married Pasiphae, the immortal daughter of the sun god Helios. Their children included Ariadne, Phaedra, Glaukos, and Androgeous. Poseidon sent Minos a beautiful white bull. When Minos refused to sacrifice it to Poseidon, the god put a curse on Pasiphae who developed a lust for the bull. She mated with it, and gave birth to the monstrous Minotaur, a creature with a man's body and a bull's head. He lived in the palatial Labyrinth at Knossos, constructed by the architect Daedalus. This last myth may be a genealogical effort by later mythographers to explain the Minoan bull ceremonies held in the central court of the palaces (Chapter 7). Minotaurs are depicted on seals from Late Minoan III and Classical Knossos. Daedalus was famous as a craftsman and inventor, who escaped Minos' rule by constructing wings so he and his son Icarus could fly away. Minoan artistic creations (Chapters 6 and 8), wall paintings, pottery, and seals, were also famous in the Mediterranean world. A Canaanite (from the Syrian area) poem speaks of the patron god of crafts-men, Kothar, as having his home on Crete.

King Minos' expansion of power brought him into conflict with the Greeks on the Mainland. He conquered Megara near Athens (Apollodorus, *Library* 3, 15.8). After his son Androgeous was killed at Athens, Minos imposed a tribute whereby every nine years the Athenians were to send seven boys and seven girls to Crete. The Athenian version of the myth recorded by Plutarch in his first-century AD book *Theseus*, says they were to be fed to the Minotaur in the Labyrinth. According to this myth, Theseus joined the group sent to Knossos, and with the aid of Minos' daughter, Ariadne, killed the Minotaur. Afterwards he and Ariadne fled from Crete. Theseus abandoned Ariadne on the offshore island of Dia, or, in another version, on the island of Naxos. Ariadne later became the wife of Dionysus. Minos' other daughter, Phaedra was said to have subsequently married Theseus, but fell in love with her step-son, Hippolytus, The story, preserved to us in Euripides' play, *Hippolytus*, ends tragically with their deaths.

ARCHAEOLOGY REVEALS THE MINOANS

Apart from ancient myths, we have come to learn about Minoan civilization through archaeological excavation. In the nineteenth century of our own era, educated Europeans believed that civilization in Greek lands had begun in the eighth century BC, at the time of the first Olympic Games (776 BC). Any literary echoes of an earlier past – of King Priam of Troy, of Agamemnon from Mycenae, or, oldest of all, King Minos of Knossos – belonged strictly to the poetic world of myth. At this time, European travelers to Greece, especially after 1827 when the Greek mainland obtained political independence from the Ottoman Empire, came primarily to see the monuments of the Classical past. All of this changed radically between 1870 and 1890 when Heinrich Schliemann's excavations uncovered spectacular evidence of an earlier civilization at Troy and Mycenae (Fig. 2.1). His archaeological finds showed that the palaces mentioned in Homer were not merely poetic inventions, but that they were part of impressive civilizations that had existed in Greece during the second millennium BC. The discovery of the Greek Bronze Age had begun.[2]

During the nineteenth century, however, Crete remained under Ottoman rule, despite numerous local uprisings. For this reason it was considered unsafe and was rarely visited by foreigners. In 1878 a group of patriotic Cretans interested in their past initiated Minoan archaeology. They established a Society of the Friends of Learning, modeled on the revolutionary society of the mainland that had led the Greek War of Independence. Under its first head, Dr. Joseph Hazzidakis, this group started a museum collection of antiquities in Heraklion with the purpose of preserving Cretan culture. That same year, Minos Kalokairinos, a member of the society, dug trenches at the fabled site of Knossos – revealing the west wing of the Minoan palace. From his finds he presented a Minoan pithos to the collection in Heraklion and to museums in Athens, Rome, Paris, and London.

2.1 Picasso, *Minotauromachy*.
Courtesy www.WallArtForLess.com

The first European archaeologist to undertake full-scale excavations on the island was the Italian Frederico Halbherr who arrived on Crete in 1894. A Classical scholar, Halbherr came in search of Classical Greek inscriptions. One month after his arrival, he discovered the famous inscribed fifth-century BC Law Code at Gortyn in the Mesara (Fig. 1.1). While early explorers were primarily interested in investigating Classical monuments, at times they encountered remains from an earlier period. Halbherr joined Joseph Hazzidakis in several early excavations, at the Idaean Cave, a legendary shrine of Zeus, at the Cave of Eileithyia at Amnissos, and in the Dictaean Cave, probably the cave identified by Hesiod (*Theogony*, 477–84) as the birthplace of Zeus.[3] In 1894 Halbherr's colleague, Taramelli, excavated a cave on Mount Ida near the village of Kamares and discovered a strange new type of pottery (of the Middle Minoan period) painted with bright colors on a dark background, that subsequently became known as Kamares ware.[4]

In 1894 the Englishman Arthur Evans made his first trip to Crete.[5] Evans was quite different from the other early explorers on the island. His first interest was in the prehistoric monuments of Crete, particularly in its pre-Greek inscriptions. Evans came from an unusually broad academic background. As a young man he had grown up in a household where his father, John Evans, was an accomplished antiquarian of prehistoric Europe and whom Arthur accompanied on his digs. John Evans was an admirer of Charles Darwin and a colleague of Sir Charles Lyell, the famous geologist, and Sir John

Lubbock (later Lord Avebury) whose influential book, *Prehistoric Times*, applied the evolutionary ideas of Darwin to archaeology. In his first trip to Crete, Evans visited Knossos, Gortyn, Phaistos, Praisos, Palaikastro, and Zakros. At Knossos he saw the excavation of Kalokairinos and was shown an inscribed Linear B tablet from the dig.

Throughout his trip in Crete Evans searched for sealstones, stone blocks and vases bearing traces of pre-Greek writing that he believed had originated on Crete. In 1897, he published his first major article on the pre-Hellenic inscriptions he had found on the island.[6] In this article he presented evidence that the people on Crete were already literate in the second millennium BC, long before the Classical period. He identified two forms of script, Hieroglyphic and Linear A, and noted that these scripts resembled the Cypriote syllabary as well as Hittite and Egyptian hieroglyphic writing. Perspicaciously, Evans began his efforts to purchase a portion of the site of Knossos from its Turkish owner.

In 1894 the European powers finally intervened in the continuing civil strife on Turkish-occupied Crete. Italian, Russian, French, and British forces landed on the island and declared Crete an independent republic. The liberation of Crete from the constraints of Turkish rule was the crucial turning point for archaeological exploration of the island. Within the next decade, British archaeologists began excavations at Knossos, the Dictaean Cave, and the Bronze Age towns at Kato Zakros and Palaikastro (Chapter 5). On the mountaintop of Petsofa, above the town of Palaikastro, John Myres uncovered a stone enclosure surrounded by the debris of burned animal sacrifices and hundreds of clay figurines.[7] This was the first known peak sanctuary on Crete. Italian archaeologists started excavations at Phaistos and at the town of Agia Triada; the French and Americans conducted excavations in east Crete. The Greek scholar Stephen Xanthoudides began his investigations of the Early Bronze Age circular tombs of the Mesara Plain in southern Crete. In the meantime, Evans returned to Crete several times and finally secured the right to excavate at Knossos.

On March 23, 1900, Evans began to dig at Knossos. In two months of digging he uncovered two full acres of a monumental Bronze Age palace. During the first four field seasons Evans' excavations employed the trained site supervisor, Duncan Mackenzie, a professional architect, as well as conservators, an artist, and gangs of upwards to 300 laborers. In order to open up the site quickly, Evans offered prizes to the gangs of workmen who were the first to reach the desired level. By 1904 Evans had revealed the entire palace at Knossos and many of the grand buildings surrounding it. Within the first week of excavation Evans found what he was looking for most – clay tablets inscribed with pre-Greek writing. By the end of the first season he had found over a thousand tablets. As the excavations progressed, marvelous discoveries came to light – a throne room with its stone throne still in place, a vast central court, elegant halls, grand staircases, and storerooms complete with rows of massive storage jars.

On April 5, 1900, Evans wrote in his notebook:

> A great day! Early in the morning the gradual surface uncovering the Corridor ... revealed two large pieces of Mycenaean [Evans' term for LM III] fresco ... One represented the head and forehead, the other the waist and part of the skirt of a female figure holding in her hand a long Mycenaean rhyton or high funnel shaped cup ... The figure was life size, the flesh colour of a deep reddish hue like that of figures on Etruscan tombs and the Keftiu of Egyptian painting. The profile of the face was of a noble type: full lips, the lower showing a slight peculiarity of curve below. The eye was dark and slightly almond shaped. In front of the ear is a kind of ornament and a necklace and bracelet are visible. The arms are beautifully modeled ... It is far and away the most remarkable human figure of the Mycenaen Age that has yet come to light.[8]

At the Archaeological Congress held in Athens in 1905 Evans proposed a chronological framework for Cretan prehistory, based on the changing types of pottery found in the different stratigraphic levels at Knossos, into an Early, Middle, and Late period (each period further subdivided into three parts). This scheme was subsequently adopted for the rest of the Aegean. With this idea, Evans was following the contemporary "Three-Ages" system of human history (Stone, Bronze, and Iron Ages) in nineteenth-century European archaeology as well as the Old, Middle, and New Kingdom scheme of Egyptian history. Evans was able to date these phases of Cretan Bronze Age civilization mainly on the basis of Egyptian objects (which, in turn, could be dated by the written King Lists from Dynastic Egypt) which he found at Knossos and on Cretan pottery recognized in Egypt. Evans named this Cretan civilization "Minoan" after the legendary King Minos, to separate it from the "Mycenaean" culture found by Schliemann on the mainland. He made this distinction not on any linguistic grounds but because the architecture he was finding on Crete was so different from that discovered at Mycenae. Most distinctively "Minoan" of all his finds were the exquisite frescoes and vases painted with graceful flowers and lively sea creatures and birds. Minoan art portrays the natural world with such vividness that it continues to awaken a powerful attraction to this day. In four years Evans had revealed to the world the earliest high civilization in Europe, bringing it out of the realm of myth.

While Evans was digging at Knossos, American explorers began to investigate prehistoric sites in east Crete. The most important of this first generation of American explorers was Harriet Boyd.[9] A student at the American School of Classical Studies at Athens in 1900, this twenty-nine-year-old woman came to Crete with no prior field experience and eventually claimed an archaeological site, Gournia, for the American School of Classical Studies. Miss Boyd excavated Gournia in 1901, 1903, and 1904, employing three site supervisors, from ninety to a hundred workmen (equally divided between Muslims and Christians), nine women to wash sherds, a cook, housemaid, site guard, and chief administrator. Costs then were minimal. In 1901 the unskilled workers were paid 15–30 cents a day, skilled workmen 40 cents a day, and the excavation administrator $20 a month. Four years after the close of the excavation, her final publication, *Gournia, Vasiliki and Other Prehistoric Sites on the Isthmus of Hierapetra, Crete* (1908), appeared. This groundbreaking quarto-sized volume revealed a Minoan town built with cobbled streets, blocks of houses filled with many personal possessions, a central public square, and a "governor's" palace.

In 1913 Crete finally achieved its long-desired political union with Greece. During the ensuing First World War, Greek archaeologists continued to explore the island. Joseph Hazzidakis discovered the palace at Malia and dug a cave at Arkalochori where the Minoans had hidden many bronze weapons.[10] Stephanos Xanthoudides uncovered a coastal villa at Nirou Chani near Amnissos.[11]

Following the war, French archaeologists began excavations at the palace, town, and cemetery of Malia, a project still in progress today (Chapter 5). The British archaeologist John Pendlebury explored the upland plain of Lasithi and excavated a portion of the twelfth–eleventh-century BC refuge site on the mountain peak of Karphi.[12] Pendlebury, who had an unrivaled knowledge of the Cretan landscape, published an excellent archaeological book, *The Archaeology of Crete*, in 1939. This handbook was the first to present a description of the archaeological evidence of Crete – architecture, pottery, metal, figurines, seals, inscriptions – systematically, period by period.

In 1925 Spyridon Marinatos, the new head of the Greek Archaeological Service in Crete, began a wide program of excavation. Upon his marriage, he and his bride, Maria Evangelidou, celebrated their honeymoon by walking from one end of the island to the other, some 260 km! His publications were admirably detailed for their time and included scientific analyses of animal bones and bronzes. Marinatos also excavated several elite mansions, now popularly labeled "villas." While working at a coastal villa at Amnissos which had been destroyed late in the seventeenth century BC, Marinatos noted that one of the huge wall blocks there had been shifted out of place, as if by a massive natural force. In a prescient article in 1939 he connected the destruction of Amnissos and other Cretan sites with the Bronze Age volcanic eruption of Thera (modern Santorini), an island 100 km north of Crete (Chapter 8).[13]

The fruit of Arthur Evans' work appeared between 1921 and 1935, in the four-volume *The Palace of Minos*. It is no overstatement to say that the basic character of Minoan culture as it is understood today was essentially a creation of Arthur Evans in these volumes. Lavishly illustrated, *The Palace of Minos* ranged widely across many topics, including Minoan society, writing, technology, religion, art, and international relations. His brilliant study became the de facto encyclopedia of Minoan civilization – the index to the volumes lists some 10,000 separate entries! In these volumes Evans' genius, partly intuitive and partly the result of his wide archaeological knowledge, was his ability to interpret the artifacts he found and from them to reconstruct ancient Minoan society.

Inevitably, Evans saw Minoan civilization through the eyes of his own age. Thus Evans envisioned a King Minos who ruled a Sea Empire, similar to that of Victorian England. Today one notices how closely his interpretation of the Knossos palace – in terms such as Porter's Lodge and State Reception Halls – resemble Oxfordian and Victorian nomenclature.[14] Living in an era of aggressive colonialism, Evans naturally attributed Minoan cultural development largely to diffusion, that is, to the influence of ideas from more developed cultures to less developed ones. Throughout *The Palace of Minos*, Evans saw Minoan civilization developing under the direct influence of the older civilizations of the Near East – *ex oriente lux* – much as the Eastern nations were being reshaped by the great colonial powers during his own lifetime.

During the Second World War, Crete was occupied by the Axis powers. With the onset of war, the British archaeologist John Pendlebury joined the underground movement on Crete. On May 21, 1941, he was captured and executed by German soldiers.

After the war, Greek archaeologists greatly expanded their research on Crete. The new head of antiquities on Crete, Nikolaos Platon, dug widely, especially in east Crete. In 1961 he discovered a new Minoan palace at the coastal site of Kato Zakros.[15] Platon's excavations there revealed what had been missing at Knossos, Malia, and Phaistos, an unplundered Minoan palace. Destroyed by fire in Late Minoan IB (*c.*1450 BC) and unoccupied after that, the palace still contained most of its rich contents – ivory tusks, copper ingots, inscribed tablets, a storeroom full of cult paraphernalia and workshops stocked with raw materials. Because all of its contents were found preserved in its rooms, the palace at Zakros gives us the best idea of how a Minoan palace actually functioned. Costis Davaras, the Ephor of East Crete, also excavated at numerous sites, including several peak sanctuaries and a Cycladic-like cemetery at Agia Photia.[16] In 1964 John and Ephi Sakellarakis began uncovering a major, palatial settlement at Archanes and its hilltop cemetery at nearby Phourni.[17]

The pace of foreign excavation and publication also increased following the war. The Italians reopened extensive excavations at Phaistos, the French at Malia, and the British at Knossos (Chapter 5). Peter Warren's excellent publication of the coastal site of Myrtos was the first clear account of an Early Minoan settlement.[18]

Fundamental new studies of Minoan civilization appeared. Martin Nilsson's *The Minoan-Mycenaean Religion, and Its Survival in Greek Religion* (1950) collected and carefully interpreted the archaeological evidence for Minoan religion. In 1953 Michael Ventris showed that the Linear B tablets from Knossos and the Mainland were written in Mycenaean Greek.[19] Ventris deciphered the writings by guessing that the varying final signs in a series of repeated words were probably suffixes. On the theory that these suffixes shared a single consonant but different vowels (such as domin*us*, domin*i*, domin*o*), he listed these various syllabic signs in their reoccurring orders to try to isolate the common vowels in the suffixes (dominus, agricolus, bellus). Finally, turning to a common category of three-sign words which were probably place names (because of their position in the tablets), he began matching them to prominent Cretan place names. Three names, *a-mi-ni-so* (Amnisos), *ko-no-so* (Knossos), and *tu-li-so* (Tylissos) seemed for various reasons to fit. With this start, he was able within a month to decipher Linear B as Greek. These translations revealed myriad details of the Greek-speaking mainland Greek administration in the fifteenth–fourteenth-century BC palace at Knossos (Chapter 9). Using Linear B, many of the commodities listed in the earlier, Minoan Linear A tablets can now be understood even though the language and the religious inscriptions still remain undeciphered to this day. More recently, much valuable research has clarified basic aspects of Minoan culture, including, to name only a few, materials (pottery, stone vases, metal), architecture, religion, war, and trade.[20]

Within the last two generations, several developments have changed our perception of Minoan civilization. First, archaeological excavation has increased exponentially. Important new sites (Chapters 4 and 5) have been partly excavated and published. These include towns (e.g. Chania, Knossos, Monasteraki, Malia, Petras, Palaikastro, and Zakros), villages (e.g. Myrtos, Trypeti, and Myrtos/Pyrgos), and farms (Achladia, Chelinomouri). New shrines have been excavated, including peak sanctuaries (e.g. Kophinas, Atsipades, and Vrysinas) and caves (e.g. Skotino and Peleketa). In 1979 the remains of a human sacrifice were unearthed in a Middle Minoan building on the slope of Mount Jouktas.[21] Excavations outside Crete, on the Aegean islands, on the Greek mainland as well as Anatolia, Syria, Egypt, and Italy have also yielded important new archaeological evidence for Minoan trade and international contacts, including Minoan-like frescoes in Egypt and the Levant (Chapter 6). In 1967 Marinatos began uncovering the well-preserved Late Bronze Age town on Thera modern Santorini, "The Pompeii of the Aegean." Stripping off layers of volcanic ash, his excavations dramatically unsealed a town of prosperous houses, jammed with finds, including much imported Cretan pottery and Minoan-style frescoes.[22] In 2015 a rich warrior grave dated to *c.*1500 BC was discovered at Pylos on the Greek mainland, filled with

Minoan objects including gold rings and over fifty seals and vases. The first publication of a Minoan shipwreck has just appeared.[23]

Second, recent excavators have adopted a broader approach to the past, with a new emphasis on scientific methods, involving geology, ethnography, physical anthropology, soil studies, and scientific methods of dating and determining the origin of pottery (and the nature of their contents) and metals. They have given us a much clearer picture of certain basic aspects of Minoan culture, such as chronology, the environment, population, food, and trade. Regional surface surveys have filled in the gaps between major sites, documenting how the rural landscape of Minoan Crete was densely settled by towns, villages, hamlets, and farms. Survey evidence is informative about population, land use, and regional economic networks. Archaeological survey is usually strenuous and sometimes can be embarrassing, as an incident from my experience illustrates. After days of walking under the heat of the Cretan sun, my leather boots were dry and beginning to crack. So I had an inspiration – I went to the village butcher and obtained several handfuls of chicken fat which I applied to my boots. The leather responded beautifully, becoming pliant and soft. The next day I set off for work and I was followed by every dog in the village who wanted to lick my boots!

Third, Aegean archaeology, originally a discipline of the humanities, has during the last forty years adopted theoretical approaches drawn from the social sciences. Current scholarship now often focuses on certain theoretical issues derived from anthropology, such as social organization and inequality, gender, agency, and new ways of explaining cultural change.[24] An important early example of this new emphasis on theory was C. Renfrew's influential volume *The Emergence of Civilization* (1972). Reacting against Arthur Evans' and Gordon Childe's diffusionist claims that powerful ideas from the kingdoms of Egypt and the Near East determined the nature of Aegean civilization, he imagined Aegean culture as a self-contained system made up of internal subsystems, like the gears in a clock, and that it was the interaction of these subsystems – subsistence, technology, social, symbolic, and trade – that were the prime movers of cultural change within Aegean society.

Following Renfrew's publication, several studies have been written from Renfrew's neo-evolutionary perspective, assuming Minoan palatial culture is solely a product of incremental internal evolution from the Neolithic and Early Bronze Age onwards. More recently, a second and more realistic approach has become popular: based on a model, called world system theory, which sees Aegean society as part of a network that included Egypt and the Near East. According to this model, large-scale cultural transformations result from the flow of materials, customs, and ideologies between core areas (large urban areas with an active economy) such as Egypt and Mesopotamia and less developed areas that supplied the large core areas with raw materials, and with time were transformed in this interactive process.[25] Initially, this process began in the Near East, and by the end of the third millennium the Aegean entered, rather suddenly, into this world system network. Studies of this type, including this volume, differ from earlier diffusionism in that they recognize that Minoan borrowing of foreign techniques and forms were quite often significantly changed from their original form and meaning to suit local ideas and practices.

A RETURN TO MYTH: VISIONS OF MINOAN CRETE IN THE TWENTIETH CENTURY

With time, Arthur Evans' influential work at Knossos has transcended the discipline of archaeology.[26] Since it is human nature to try to read the past in order to understand the present, Evans' portrait of Minoan Crete painted in *The Palace of Minos* has become widely influential and has come to play an important role in shaping a cultural perspective on our own era.

Following the devastating violence of two world wars, intellectuals began to search for positive developments in human history. Evans' reconstruction of Minoan Crete as a peaceful, well-ordered civilization provided a welcome alternative vision to the recent violence. For example, in 1916 James Joyce published his autobiographical book, *Portrait of an Artist as a Young Man*, whose hero, an artist whose last name was Dedalus, is seeking to escape his past and create a new life. The writer Henry Miller traveled to Crete on the eve of the Second World War, and upon his visit to Knossos, declared: "Knossos in all its manifestations suggests the splendor and sanity and opulence of a powerful and peaceful people . . . In many ways it is far closer in spirit to modern times, to the twentieth century, I might add, than other later epochs of the Hellenic world . . . Knossos was worldly in the best sense of the word."[27] Minoan Crete came to offer an example of potential future happiness for the twentieth century.

The Cretan myths of Europa and the Bull, the Minotaur in the Labyrinth, and Daedalus and Icarus incorporated in *The Palace of Minos* also became popular subjects in art and literature. In Picasso's art, a series of scenes depict female bull leapers and a violent, menacing Minotaur. In his *Minotauromachy* of 1935 (Fig. 2.1), Ariadne and a bare-breasted toreador face the approaching Minotaur, Picassos' symbol of the brutality of the totalitarian state.[28] In 1948, the poet laureate of England, Robert Graves, published a book, *The White Goddess*, that traced European mythologies back to an original Mother goddess, modeled in part on the Great Mother goddess described repeatedly in Evans' *Palace of Minos*.[29] The book became an instant classic, and along with Evans' volumes formed a basis for the subsequent anti-war movement and an inspiration for modern feminism.[30] So, too, Minoan Crete, with its myths of sexually emancipated women, such as Europa, Ariadne, and Phaedra, and its sensual artistic appreciation of women, has acquired a wide popularity in our own culture today.[31]

NOTES

1   For the mythical tradition of Minoan Crete, see C. Boulotis, "From Mythical Minos to the Search for Cretan Kingship," in M. Andreadaki-Vlasaki, G. Rethemiotakis, N. Dimopoulou-Rethemiotaki, eds., *From the Land of the Labyrinth, II*, New York: Onassis Foundation, 2008, 44–55.

2   L. Fitton, *The Discovery of the Greek Bronze Age*, Cambridge, MA: Harvard University Press, 1996.

3   The Idaean cave: F. Halbherr, *Monumenti Antichi* 2 (1888) 690ff. Amnissos: J. Hazzidakis, *Parnassos* 10 (1886) 339–42; F. Halbherr, "Amnissos," *The Antiquary* 27 (1893) 112. Dictaean Cave: F. Halbherr, "Scoperte nell'antro di Psychro," *Museo Italiano de antichita Classica* 2 (1888) 905–12.

4   A. Taramelli, "A Visit to the Grotto of Camares on Mount Ida," *AJA* 5 (1901) 437–51.

5   A. Brown, *Arthur Evans and the Palace of Minos*, Oxford: Ashmolean Museum, 1983. A. MacGillivray, *Minotaur: Sir Arthur Evans and the Archaeology of the Minoan Myth*, New York: Farrar, Straus and Giroux, 2000.

6   A. Evans, "Further Discoveries of Cretan and Aegean Script, with Libyan and Proto-Egyptian Comparisons," *Journal of Hellenic Studies* 17 (1897) 327–95.

7   J. Myers, "The Sanctuary – Site of Petsofa," *BSA* 9 (1902–3) 356–87.

8   J. Evans, *Time and Chance: The Story of Arthur Evans and his Forbearers*, London: Longmans and Green, 1943, 331.

9   A biography of this remarkable woman was published by her daughter, M. Allsebrook, *Born to Rebel: The Life of Harriet Boyd Hawes*, London: Short Run Press, 1992.

10 J. Hazzidakis, "An Early Minoan Sacred Cave at Arkalochori," *BSA* 19 (1912–13) 35–47.

11 S. Xanthoudides, "Μινωικν μεγαρον Νιρου," *Archaiologiki Ephemeris* (1922–3) 1–25.

12 Survey: J. and H. Pendlebury and M. Money-Coutts, "Excavations in the Plain of Lasithi, I," *BSA* 36 (1935–6) 9–13. Karphi: J. and H. Pendlebury and M. Money-Coutts, "Excavations in the Plain of Lasithi. III Karphi," *BSA* 38 (1937–8) 57–148.

13 S. Marinatos, "The Volcanic Destruction of Minoan Crete," *Antiquity* 13 (1939) 425–439.

14 J. McEnroe, "Sir Arthur Evans and Edwardian Archaeology," *Classical Bulletin* 71 (1995) 3–18.

15 N. Platon, *Zakros: The Discovery of a Lost Palace of Ancient Crete*, New York: Charles Scribner's Sons, 1971.

16 C. Davaras and P. Betancourt, *The Hagia Photia Cemetery*, I–II, Philadelphia: Instap Academic Press, 2004–12.

17 Y. Sakellarakis and E. Sapouna-Sakellarakis, *Archanes: Minoan Crete in a New Light*, I–II, Athens: Ammos Publications, 1997.

18 P. Warren, *Myrtos: An Early Bronze Age Settlement in Crete*, Oxford: Thames and Hudson, 1972. Many of Evans' finds can now be seen at Oxford in the Ashmolean Museum, see Y. Galanakis, ed., *The Aegean World: A Guide to the Minoan and Mycenaean Antiquities in the Ashmolean Museum*, Athens: Kapon Editions, 2013.

19 M. Ventris, and J. Chadwick, *Documents in Mycenaean Greek*, Cambridge: Cambridge University Press, 1956.

20 J. Driessen, "Recent Developments in the Archaeology of Minoan Crete," *Pharos* 20 (2014) 75–115, gives an overview.

21 Y. Sakellarakis and E. Sapouna-Sakellarakis, "Drama of Death in a Minoan Temple," *National Geographic* 159 (1981) 205–22.

22 S. Marinatos, *Excavations at Thera, I–V*, Athens: The Archaeological Society at Athens, 1968–72.

23 E. Hadjidaki, *The Minoan Shipwreck at Pseira, Crete*, Philadelph: INSTAP Press, 2019.

24 Several scholarly series of publications, *Aegaeum*, *Studies in Mediterranean Archaeology*, and the online website, *Aegeanet*, have been quite important in this process.

25   A. and S. Sherratt, "From Luxuries to Commodities: The Nature of Mediterranean Bronze Age Trading Systems," in N. Gale, ed., *Bronze Age Trade in the Mediterranean*, SIMA 90, Jonsered: Astroms Forlag, 1991, 351–86. See also C. Colburn, "Eastern Imports in Prepalatial Crete," *AJA* 112 (2008) 203–24. See fig. 9 for the Egyptian fresco. Two good overall explanations of this subject are: P. Warren, " Minoan Crete and Pharaonic Egypt," in W. Davies and L. Schofield, eds., *Egypt, the Aegean and the Levant*, London: British Museum, 1995, 1–18; P. Warren, "Crete and Egypt: The Transmission of Relationships," in A. Karetsou, ed., *Kphth–Aigyptos*, Athens: Kapon Editions, 2000, 24–8.

26   C. Gere, *Knossos and the Prophets of Modernism*, Chicago: University of Chicago Press, 2009.

27   H. Miller, *The Colossus of Maroussi*, New York: New Directions, 1941, 121–22, quoted in Gere, *Knossos and the Prophets of Modernism*, 153.

28   Gere, *Knossos and the Prophets of Modernism*, 79–9 and fig. 19, *Minotauromachia* by Picasso.

29   J. Evans, *Index to the Palace of Minos*, New York: Biblo and Tannen, 1964, sv "Goddess, Minoan" 59–61, cites over a hundred references to the Minoan Goddess in *The Palace of Minos*!

30   Gere, (=*Knossos and the Prophets of Modernism*, 151–3.

31   T. Ziolkowski, *Minos and the Moderns: Cretan Myth in Twentieth- Century Literature and Art*, Oxford: Oxford University Press, 2008, 27–66; 119–21; 121–6. See also N. Momigliano and A. Farnoux, eds., *Cretomania, Modern Desires for the Minoan Past*, Abingdon: Routledge, 2017.

THREE

CRETE BEFORE THE PALACES

Earliest Prehistory to EM II (130,000–2200 BC)

EARLY PREHISTORY

Recently, archaeologists have discovered the earliest signs of people living on Crete – by the Middle Paleolithic period, perhaps as early as 130,000 BC.[1] Small groups were able to cross the Mediterranean by boat and lived perhaps seasonally along the coast in rock shelters and caves located next to freshwater streams. Many of these new sites, identified by their distinctive local quartz tools, have been identified on the south coast near the village of Prevali (Fig. 3.1). These hunter-gatherers may have been responsible for the extinction of certain Pleistocene animals, such as the pigmy hippo, elephant, and deer, that are present in the earlier fossil record of Crete, but had disappeared by the later Neolithic period.

THE FIRST SETTLERS

A wave of permanent settlers arrived in Crete from the Anatolian coast (Fig. 3.1) from *c.*7000 BC at the time that the coastal plains of southern Anatolia and the Levant were being settled by Neolithic farmers. During most of the long Neolithic period (*c.*7000–3100 BC), settlements on Crete remained few, for example at Knossos, Lera Cave near Chania, and the Gerani Cave near Rethymnon.

The best known settlement on Crete of this period is Knossos.[2] Located a little more than 3 km from the north coast on a hill next to two streams, this

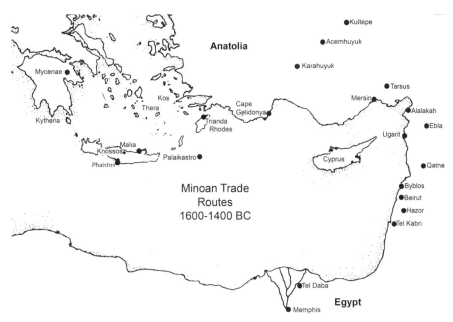

3.1 Map of the Eastern Mediterranean.
Map by the author

Neolithic settlement grew over some 2,000 years, rising to form an artificial mound, similar to those known at the Near Eastern archaeological sites. These first settlers brought with them a fully developed farming economy which included wheat, barley, lentils, sheep, goats, pigs, some cattle, and dogs, an assemblage similar to that at contemporary Neolithic sites in Anatolia and Syria.[3] The native Anatolian mountain goat (ancestor of the Cretan wild goat, the *agrimi*) and deer may also have been brought to the island at this time. In terms of its shapes and decoration, the Early Neolithic pottery of Knossos is a developed form of the ceramics used at early sixth-millennium sites, such as Mersin and Byblos, in Cilicia and the Levant (Fig. 3.1). The Knossian pottery, however, exhibits certain elaborations, mainly relief decoration and elegantly modeled handles that were probably an Aegean development.

In its earliest phases, Knossos seems to have remained quite small, but by the Late Neolithic period (5300–4500 BC) the settlement had grown to the size of a village extending over 4 hectares with around 300–600 settlers.[4] An excavated house at Late Neolithic Knossos had a dozen rooms, a built-up hearth on the floor, storerooms with large pots, stone mace heads, obsidian imported from the Cycladic island of Melos, a copper ax, and debris from meals, including cattle, goat, and pig bones, seashells, and an almond shell.[5] Figs, grapes, and nuts were also part of the local diet. Red deer, *agrimi*, and hare were hunted. Two rooms in houses at Knossos with hearths and clay female figurines (Fig. 3.2) may have been used for religious rites, on analogy with

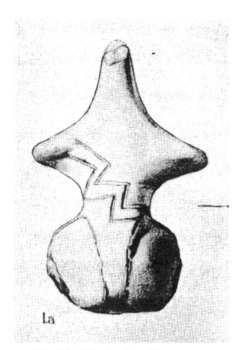

3.2 Neolithic Figurine from Knossos. Evans (1921), 46, fig. 12.1a

so-called domestic shrines in similar Cypriote household spaces.[6] The earliest clear evidence we have for religion in Crete are Neolithic figurines. Made of clay, stone, and marble, they are mostly female although a few males and animal examples also exist. These females can be nude or clothed, steatopygous, naturalistic, or stylized. The figurines found at Knossos all come from household contexts. Who do these figurines represent? This question has attracted much attention and fierce controversy. Evans identified the female figurines as an oriental Mother goddess, but other scholars favor multiple Minoan deities (Chapter 7).

In southern Crete, Phaistos and Gortyn were established in this period on high ridges above the Mesara Plain. The Neolithic settlement at Phaistos was at least 3 hectares in size.[7] A circular-shaped house, similar to examples in Cyprus, possessed a fragment of red-banded plaster (possibly from a wall), stone mortars, a quern (stone for grinding grain), obsidian blades and flakes, and pottery.[8] A spouted stone trough may have functioned as an oil press.[9] Late Neolithic levels at Phaistos also produced spinning and weaving equipment, domestic stone and bone tools, pierced cardium shells, many obsidian blades and scrapers, and a copper borer. Two clay steatopygous female figurines found with seashells, miniature vases, magnetic iron, and a red-painted triton shell may well have been part of a domestic shrine.[10] Both at Phaistos and Knossos two open areas located under the area of the later Minoan palace were used by large groups of people who gathered to share food and wine, a sign that ceremonies carried out in the Minoan palaces had an earlier precedent.[11]

The population on the island expanded dramatically toward the end of the Neolithic period (3100 BC). Small new groups of immigrants from the Cyclades, Dodecanese, and coastal Anatolia arrived and established hundreds of new sites, particularly along the coasts.[12] Many of these settlements were on defensible hilltops, protected by fortification walls. In east Crete, the steep cliff of Katalimata was occupied in the Final Neolithic period as a refuge by locals in the face of new arrivals.[13] Further east, at Magasa, in the hills above Palaikastro, settlers walled in a rock shelter and built a rectangular stone hut. The hut floor produced stone axes, pumice, bone awls (pointed tools), obsidian debris, seashells, querns, cooking pots, and the bones of sheep and goat. The inhabitants seem to have lived there during the summer with their flocks and produced cheese from boiled milk, sewed skins, and ground their locally harvested grain to make bread.[14] The rise of the amount of olive pollen in later Neolithic cores from Crete suggests the olive had become domesticated and was cultivated, offering a wider diet.[15] Climate became less moist late in the Neolithic period (3500–3100 BC). The spread of large and small settlements across the landscape would also have begun to create regional economic networks.

During the Late Neolithic period, Crete made closer contacts with the outside world. Obsidian was imported from the island of Melos and from southern Anatolia. A Late Neolithic site at Pelekita Cave near Zakros produced a phallus-shaped idol similar to examples in Cyprus.[16] Cretan pottery shows many similarities with the ceramics of the Dodecanese, Cyprus, and western Anatolia. Cretan Late Neolithic seated female figures, modeled with exaggerated breasts and hips, are a type found throughout the eastern Mediterranean and southern Europe during this period.[17]

EARLY MINOAN I: NEW DEVELOPMENTS

The Early Bronze Age ushers in a series of new developments on Crete. Local population continued to grow, accompanied by the arrival of immigrants. The Cretan diet became more diverse. During this time certain families began to accumulate ostentatious wealth. Gold jewelry and new types of metal tools and weapons, made in imported metals, copper, bronze, and silver were created. Each region of Crete began to produce a distinctive local style of pottery that was often traded to other parts of the island. Overseas trade increased.

A few centers, such as Knossos and Phaistos, grew to the size of a large village, numbering well over 500 people. Knossos, for instance, was about 6.5 hectares.[18] An excavated Early Minoan I (EM I) farmstead at Debla, at an elevation of 542 meters within the White Mountains, south of Chania, produces evidence that during the summer months the local inhabitants lived in two stone huts. They harvested barley, emmer wheat, and oats, and grazed herds of sheep and goats.[19] South of the Mesara Plain in the Asterousia Mountains, the occupants of the Miamou cave, first inhabited in the Neolithic period, subsisted on their flocks, hunted deer and hare, and farmed seasonally.[20] North of Herapetra, on a high hilltop of Aphrodite Kephala overlooking the plain of Herapetra, a single house with a walled courtyard was able to accumulate and store produce such as olives, almonds, grapes, and figs, and probably cheese.[21]

Better food sources certainly contributed to population expansion. Already in the Late Neolithic period there is evidence that the size of sheep flocks had grown.[22] Farmers learned how to convert milk, by boiling, into a storable form, such as yogurt and cheese, making larger herds economically valuable, and thus producing more food.[23] Milk products are important because they give at least four or five times more nutrients – protein, fat, and sugar – than a meat diet does. Olive cultivation also spread. Olives were a crucial supplement to cereals because they yield twice the amount of calories per acre as cereals or pulses do. Early Minoan agriculture became diversified, consisting of barley, wheat, olives, and grapes as well as certain legumes. These crops, especially olives that can grow on poorer, dry soils, made it possible for settlers to move to more marginal environments away from the well-watered plains. In the Early Minoan period the countryside became much more densely settled. Grazing and cutting down the virgin vegetation cover also set in motion the first large period of soil erosion of the Cretan landscape.[24]

The regions of Early Minoan Crete display different cultural practices. Funerary customs, for example, vary markedly from region to region. In north central Crete, settlers continued to bury their dead collectively in caves and in rock crevices, as at Kyparissi and at Pyrgos near Heraklion that contain jumbled skeletons, some burned by fumigation during later burials, clay jugs, pyxides, cups and chalices (tall footed cups), Cycladic-type schematic stone idols, bronze daggers and awls, obsidian blades, and a few pieces of jewelry (two gold bracelets and a gold spiral earring).[25]

In east Crete the north coast cemetery at Agia Photia first settled in EM I, near Siteia, provides a different picture.[26] This necropolis (EM I–IIB, 3100–2200 BC) consisted of at least 252 tombs, most of which were small oval chambers dug into the shallow bedrock with a north- and seaward-facing doorway closed with an upright slab (Fig. 3.3). These tombs resemble Cycladic

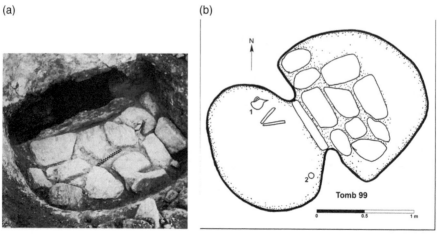

(a)   (b)

3.3 Photo of Entrance and Plan of Early Minoan Tomb 99.
Davaras and Betancourt (2004), 93, figs. 215, 217

types. Individuals were laid out on a floor strewn with sea pebbles and were accompanied by their possessions, including clay vases, obsidian blades, a few stone vases, an Egyptian type of marble cosmetic palette, stone axes, grind-stones, pieces of abrasive pumice, a few crucibles and metal objects such as bronze weapons, fishhooks, pins, chisels, bracelets, and lead animal-shaped pendants. Analyses of bronze examples from the tombs at Agia Photia point to a Cycladic source for the metal.[27] A bowl, *pyxis* (a cylindrical Cycladic type of vase), and jug containing food and liquid were often placed next to the deceased. Miniature clay copies of larger pots, cups, jars, and *pyxides* were symbolic grave gifts for the dead. Outside the doorway on the paved exterior antechamber the deceased was left with a large chalice filled with a liquid offering.[28] Large numbers of Cycladic vases in the cemetery suggest that Agia Photia was an immigrant settlement from the Cyclades.

In the southern part of Crete, communities constructed giant circular *tholos* tombs (Fig. 3.4), whose interior diameter ranged from 4.5 to 8 m, for collective burials. These structures, often called beehive tombs because of their shape, were meant to mark the permanent status of the many newly established settlers in the Mesara Plain. They are by far the most impressive architectural monuments in Early Minoan Crete. Around a hundred such tombs are now

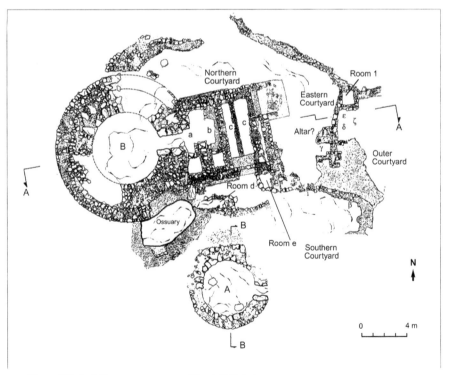

3.4 Plan of Early Minoan cemetery at Moni Odigitria.
Vasilakis and Branigan (2010), fig. 14

known, almost all located in southern Crete. Unfortunately many have been, and continue to be looted by local tomb robbers. The massive tomb walls are of *cyclopean* masonry, constructed using courses of giant boulders weighing up to a ton or more, built up to 1.8 m in height that supported a corbelled vaulted roof.[29] The doorway of these tombs, which consisted of two upright slabs supporting a massive stone lintel, usually faced east.

In contrast to the individual burials in northern Crete, these *tholos* tombs contained many hundreds of communal burials, in some cases lasting for over a period of 1,000 years. Quite a few Early Minoan settlements possessed more than one *tholos* tomb, which suggests that each tomb served a separate familial or kinship group within a larger community. It seems likely that these circular tombs were viewed as 'houses for the dead', that is, imitations of an ancestral house.

EARLY MINOAN II: AN INTERNATIONAL ERA

Minoan trade expanded in this period, creating greater prosperity on the island. While Crete has some sources of low-grade metals, richer sources existed to the north in the Aegean and east in the Levant. Cycladic islanders brought copper to Crete from Kythnos, Seriphos, Siphnos, and Lavrion on the east coast of Attica (Fig. 1.2). Copper ores imported from the Cycladic island of Kythnos and Lavrion were being smelted at Chrysokaminos, near Gournia (Fig. 1.1).[30] A workshop at coastal Poros, in Heraklion, a port for Knossos, produced masses of Melian obsidian and Cycladic pottery, tools, crucibles for silver and copper, a mold, a dagger, and an ingot of Near Eastern shape.[31] Much of the pottery from this workshop is Cycladic in style, suggesting the artisans were from the islands. Specialized tools and weapons, such as chisels, knives, axes, and daggers become common. Within Crete local vases were exported between regions on the island. Mesara workshops, for example, sent their pottery to Knossos.[32] In return they obtained obsidian, abrasive stones (possibly emery from Naxos), and copper imported from the Aegean.

By the mid-third millennium BC, all of the Aegean world entered an unprecedented era of economic interconnections and prosperity.[33] The Early Helladic culture of the mainland developed large urban settlements. Urban Manika in Euboia, for example, measured, over 50 hectares in size. Some were politically organized around a central community building. In the Cyclades the small island settlements were especially prosperous from conducting widespread maritime trade, especially in local metals, including tin obtained via Anatolia.

Crete shared this prosperity. At Vasiliki and Mochlos one or two aristocratic households can be recognized by their impressive architecture and costly imported tomb contents. The gold jewelry, diadems, bracelets, earrings, floral pendants, and hair sprays in the shape of flowers found in three rich Mochlos tombs were meant to be worn in daily life and would have distinguished their owners from most of the local population who were farmers, shepherds, and fishermen. An artisan middle class, made up of metalworkers, potters, masons, and seal and stone carvers may have become full-time professionals by this point. Each region manufactured distinctive local products that were exported to other areas of Crete. In east Crete, for example, Gournia made and exported its pottery, which we call Mirabello ware, along the north and south coasts.

Located on well-watered plains, Knossos, Phaistos, and Malia reached the size of small towns (2–5 hectares) at this time, with populations between 700 and 2,000.[34] Knossos was close to 6.5 hectares in extent, and possessed substantial houses in the area of the later palace. In EM IIA the slopes of the hill at the center of the settlement were leveled and terraced to create an open area for buildings, reached by a stone-paved ramp. These towns would have been regional centers, since their open central areas were used for large gatherings that involved drinking and eating. At Malia the EM II settlement was around 2.5 hectares in size with an estimated population of 690–1,000 persons.[35] Burials were made in rock crevices along the nearby seashore.

In the countryside, new settlements were established on defensive hilltops and fortified, pointing to increasing competition and conflict among local groups on the island. The hamlet of Trypeti, for example, placed on a hill by the south coast near Lebena was a small community that lived off a mixed economy relying mainly on farming (barley, wheat, peas, vetch, and figs) and the rearing of livestock, which was supplemented by fishing, gathering mollusks, clams, and snails, and hunting hare and birds.[36] Other EM II settlements, like Vasiliki and Mochlos, were the size of small villages. At Mochlos the size of the cemetery and the estimated area of settlement (0.8 hectares) points to a community of perhaps fifteen families, or about ninety persons.

Only two EM II settlements on Crete, Myrtos Fournou Koriphi and Vasiliki, have been excavated to any extent. Myrtos, an EM II rural hamlet of 30–40 people, was established on a steep and defensible hilltop, called Fournou Koriphi, overlooking the south coast (Fig. 1.1).[37] A cluster of five or six households was surrounded by a fortification wall with a tower on its seaward side (Fig. 3.5). Houses were small, one-story constructions of stone and mudbrick, each with an outside work area. In the center of the hamlet an open area about 14 by 18 m served as a public space. Two flat-faced stone *kernoi*, stones with a series of small depressions, may have served for religious offerings and/or as game boards. One house had a small domestic shrine that consisted of a low bench on which was placed a clay statuette of a female, holding a jug (possibly for water) to her breast. She has become known as the "Lady of Myrtos" (Fig. 3.6).[38] The jug functioned as a pouring spout. Similar prepalatial anthropomorphic vases, found in tombs at Koumasa, Trapeza Cave,

Arc-shaped building

3.5 Plan of Early Minoan II settlement at Myrtos Fournou Koriphi.
Myers and Cadogan (1992), 198, fig. 27.1

and Malia are also female-shaped, presumably representing a maternal deity
who pours liquid from a spout or from her breasts. The villagers at Myrtos
grew olives, vines, barley, and wheat, and kept herds of sheep and goats.
Limpets were gathered from the shore and fish taken from the sea. Textiles
were woven on looms, handmade pottery made on circular turntables, and
blades knapped from Melian obsidian. Pottery was imported from the Mesara
Plain and the north coast.

3.6 Early Minoan II figurine, "Lady of Myrtos," Myrtos Fournoi. Korip AN HMC/ TAP. BSA.
Photo by the author

The second excavated site is the hamlet at Vasiliki, in the northern Isthmus of Herapetra (Fig. 3.1). Located on a hill by a spring and a stream, Vasiliki consisted of at least six small houses in EM IIA (2700–2400 BC), belonging to a group of interrelated families.[39] After a destructive episode at the end of EM IIA, the community seems to have been fundamentally reorganized. In Em IIB (2400–2200 BC), two large houses, constructed on stone foundations with mud-brick walls, were built on the hilltop next to a stone-paved courtyard (Fig. 3.7). Smaller buildings existed on the slope below. These two hill-top houses, called the "Red Houses," are distinctive in their construction, size, and plan. They are elite residences possessing two stories, elegant red plastered and polished floors and walls, and cobbled stone courtyards. Both houses had one or two main central rooms and thick-walled annexes made up of small rooms, which were probably storage and food-processing areas. The eastern of the two houses may have had an inner courtyard; in its center a deep well or cistern was cut into the bedrock. The two houses produced obsidian, bronze tools, a mold for a double ax, loomweights, many storage jars, a marble figurine with folded arms, a stone seal, and a large vase stamped with another seal. Slightly later, two small annexes that may have been storage rooms and workshops (Fig. 3.7, West House) were added to the west of the two houses. The cobbled courtyard at Vasiliki had at least five stone *kernoi*, set into it (Fig. 3.8). From the finds at Vasiliki we know that inhabitants farmed cereals and olives, kept livestock, wove textiles, and made their own bronze tools. They had access to imported copper, probably from the nearby foundry site of Chrysokaminos on the north coast, and to obsidian, from the Cycladic island of Melos.

The cemeteries of EM II Crete are better known than the settlement sites. At Mochlos on the north coast of Crete the cemetery consisted of at least fourteen tombs in the shape of miniature rectangular houses. (Fig. 3.9).[40] One of the largest tombs (IV–VI) in the cemetery was about 4.5 by 7.5 m, and

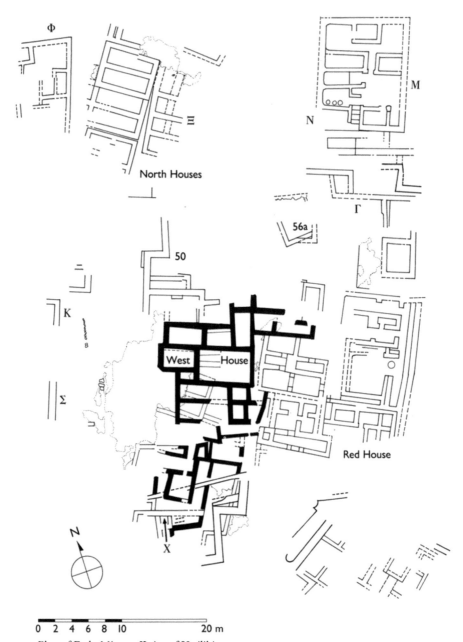

3.7 Plan of Early Minoan II site of Vasiliki.
Myers and Cadogan (1992), 276, fig. 41.1

consisted of a two-room roofed compartment, with an additional room added
on later. In the lower part of the cemetery, smaller, single- or double- room
tombs were set in rows on the slope. The larger tombs possessed bronze
daggers, knives, toilet articles, and obsidian blades as well as gold jewelry,
including diadems (Fig. 3.10), hair pins in the shape of a daisy or crocus,

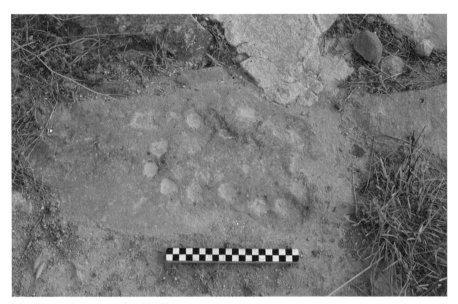

3.8 Kernos in courtyard at Vasiliki.
Photo by the author

armbands, rings, necklaces, and pendants of amethyst, rock crystal, carnelian, and lead. The simple, rubble-walled tombs were poorer: they contained a few pots, a stone quern, and a stone vase or two. The disparate contents and size of these tombs in the cemetery suggest that the community at Mochlos was made up of two to four wealthy families and at least ten poorer ones.[41]

The cemetery of Moni Odigitria is typical of EM II burial complexes in southern Crete (Fig. 3.4).[42] In its original form, it consisted of two large *tholos* tombs with a cobble courtyard. (The Annex a, b, c, c in the courtyard is later.) These two tombs probably served two separate social groups living in nearby settlements. The dead were placed in the tombs with some of their possessions: cups, triangular clay game pieces, a copper dagger, obsidian blades, a sealstone, a stone vase, and a necklace of stone beads. The *tholoi* were periodically cleared out and fumigated. Pouring vases called *rhyta*, in the shape of bulls, sheep, and a pig, were used to make libations to the dead. Their shapes seem to suggest that the poured libation was regarded as a symbolic substitute for sacrifice of the actual animal. Similar vases are also known in Egypt and at Byblos. One part of the outer courtyard contained piles of cooking pots and bowls, suggesting that sizable groups of people gathered to eat and drink there. Another area of the court was leveled and left open, probably for community ceremonies.

Tombs and their contents help us to understand the Minoans' ideas about the dead and the afterlife. At Phaistos and Mochlos, the dead were buried in tombs on a slope facing and visible from the settlement, as if the dead were

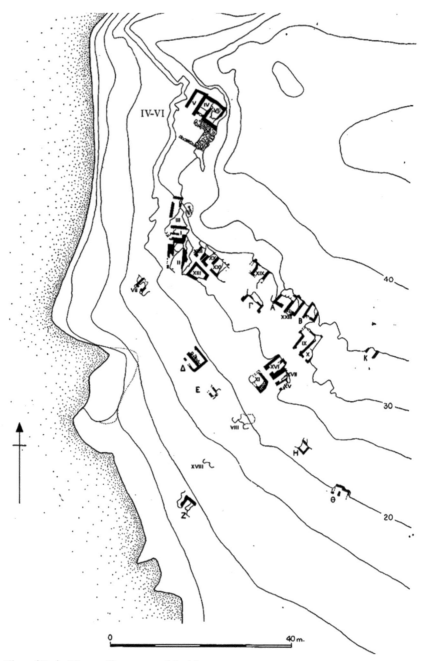

3.9 Plan of Early Minoan Cemetery at Mochlos.
Soles (1992), 272, plan 3

considered a continuing part of the living community. Settlements near the
coast, such as Malia and Gournia, often chose to bury their dead on the
shoreline. The sea may have had a special meaning, perhaps as the pathway
to the Afterworld, as the Nile did for Egyptians. *Tholos* doorways also normally

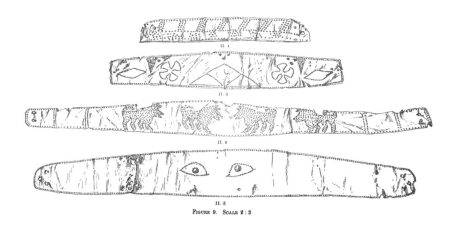

FIGURE 9. SCALE 2 : 3

3.10 Gold diadems from Mochlos.
Seager (1912), fig. 9

faced east, suggesting the afterlife of the dead may have been connected with the direction of the rising sun.[43] Some tombs had seashells or beach pebbles, and boat models, as if the soul was thought to journey a distance across the water to reach another world, as was believed in Egypt.

The deceased were provided with their daily belongings and special objects for their continued use in the afterlife. A man's burial might include his dagger and seal, as well as a clay jug, cup, bowl, and stone vase, for food and drink. A woman might take to the grave her necklace, tweezers, and perhaps a figurine, as well as the usual vases. Stone figurines have been found in tombs. Most are recognizably female, while the more schematic, oblong, or phallic ones are probably male. These figurines show signs of use and repair, indicating they were the personal items of those buried there. Small, flat examples may have been worn as personal amulets. They have been interpreted as images of a protective deity, since small examples were worn as pendants, a practice learned from the Cyclades.[44] These figures are variations of Early Bronze Age types known throughout the Eastern Mediterranean. Stone vases were expensive funerary offerings used for cosmetics. In two cases the dead were buried with a model house, perhaps meant as a residence for the soul, like Egyptian funerary model "soul houses."

Communal ceremonies for the dead were held outside the tomb. Food or drink were provided in a pedestaled bowl which was closely modeled on an identical Egyptian bowl sitting on a stand.[45] Actual food, left for the dead, has been identified in a few tombs, including the remains of pig, sheep or goat, dog, hare, birds, shellfish, and olives. Close parallels for this practice exist in the

3.11 Clay *rhyton* depicting a bull ritual from a Koumasa tomb. HM 4126. HMC/TAP. Photo by the author

3.12 Early Minoan II Vasiliki ware teapot. MMA. MMA 07.232.14

3.13 Jug, from Agios Onouphrios cemetery near Pha. HM 5. HMC/TAP. Photo by the author

Near East and Old Kingdom Egypt where offerings of food and drink were made in the antechamber of Egyptian mastabas. Two *rhyta* in the shape of a bull, from tombs at Koumasa and Porti near Miamou, show men actually hanging on to and wrestling with a bull (Fig. 3.11). If the Minoan bulls were to be sacrificed to the dead, as seems likely, it seems the men of the community were expected to ceremonially subdue them first. These representations may be early examples of the more refined 'bull-leaping' scenes depicted in Late Minoan art (Chapter 7). Clay models of dancing groups (Figs. 4.11 and 5.6) from tombs hint that these courtyards may also have been used for ceremonies involving dancing.

New and luxurious forms of ceramic shapes, metalwork, and stone vases appear in the EM II period. At Gournia, in east Crete, potters produced a distinctive style of pottery called Vasiliki ware, composed of deliberate patterns of orange flames and patches of color that imitate the mottling of Near Eastern copper vases (Fig. 3.12). At the same time, workshops in the region of the southern Mesara Plain were making very different types of vases, called Agios Onouphrios ware (Fig. 3.13). Sites along the north coast, at Mochlos, Poros, and Petras Agia Photia acquired and worked metal and obsidian imported from the Aegean. In the EM II period, jewelry and seals made of imported gold, silver, and ivory first appear. An elite tomb (Gamma) at Phournoi (Archanes) produced ivory seals, Cycladic figurines, copper, silver, and gold objects including jewelry, and daggers. Most Early Minoan seals were carved in animal bone and soft stones, and bear a simple design of hatched, wavy, or random lines on their stamp face.[46]

Drawing on Cycladic knowledge of metallurgy, Cretan bronze smiths made a variety of daggers, short swords, spears, and arrowheads for wealthy patrons.

In the EM II period a Cretan male had a choice of two varieties of hand weapon, the short, triangular dirk or the slimmer, sword-like dagger. What is revealing about Early Minoan Crete is the proportion of known weapons to tools. In southern Greece, the ratio of known weapons to tools found in tombs is 14:39, in the Cyclades the ratio is 15:53, but in Crete the relationship is 80:7![47] Already in this period Minoan society seems to have had a combative nature, probably the result of conflicts between local groups.

One of the sources of EM II prosperity was its expanded overseas trade relations, in large part via Cycladic shipping. Necessary raw materials, such as Melian obsidian used for cutting blades and copper from Kythnos and Lavrion used for tools and weapons, were imported to the island. The port of Poros-Katsambas (Heraklion) was a center for obsidian and metalworking that probably included Cycladic workers.[48] Cycladic settlers at Agia Photia brought obsidian, silver, copper, and metallurgical technology to eastern Crete. Cretans established a colony on the island of Kythera, probably as a trading station, for possible sources of lead, silver, and gold from the Peloponnese. Gold and ivory were imported from the Near East for their value as exotic rarities. At EM II Mochlos, gold jewelry, diadems, leaf pendants, floral sprays, and beads are found in the cemetery. Several seals from Archanes are of imported Near Eastern ivory. Wealthy individuals wore gold jewelry as a sign of their elite social status. Copper artifacts from the Agia Photia and the Mesara tombs have been shown by analyses to come from the Cycladic island of Kythnos as well as from Lavrion and perhaps Cyprus.[49] Recent excavations at the windy coastal site of Chrysokaminos near Mochlos have revealed a place where copper ores from Kythnos were smelted in clay furnaces.[50] Minoan overseas exports, however, are rare – perhaps they were perishable goods, such as textiles and oil.

During the EM II period Cretan seafarers also sailed to the great cities along the eastern seaboard of the Mediterranean. An Egyptian poem, "The Lamentation of Ipuwer" that describes the dissolution of Egyptian society toward the end of the third millennium BC, complains that Egypt is no longer visited by the men of Keftiu, the Egyptian name for Crete. Ipuwer names the Keftiu men in the context of the Egyptian loss of imported oil, suggesting that oil may have been a Minoan export. Textiles are also possible. Tenth Dynasty tombs in Egypt depict a double-heart spiral pattern that is likely a Minoan textile motif.[51] Near Eastern objects found in Early Minoan contexts also bear witness to Minoan overseas contacts. A trader from Mochlos brought home a mid-third-millennium silver cylinder seal from Syria.[52] A piece of Egyptian hippopotamus tusk (used for carving ivory seals) and a few Egyptian stone vases are known from Knossos.[53] Cretan traders to the Near East seem to have focused on obtaining metals, ivory, and exotic materials.

Minoan interest in the Near East, however, was not confined to physical goods. Already by this period the Minoans had begun to learn about and adapt ideological practices from Egypt, mainly visible in the funerary sphere. EM II amuletic motifs, such as the scarab beetle, monkey, and scorpion, worn by the living, suggest that the Minoans may have believed in some of Egyptian magic – the scarab promises renewed life, the monkey fertility, and the scorpion apotropaic protection against the creature's sting. Two Minoan foot-shaped seals from EM II tombs imitate the popular Near Eastern/Egyptian foot amulet believed to protect the owner's use of his leg in life and in the Afterworld.[54] Miniature Egyptian funerary stone vases were imported and used, like the Egyptian examples, as funerary offerings.[55]

END OF THE EARLY BRONZE AGE

The end of the EM II period (2200 BC) was marked by the destruction and abandonment of many settlements on Crete. Malia, Vasiliki, Myrtos Fournou Koriphi, and Pyrgos/Myrtos were destroyed by fire. The settlers of Myrtos Fournou Koriphi probably moved inland, to a more defensive site up in the foothills overlooking the coast.[56] Other sites, Agia Photia and Palaikastro, were deserted. Some sites on the Cycladic islands, including Thera, were also deserted. The Greek mainland was severely disrupted by the arrival of new groups of people. Major settlements on Crete continued, but little is known about them during this interim period.

These events in the Aegean are part of a wider pattern visible throughout the eastern Mediterranean at this time. Sites in southern Anatolia, Levant, and Egypt (First Intermediate Period) were also destroyed, abandoned, or show other signs of disruption. Scientific studies and contemporary written records in the Near East document a period of drought, population loss, and migration.[57] Urban centers at Byblos, Ugarit, Ebla, Tarsus, and Kultepe were destroyed by fire at the end of the Early Bronze Age period. During the period 2250–2000 BC there are few signs of trade, until after 2000 BC. Only with the establishment of the later Eleventh Dynasty (2066–1994 BC) and Middle Kingdom in Egypt (1994 BC) do the numbers of Egyptian objects begin to reappear in the Levant at sites such as Byblos. In Anatolia, trade revived at Kultepe in the Karum Kanish II period with the establishment of Assyrian merchant colonies by c.1950 BC.

NOTES

1   T. Strasser, "Stone Age Seafaring in the Mediterranean," *Hesperia* 79 (2010) 145–90. T. Strasser et al., "Palaeolithic Cave Art from Crete, Greece," *Journal of Archaeological Science: Reports* 18 (2018) 100–8. These early people carved scenes of deer on Asphendou Cave in west Crete some 11,000 years ago.

2   J. Evans, "Neolithic Knossos: The Growth of a Settlement," *PPS* 37 (1971) 95–117.

3   C. Broodbank, and T. Strasser, "Migrant Farmers and the Neolithic Colonization of Crete," *Antiquity* 65 (1991) 233–45. V. Isaakidou, "The Fauna and Economy of Neolithic Knossos Revisited," in V. Isaakidou and P. Tomkins, eds., *Escaping the Labyrinth: The Cretan Neolithic in Context*, Sheffield Studies in Aegean Archaeology 8, Oxford: Oxbow, 2014, 90–114.

4   T. Whitelaw, "The Urbanization of Prehistoric Crete: Settlement Perspectives and Minoan State Formation," in I. Schoep, P. Tomkins, and J. Driessen, eds., *Back to the Beginning: Reassessing Social and Political Complexity on Crete during the Early and Middle Bronze Age,* Oxford: Oxbow, 2012, 114–76.

5   A. Evans, *The Palace of Minos, II*, London: Macmillan, 1927, 19, and fig. 8a.

6   A. Evans *Palace of Minos, I*, London: Macmillan, 1925, 43–52. Peltenburg has identified similar shrines in Neolithic Cyprus. E. Peltenburg, *Early Society in Cyprus*, Edinburgh, Edinburgh University Press, 1989, 108–26.

7   L. Vagnetti, "L'Insediamento Neolithico di Festos," *Asatene* 50/51 (1975) 7–138.

8   Vagnetti, "L'Insediamento Neolithico di Festos," 27–9. Compare the Cypriote houses at Lemba-Lakkous in V. Karageorghis, *Cyprus,* London: Thames and Hudson, 1982, 33, fig. 18.

9   L. Vagnetti, "L'Insediamento Neolithico di Festos," 24, fig. 16 and 117, fig. 134.

10 L. Pernier, *Il Palazzo Minoico di Festos, I*, Rome, 1935, 105, fig. 48. Evans, *The Palace at Knossos, II*, 12 and figs. 3bb and 3cc.

11 S. Todaro and S. DiTonto," The Neolithic Settlement of Phaistos Revisited," in V. Isaakidou and P. Tomkins, eds., *Escaping the Labyrinth: The Cretan Neolithic in Context*, Sheffield Studies in Aegean Archaeology 8, Oxford: Oxbow, 2014, 177–90 and S. Todaro, "Craft Production and Social Practices at Prepalatial Phaistos," in Schoep et al., *Back to the Beginning*, 195–235. J. Hansen, "Agriculture in the Prehistoric Aegean," *AJA* 92 (1988) 39–52, weighs the evidence of Early Minoan wine production.

12 K. Nowicki, *Final Neolithic Crete and the Southeast Aegean*, Berlin: De Gruyter, 2014.

13 K. Nowicki, *Monastiraki Katalimata. Excavation of a Cretan Refuge Site, 1993–2000*, Philadelphia: Instap Academic Press, 2008, 41–5; 72–6.

14 R. Dawkins, "Excavations at Palaikastro. IV," *BSA* 11 (1904–5) 260–61.

15 O. Rackham and J. Moody, *The Making of the Cretan Landscape*, Manchester: Manchester University Press, 1996, 124–5.

16 The figurine from Pelekita Cave appears in C. Davaras, "Chronika," Αρχαιολογικον Δελτιον 34 B2 (1979) pl. 215c. Compare to the Cypriote figurine in E. Peltenburg, *Early Society in Cyprus*, Edinburgh: Edinburgh University Press, 1989, 112, fig. 15.2 from Agios Epiktitos-Vrysi.

17 S. Weinberg, "Neolithic Figurines and Aegean Interrelations," *AJA* 55 (1951) 121–33. P. Ucko, *Anthropomorphic Figurines of Prehistoric Egypt and Neolithic Crete*, London, 1968.

18 T. Whitelaw (supra n 4), "The Urbanization of Prehistoric Crete."

19 P. Warren, J. Tzedakis, and J. Greig, "Debla.: An Early Minoan Settlement in Western Crete," *BSA* 69 (1974) 293–342.

20 A. Taramelli, "The Prehistoric Grotto at Miamu," *AJA* 1 (1897) 287–312.

21 P. Betancourt, *Aphrodite's Kephali: An Early Minoan I Defensive Site in Eastern Crete*, Philadelphia: Instap Academic Press, 2013.

22 A. Sarpaki, " The Economy of Neolithic Knossos," in N. Efstratiou, A. Karetsou, and M. Ntinou, eds., *The Neolithic Settlement of Knossos in Crete*, Philadelphia: Instap Academic Press, 2013, 63–94.

23 A. Sherratt, *Economy and Society in Prehistoric Europe: Changing Perspectives*, Edinburgh: Edinburgh University Press, 1997.

24 K. Pope, "Geology and Soils," *Hesperia* 62 (1993) 202–24.

25 Kyparissi: S. Alexiou, "Πρωτομινωικαι παρα το Κανλι Καστελλι Ηρακειο," *Κρητικα Χρονικα* 5 (1951) 275–94. Pyrgos: S. Xanthoudides, "Μεγας πρωτομινοικος ταφος Πυργου," *Αρχαιολογικον Δελτιον* 4 (1918) 136–70.

26   C. Davaras and P. Betancourt, *The Hagia Photia Cemetery, I–II*, Philadelphia: Instap Academic Press, 2004–12.

27   N. Gale, "The Provenance of Metals for Early Bronze Age Crete–Local or Cycladic?" *Πεπραγμενα του ΣΤ' Διεθνους Κρητολογικου Συνεδριου I*, Chania, 1990, 299–316.

28   D. Haggis, "The Typology of the Early Minoan I Chalice and the Cultural Implications of Form and Style in Early Bronze Age Ceramics," in R. Laffineur and P. Betancourt, eds., *TEXNH*, Aegaeaum 16, Liege: University of Liege, 1997, 296–99.

29   P. Warren, "The Roofing of Early Minoan Round Tombs: The Evidence of Lebena Tomb II (Gerokampos) and of Cretan Mitata," in P. Betancourt, M. Nelson, and H. Williams, eds., *Krinoi kai Limenes*, Philadelphia: Instap Academic Press, 2007, 9–16.

30   P. Betancourt, ed., *The Chrysokamino Metallurgy Workshop and Its Territory* (Hesperia Supplement 36), Princeton: Princeton University Press, 2006.

31   N. Dimopoulou-Retheniotakis, D. Wilson, and P. Day, "The Earlier Prepalatial Settlement of Poros-Katsambas: Craft Production and Exchange at the Harbor Town of Knossos," in P. Day and C. Doonan, eds., *Metallurgy in the Early Bronze Age Aegean*, Sheffield Studies in Aegean Archaeology 7, Oxford: Oxbow, 2007, 84–97. D. Wilson, "Early Prepalatial Crete," in C. Shelmerdine, ed., *The Aegean Bronze Age*, Cambridge: Cambridge University Press, 2008, 77–104.

32   D. Wilson and P. Day, "Ceramic Regionalism in Prepalatial Central Crete: The Mesara Imports from EM IB to EM IIA Knossos," *BSA* 89 (2000) 21–63.

33   For the Mainland, see O. Dickinson, *The Aegean Bronze Age*, Cambridge: Cambridge University Press, 1994. The Cyclades are discussed in R. Barber, *The Cyclades in the Bronze Age*, London: Duckworth, 1987, and C. Broodbank, *An Island Archaeology of the Early Cyclades*, Cambridge: Cambridge University Press, 2000.

34   T. Whitelaw, "The Urbanization of Prehistoric Crete."

35   H. and M. van Effenterre, "Fouilles executes a Mallia: Le centre politique," *Etudes Cretoises* 17, Paris: Geuthner, 1969, 18–24.

36   A. Vasilikis, 'Ο Πρωτομινωικος Οικισμος της Τρυπιτης," Αρχαιολογια, 30 (1989) 52–6.

37   P. Warren, *Myrtos: An Early Bronze Age Settlement*, *BSA* Supplement 7, 1972. T. Whitelaw, "House, Households and Community in Early Minoan Fournou Korifi: Methods and Models for Interpretation," in R. Westgate, N. Fisher, and J. Whitley, eds., *Building Communities*, British School at Athens Study 15, London: Short Run Press, 2007, 65–76.

38   A similar bronze figurine has been discovered at Alaca Hoyuk in Anatolia. K. Bittel, *Die Hethiter*, Munich: Beck, 1976, 46, fig. 29.

39   A. Zois, *Vasiliki I*, Athens: The Archaeological Society at Athens, 1976. Summary in V. Watrous, "Crete through the Protopalatial Period," *Aegean Prehistory: A Revue*, *American Journal of Archaeology* Supplement 1, 2001, 169–171.

40   J. Soles, *The Prepalatial Cemeteries at Mochlos and Gournia*, Hesperia Supplement 24, 1992.

41   J. Soles, "Social Ranking in Prepalatial Cemeteries," in E. French and K. Wardle, eds., *Problems in Greek Prehistory*, Bristol: Bristol Classical Press, 1988, 49–62.

42   A. Vasilikis and K. Branigan, *Moni Odigitria: A Prepalatial Cemetery and Its Environs in the Asterousia, Southern Crete*, Philadelphia: Instap Academic Press, 2010. The site was looted before the excavation. Many of its finds are on display today in the Mitsoutakis Collection in the Archaeological Museum in Chania.

43   L. Goodison, *Moving Heaven and Earth: Sexuality, Spirituality and Social Change*, London: Women's Press, 1990, 98–100, and 207–9.

44   K. Branigan, "Cycladic Figurines and Their Derivatives in Crete," *BSA* 66 (1971) 57–78.

45   Compare the vase in Soles, *The Prepalatial Cemeteries*, 26, fig. 10, upper right with W. Emory, *Archaic Egypt*, Baltimore: Penquin, 1961, 243, fig. 142.

46   O. Krzyszkowska, *Aegean Seals: An Introduction*, British Institute of Classical Studies Supplement 85, London: University of London, 2005, 57–78.

47   These numbers are derived from the catalogues in K. Branigan, "Copper and Bronze
     Working in Early Bronze Age Crete," *SIMA* 19 (1968), and K. Branigan, *Aegean Metalwork
     of the Early and Middle Bronze Age*, Oxford: Oxford University Press, 1974.

48   N. Dimopoulou, "The Neopalatial Cemetery of the Knossian Harbor Town at Poros:
     Mortuary Behavior and Social Ranking," in *Eliten in der Bronzezeit*, Mainz: Verlag der
     Romisch-Germanisches Zentral Museums and Rudolf Halbet Verlag, 1999, 27–36.

49   N. Gale, "The Provenance of Metals for Early Bronze Age Crete–Local or Cycladic?"
     Πεπραγμενα του ΣΤ' Διεθνους Κρητολογικου Συνεδρριου I, Chania, 1990, 299–316.

50   Betancourt, *The Chrysokamino Metallurgy Workshop*.

51   E. Barber, *Womens' Work: The First 20,000 Years*, New York: Norton, 1994, 109.

52   J. Aruz, "The Silver Cylinder Seal from Mochlos," *Kadmos* 23 (1984) 186–7. J. Aruz, *Marks
     of Distinction: Seals and Cultural Exchange between the Aegean and the Orient ca 2600–1360 BC*,
     CMS Beiheft 7, Mainz: Verlag von Zabern, 2008, 40, fig. 59.

53   O. Krzyszkowska, "Wealth and Prosperity in Prepalatial Crete: The Case of Ivory," in
     O. Krzyszkowska and L. Nixon, eds., *Minoan Society*, Bristol: Bristol Classical Press,
     1983, 166.

54   Aruz, *Marks of Distinction*, cat. 139 and 140. Aruz lists three other seals that imitate the shape
     of NE types (cat. 137, 138, 142) in EM II tomb contexts.

55   An exhibition of Egyptian objects found on Crete was on display in the Heraklion
     Archaeological Museum in 1999 and 2000. Examples (nos. 11, 13a, 13b, 21) appear in the
     catalogue: A. Karetsou et al., *Crete–Egypt: Three thousand years of Cultural Links*. Herakleion
     and Cairo: Hellenic Ministry of Culture: Ephorates, 2001. Essays: A. Karetsou, ed.,
     ΚΡΗΤΗ-ΑΙΓΥΠΤΟΣ. Πολιτισμικοι δεσμοι τριων χιλιετιων, Athens: Kapon Editions, 2000.

56   K. Nowicki, "Myrtos Fournou Koriphi: Before and After," in O. Krzyszkowska, ed.,
     Cretan Offerings: Studies in Honour of Peter Warren, BSA Studies 18, 2010, 223–38.

57   H. Weiss, "Altered Trajectories: The Intermediate Bronze Age in Syria and Lebanon
     2200–1900 BCE," in A. Killebrew and M. Steiner, eds., *Oxford Handbook of the
     Archaeology of the Levant*, Oxford: Oxford University Press, 2014, 367–87. F. Hoflmayer,
     ed., *The Late Third Millennium in the Ancient Near East*, Chicago: University of Chicago
     Press, 2017. S. Manning, "Comments on Climate, Intra-regional Variations, Chronology,
     the 2200 B.C. Horizon of Change in the Eastern Mediterranean Region, and Then Socio-
     political Change in Crete," in Hoflmayer, *The Late Third Millennium in the Ancient Near
     East*, 451–80.

FOUR

THE RISE (EM III–MM IA) AND FIRST PHASE OF MINOAN PALATIAL CIVILIZATION (MM IB–II)

LATE PREPALATIAL CRETE, EM III–MM IA: RECOVERY AND RAPID GROWTH

This is the formative period of Minoan high civilization. Many important cultural changes began in Middle Minoan IA (MM IA, 2100–1950 BC) and reach a lasting cultural form in MM IB.

At the end of the third millennium BC the eastern Mediterranean entered a period of renewed prosperity and expanded international contacts that included Egypt, the Levant, and Crete. Unlike the sparsely populated Cyclades and the mainland,[1] Crete experienced vigorous growth and important social change at this time. This period in Crete, known as the Late Prepalatial period (MM IA) corresponds to the early Middle Kingdom (Dynasties 11 B and early 12, c.2066–1929) when Egypt regained political stability and foreign trade among the Near Eastern states began to flourish. Certain social developments – immigration, increased population, overseas contacts, wealth, and social competition – provided the necessary conditions for the formation of Minoan palatial society.

At this time Crete received newcomers to its shores. Signs of these immigrants are visible in the establishment of new sites near the coastlines (Fig. 4.1). At Agia Photia on a hill on the north coast near Siteia, a large new architectural complex of residences and work areas was constructed in MM IA.[2] This cluster of thirty-seven rooms (Fig. 4.2) opened out on to a court and was surrounded

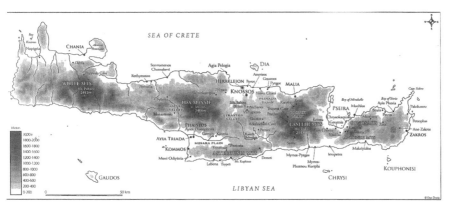

4.1 Map of Middle Minoan I–II.
Schelmerdine (2008), map 4, redrawn by Amanda Killian

by an impressive fortification wall with four apsidal towers similar to Cycladic examples. The Cretan countryside was gradually resettled during this period, but usually at defensive locations. For example, a house at Chamaizi near Siteia was built on top of a steep, defensive hilltop and protected by a heavy exterior wall.[3] At Vasiliki five new houses were built on the hilltop, surrounded by massive fortification walls and a tower.[4] The defensive nature of MM IA settlements suggests uneasy relations between different groups on the island. New funerary practices, that is, cist graves (a Cycladic form of burial), *pithos* burials (common in western Anatolia), and *larnakes* (an Egyptian type of coffin) appear along the north coast, signaling the arrival of immigrants and new ideas.

Towns like Knossos, Phaistos, and Malia expanded rapidly during this period. Some of this new urban population probably came from rural settlers seeking safety. Knossos has been estimated to have reached 20 hectares with 6,000–11,000 inhabitants.[5] Malia's population had grown to at least 5,000 people and had fortified its coast with a large wall. Phaistos was about 27 hectares in size with a population of 7,500–10,000. The center of the city at Phaistos, where a palace would be built about 200 years later (1900 BC), consisted of a paved street leading to a cobbled area, and several small pottery workshops. This area was used by groups for communal feasting.[6] Many smaller village-sized sites, like Mochlos, Agia Triada, Platanos, and Palaikastro certainly continued to be occupied.

Minoan overseas exports and imports increased sharply in this period.[7] Exported Cretan pottery has been recognized at Aegina, the Greek mainland, and Cyprus. Cyprus was especially important because it was a source of copper and on route to Cilician silver. On Crete, Cypriote pottery first appears in MM IB at Kommos.[8] *Tholos* tombs in the Mesara in southern Crete possessed many Egyptian goods, such as stone vases and seals modeled on Egyptian types, that indicate Cretans' contact with Egypt.[9] A workshop on the south coast

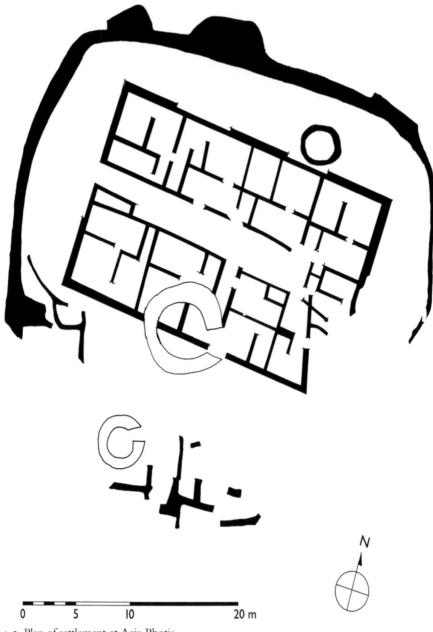

4.2 Plan of settlement at Agia Photia.
Myres et al. (1992), 66, fig. 6.1

produced a group of some one hundred preserved stone seals of burned *steatite*, called 'White Pieces', that mimic Egyptian faience material as well as motifs such as the scarab, bee, and claw (Fig. 4.3).[10] The Minoans also fashioned stamp cylinder seals, an Eastern shape, made of hippopotamus ivory imported from Egypt and Syria. Seals depict many foreign motifs (Chapter 8). Imported

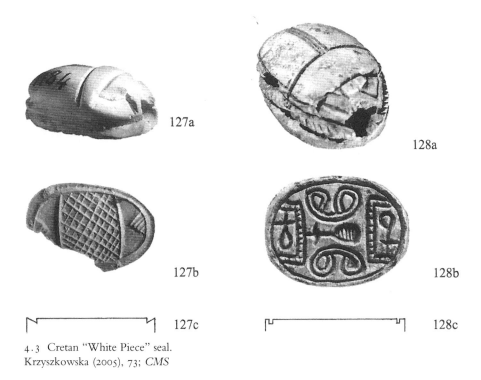

127a

128a

127b

128b

127c

128c

4.3 Cretan "White Piece" seal.
Krzyszkowska (2005), 73; *CMS*

Egyptian scarabs reached Lebena on the south coast and to Archanes; they were also locally copied.[11]

Rich finds from tombs of this period point to increased wealth in Minoan society. Tholos Tomb Gamma, at Phournoi, for example, possessed many imported materials, such as obsidian, ivory, gold, silver, lead, and Cycladic figurines. A second tomb there, Building 13, yielded an Egyptian scarab, gold and ivory pendants, and necklaces of imported sard, amethyst, and faience. At Mochlos, gold bracelets, diadems, earrings, and beads from tombs have parallels at Byblos, Egypt and Kultepe, Anatolia. Ethnographic study (see Introduction) of traditional societies has shown that the acquisition of foreign objects provides social status and can play a powerful role in societal change. Those who possessed knowledge of foreign places were regarded as powerful and close to the gods.[12] Seals (Chapter 8) functioned as markers of individual ownership, kinship identity, and in the case of the foreign images cited above, of foreign knowledge.

Collective communal and family burials, typical of the Early Minoan period, continued in some parts of Crete. At this time, however, certain wealthy family groups have left traces of ostentatious ceremonies conducted outside their tombs, publically commemorating their ancestral ties, and hence displaying their prominent social status. At Mochlos, for example, one of the larger tombs (IV/V/VI) in the cemetery is provided with an exterior platform on its

4.4 Reconstruction of Offerings being made at Gournia Tombs 1 and 2.
Soles (1992), 4, fig. 1

south side on which were placed funerary gifts.[13] At Gournia, Tomb 2 was
built with a unique platform for a *kernos* on its south face to receive offerings
(Fig. 4.4). The Gournia house tombs contrast with the simple graves at
Sphoungaras in the valley below, suggesting a class distinction. On the south
coast of Crete at Myrtos/Pyrgos a processional way, visible to the settlement
below, linked the elite building on the hilltop with a large tomb that contained
exclusively male burials and elite offerings. Next to the tomb, a *kernos* was set
in the pavement for offerings.[14] The paved processional ramp to the tomb
resembles similar examples in Egypt leading to royal tombs.

Social competition among elite Minoan family groups is especially obvious
in the Phournoi cemetery at Archanes.[15] Five tombs, Tholos E, Gamma, and
Buildings 6, 7, and 13, belonged to separate households in Archanes. A massive
tholos (B) was built over an earlier structure, greatly increasing its size. Not to
be outdone, Building 6 next to it was constructed on the highest spot of the
cemetery and was provided with a paved platform on a raised terrace in front
of its entrance, which was used for conspicuous ritual offerings (conical cups,
kernoi, and a figurine). In the succeeding Protopalatial period (1900–1700 BC),
the family associated with the adjacent Tholos B built five annexes forming an
even larger two-story funerary structure. What is equally striking about these
public funerary displays is their deliberate use of expensive foreign objects.
One of the stone vases left outside the Mochlos Tomb (IV/V/VI), for
example, is a miniature imitation of an Egyptian amphora.

At Malia, burial finds illustrate the emergence of a local royal group. Most
burials at Malia were made in rock crevices, in *pithoi* and *larnakes*, cists and
house tombs, suggesting the Malia community consisted of diverse social
groups. In contrast to these tombs, a large new walled funerary complex
(Fig. 4.5) was built at Chrysolakkos some 500 meters north of the later
palace.[16] The initial (MM IA) phase of the tomb has a western paved court
bounded by an irregular wall, made of mudbrick and capped by half-rounded

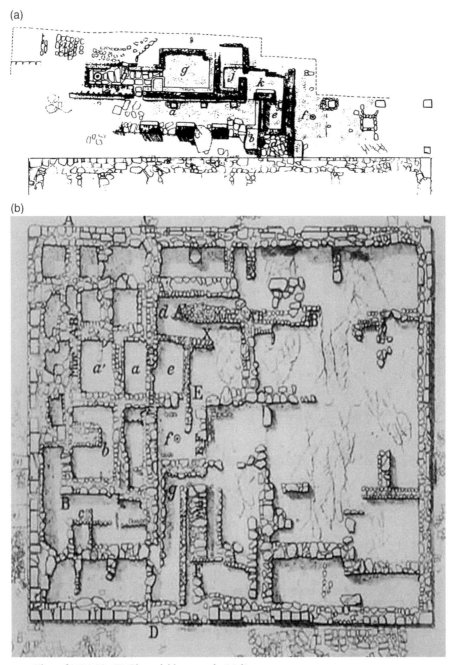

4.5 Plan of MM IA–IB Chrysolakkos, tomb, Malia.
Soles (1992), figs. 68 and 69

stone caps, an Egyptian technique unparalleled elsewhere in Crete. Along its
eastern side ran a corridor with alternating *orthostates* and niches, and doors that
joined five paved rooms (h, g, j, k, e) fitted with benches, a clay hearth, a large
kernos and an altar (b) forming a funerary shrine. Two of the rooms served as

shrines – both had an altar and one also a *kernos* set in the floor. The plan of this building and its corridor closely resemble the Egyptian "corridor chapel" with alternating niches for wooden panels, placed in front of Egyptian burial mastabas.

The later, second phase of Chrysolakkos is better preserved. It is a monumentalized rectangular house tomb constructed of elite *ashlar orthostate* masonry, an Egyptian architectural form reserved for Old Kingdom royal tombs. In this case, the impressive foreign masonry and plan of the tomb must have been meant as a display to enhance the prestige of the kin group buried inside. Inside Chrysolakkos, many chambers held burials. One room had a clay hearth and another a large stucco altar. Chyrsolakkos' grave goods were mostly robbed, hence the name of the tomb today is *Chrysolakkos* which means "Gold Pit." Burials inside included the famous gold bee pendant (Fig. 8.21) and unique pointed-bottom cups, an Egyptian type. The Chrysolakkos tomb shows a newly elevated social group at Malia distinguishing itself within its local community by using monumental architectural forms based on elite foreign Egyptian models.

These developments on Crete set the stage for fundamental changes apparent in Minoan society in the succeeding Protopalatial period.

CRETE DURING THE FIRST PALACES (PROTOPALATIAL PERIOD)

During this period certain aspects of Minoan society – economic, social, and religious – exhibit fundamental changes that mark the maturity of Minoan culture. Economic developments are considered first as they provide a context for social changes.

The Protopalatial Economy: Expansion in the Aegean and Near East

For the first time, large amounts of Minoan pottery now appear on many Aegean sites, at Mycenae, Aegina, Argos, Lerna, Iolkos, Keos, Thera, Melos, Naxos, Rhodes and Samos, Pefkakia, and along the Anatolian coast at Knidos, Miletos, and Iasos (Fig. 1.2). Minoan visits to the Aegean islands, observable in this distribution of Minoan pottery, followed a sailing route along the western Aegean to Attica where silver, lead, and copper were mined and were available. The main motivation for this outburst of maritime activity was the search for metals (copper, lead, silver, and gold). Bronze (copper alloyed with tin), the primary material for weapons, tools, and elite vases, was particularly important. A Minoan ship, dated to MM II, has been found off the north coast of the island of Pseira: its transport cargo consisted of many medium-sized utilitarian Mirabello ware vases – amphoras, jugs, and jars.[17] It seems to have been transporting and trading this pottery along the north coast of Crete, where natural harbors including Agia Pelagia, Nirou Chani, Malia, Mochlos, Palaikastro, and Gournia are known; natural harbors are also known on the south coast, including at Trypeti and Makriyalos (Fig. 4.1). Stone anchors of Near Eastern type found at Kommos and Chania come from large cargo ships. Minoan administrative documents, stamped *roundels*, and *noduli* have been discovered as far north as the island of Samothrace in the northern Aegean.[18] Minoans sent a permanent colony to the site of Kastri on Kythera off the south coast of the Peloponnese (Chapter 6).[19]

Crete also began to be actively involved in international trade outside the Aegean. Countries in the eastern Mediterranean at this time were closely connected by trade networks. Assyrian merchants began to send caravans with silver, gold, tin, and textiles to Syria and Anatolia. Minoan craftsmen created specialized luxury objects for foreign exchange. In the Near East, clay vases were plain and strictly functional, so the colorful decorative fine wares produced by Minoan potters were a popular export item.[20] Middle Minoan vases found at Byblos and Ugarit, Beirut, Qatna, and Hazor are a sign that Minoans had successfully tapped into this Near Eastern network (Fig. 3.1). Minoan vases found on Cyprus are part of the route leading ultimately to Syro-Cilicia where copper, tin, and silver were available. Some thirty Minoan vases have also been found in the workmen's village of Lahun in Egypt and far to the south, at Qubbet el-Hawa.[21] A tablet from Mari in eastern Syria refers to an inlaid metal weapon and metal vases made in Kaptara, the Near Eastern name for Crete.[22] The king of Mari sent some of these prized goods as gifts to King Hammurabi of Babylon. A second tablet records clothing and leather shoes from Kaptara. Minoan export trade to the Near East certainly included clay vases, metal objects, and especially textiles. Wine, olive oil, and wood can also probably be added to this list.

In return, Cretan traders obtained many foreign materials not locally available – gold, ivory, precious stones, copper, silver, and tin. For the first time, many Minoan bronze objects contain tin as an alloy, obtained via Syria. A tablet from Mari (*c.*1800) in Syria records tin sent to Mari from the Caspian area for Cretans to pick up at Ugarit. Minoans also imported ivory and gold from Egypt. Many bronze objects from the Mesara tombs have been shown by analysis to be from Cyprus. The well-known silver kantharos (Fig. 4.6) from Gournia is an import from Anatolia.[23] Hippopotamus ivory was imported from Egypt for seals and inlays. An Egyptian scarab seal carved with an image of the goddess Taweret was deposited in Platanos Tholos B.[24] Many Minoan seals of this period are also carved in other stones (agate, amethyst, onyx, carnelian, sard, lapis lazuli) imported from the Near East.[25] Cypriote pottery has been found at the southern harbor of Kommos and at Knossos.[26] A cylinder seal (1850–1720 BC) found in Tomb L at Mochlos came

4.6 Anatolian silver vase from Gournia.
Boyd-Hawes et al. (2014). Pl. C, upper center

from Syria.[27] Much of the copper ore from the metal workshop in Quartier Mu at Malia was imported from Anatolia.[28] Minoan seamen traveling to Byblos and the Nile Delta brought back Egyptian amulets, probably for their perceived magical power. Craftsmen on Crete also begin to make stone vases in Egyptian shapes. At Phaistos a shrine in Room LI of the palace produced seven such vases. The ceiling design of a tomb from Egypt in the reign of Senworst I (1900–1880 BC) is a Minoan design, probably copied from Minoan textiles.[29]

The Minoans acquired more than raw materials abroad. Similarities between the sealings at Phaistos and Karahoyuk, an important commercial city in central Anatolia, suggest that the Middle Minoan administrative system may have been learned from the Near East.[30] Artistic motifs from the Near East were also borrowed by Cretan seal carvers: fantastic animals – griffins, sphinxes, and bird-headed demons – appear on Minoan seals. Their closest parallels are in Anatolia and Syria. Egypt seems to have exerted a special attraction for the Minoans. The recently published burial cave at Agios Haralambos, Lasithi, in the inland interior of Crete, was filled with Egyptian and Egyptianizing objects: scarabs, *sistra*, foot amulets, ivory objects, and beads.[31] Many scarab seals were imported to Crete,[32] and Minoans made imitations of scarabs, often with Egyptian-like designs. Minoan sealings depict the protective Egyptian deities Tawaret and Beset.[33] Three clay vases from Quartier Mu depict cats seated in Egyptian fashion among trees. A fourth features a sphinx. Other Egyptian and Syrian motifs – ape, lion, bull and battlement, griffin, bee, and hieroglyphic characters (*sistrum*, leg, double ax) – were adopted by Cretan seal carvers.[34]

Minoan Society

Society within Crete also developed in important new ways during this period – population growth, the introduction of literacy, increased social complexity, the construction of the first palace states, and nature shrines (peak and cave sanctuaries). The original stimulus for many of these innovations were learned overseas by the Minoans, but were often changed to suit local needs. The form of the Chrysolakkos tomb, discussed above, is an example of this process. The Protopalatial palaces are considered below. Nature shrines are discussed in Chapter 7.

Population

The population on Crete continued to grow. The urban centers at Knossos, Phaistos, and Malia were embellished with paved streets, open courts, and a central palace. It is estimated that Knossos at this time may have had a population reaching 17,000.[35] At Knossos, the palace was built (1900 BC) on the central hill that was terraced for houses and workshops around it. A system of streets and drains was installed. Phaistos may have reached a population of 9,300. MM II Malia grew to a size of about 50 hectares with a population of about 7,500–17,000. As these centers grew in size, they were surrounded by a cluster of new villages, hamlets, and farms that sprung up around them. At Phaistos, for example, the surrounding countryside was settled by eight villages, twenty-seven hamlets, and fifteen single farms, a tenfold increase from Early Minoan times.[36] These sites formed a halo of farms producing food for the large urban population at Phaistos. By the Protopalatial period the Cretan countryside was densely settled with farms. Rural road systems linking farms and towns were constructed across the landscape. Based on their defensive location, some small roughly built megalithic structures may have functioned as outlying guardhouses meant to provide regional centers with early warning of approaching forces.[37]

A recent archaeological survey of the remote mountainous area far above the east Cretan village of Kritsa has recorded over 300 farms and shepherds' compounds (Fig. 4.7) for this period.[38] A visitor today can see rural Minoan roads, paths, and hamlets of farmhouses preserved as if in a time capsule. The intensive settlement of rural upland areas, ideal for grazing sheep, would have produced surplus amounts of wool for textiles that could be exported overseas. Even the small waterless island of Pseira in the Mirabello Bay was extensively terraced for farming by Middle Minoan times.[39]

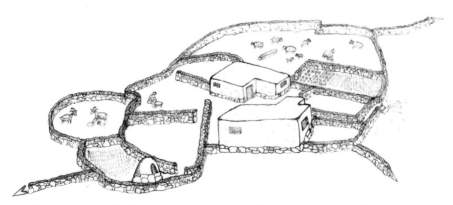

4.7 Reconstruction of Minoan shepherd's compound in mountains above Kritsa. Plan, courtesy of Sabine Beckman

Literacy

Cretan society became literate at this time, using two different scripts, hiero-glyphic and Linear A (Fig. 4.8) that probably represent two languages.[40] Based on secure contexts, it is probable that both scripts began in the Protopalatial period (1950–1700 BC) when large-scale organizations (palaces and trade networks) appeared that required writing as an administrative tool. The Cretan hieroglyphic script remains undeciphered, although a few isolated words and signs can be read. Made up of many pictographic signs, this writing system appears in MM I–II deposits in northern Crete, at Archanes, Knossos, Malia, Gournia, and Petras. It also occurs on inscribed or sealed clay docu-ments and on sealstones. It was often used by officials to list commodities; large numbers probably list livestock. The hieroglyphic script consists of ninety-six syllabic signs and thirty plus names, probably toponyms and individuals' names as well as numbers and fractions. Both hieroglyphic and Linear A were used for administrative purposes, to record incoming commodities and their dispersal by scribes in elite households and the palaces. These two writing systems have been found at a number of the larger sites. At MM II–IIIA Knossos both were

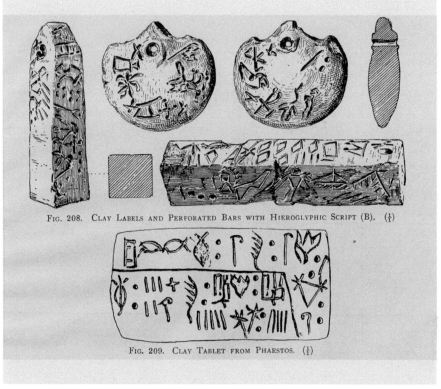

FIG. 208.   CLAY LABELS AND PERFORATED BARS WITH HIEROGLYPHIC SCRIPT (B). (⅓)

FIG. 209.   CLAY TABLET FROM PHAESTOS. (⅓)

4.8 Hieroglyphic script.
Evans (1927), 278, figs. 208 and 209

apparently in use. The hieroglyphic script went out of use in MM IIIA, being replaced by Linear A.

The Linear A writing script was first used in southern Crete, and is best known at Phaistos. While the language of Linear A remains undeciphered, many studies have pointed out similarities between Linear A and other Eastern Indo-European languages – Lycian, Hurrian, Indo-Iranian/Sanskrit – that make it virtually certain that Linear A is an Indo-European language.[41] Preserved Linear A inscriptions are either administrative, found on clay tablets in palaces and villas, or religious, present on votive objects dedicated at sanctuaries. Inscribed objects are widely distributed across Crete, indicating a relatively high level of literacy in Protopalatial Crete. Linear A consists of some ninety syllabic signs and about a hundred logograms, representing commodities such as oil, wine, figs, barley, sheep, goats, cattle, and pigs, and a smaller number of names and numbers. Special numbers indicate fractions and weights. Most other sign groups are probably toponyms and men's names followed by logograms and numbers. The word for total in Linear A (*ku-ro* or *ku-lo*), however, is almost certainly a Semitic loanword (*kl*, meaning total). Counting all (MM II–LM I) examples, some 150 tablets and more than 1,000 sealings are known in Crete. Impressions of folded parchment, leather, and string left on clay sealings show that written documents also existed, but unfortunately their materials have not survived.

Social changes in Minoan society at this time are especially apparent in new types of seals. Minoan seals were used primarily as identity markers and for administrative purposes. Objects such as vases and loomweights were stamped with a personal seal indicating the potter or owner. Lumps of clay stamped with an official's seal were also placed directly on objects such as pithoi, chests, and sacks or to seal lids and door pegs to prevent unauthorized access. *Roundels*, clay disks with seal impressions along the edge, are inscribed on one or two sides, often with a logogram standing for a commodity, like olives or wine. They were used by palace officials as a receipt for a disbursed commodity from a storeroom. *Nodules* functioned as receipts for work accomplished, for exchange of goods, for wages, or as receipts for goods delivered to storerooms. Two-hole *nodules* were probably attached to commodities as labels. The large number of seals in soft local stones found in Cretan settlements make it certain that seals were not owned solely by the upper class.

New groups of seals began to be made in MM IA and continued into the Protopalatial period.[42] One group, the Parading Lion-Spiral seals, popular in southern Crete, was often made of imported hippopotamus ivory and features lions, a foreign animal linked to kings in Egypt. Made intentionally large, this first group may have appealed to the emerging aristocracy. Other seals, found at Archanes, display hieroglyphic signs that would have been appropriate for literate owners. By MM II (1800 BC) Cretan seal craftsmen began to work with semi-precious stones, some of which, such as jasper, amethyst, agate, and carnelian, were imported from the East. New stones led to new colors, including gray, yellow, orange, red, brown, black (agate and carnelian), lilac-violet (amethyst), green, red (jasper), blue (lapis lazuli), and translucent (rock crystal). Some new shapes, such as the handled signet and three- or four-sided prism shape, appear to have been used mainly by palace officials.

Social Organization

Minoan society started to become more complex. New groups of seal hint at the development of new social classes. Seals among the administration at Phaistos were owned by palatial officials (whose seals were used repeatedly), a wealthy group below (seals that sealed more than ten times), and a group of commoners (283 seals used only one or two times). Minoan architecture also reveals at least three socioeconomic classes: residents in monumental palaces and elite *ashlar* houses ("villas"), cyclopean-built structures, and finally small rubble-built houses. Archaeological artifacts also point to a variety of professions: merchants, shipwrights, masons, potters, stone vase artisans, seal carvers, bronze workers, and jewelers, in addition to farmers and shepherds. In this period specialized workshops begin to produce a wider and more sophisticated range of clay vases, jewelry, textiles, seals, and dress weapons, for example gold-hilted daggers and silver swords for a Minoan upper class. Both the palaces and elite households, such as houses A and B in Quartier Mu at Malia, possessed workshops capable of producing these finished materials – some for export.

During this period stone vases, a sign of elite society, multiply in number and types. In MM IB, the fast potter's wheel was introduced to Crete, which revolutionized potters' ability to manufacture sophisticated shapes. A new type of pottery, that we called Kamares ware, consists of polychrome cups, goblets, and jugs often with exquisitely thin walls, impressed designs, and sharp carinations that imitate metal vases (Chapter 8). Seals of this period depict looms with hanging loomweights that probably belonged to weavers working in professional workshops.[43] In this period, two new jewelry techniques, filigree (decoration with fine wire) and granulation (decoration with soldered grains), were introduced from the Near East. The elaborate gold pendant in the shape of two bees on a honeycomb, found in the tomb at Chrysolakkos at Malia, illustrates these techniques on their wings and bodies.

A more complex social organization can also be seen in varied Minoan burial practices. Individual burials were now made in clay coffins called *larnakes* (in origin an Egyptian shape) or in different types of jars. The dead received provisions for the afterlife that were far more elaborate and included new offerings, such as certain shapes of stone vases, possibly for perfumes and

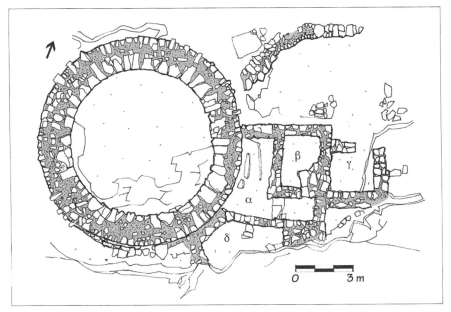

4.9 Plan of Kamilari *tholos* tomb.
SAA. ASAtene 39/40 (1961–2), pl. 1

cosmetics, seashells, and sea pebbles, and clay models of boats. Objects of Egyptian derivation are particularly noticeable – Egyptianizing clay and stone vases are common in Minoan tombs. In the south, the Mesara *tholos* tombs contained many new types of objects. At Platanos, for instance, burials in Tholos A and B were accompanied by personal possessions such as clay and stone vases, over thirty bronze daggers, a short sword, two double axes, thirty seals, an Old Babylonian cylinder seal, three Egyptian scarabs, stone cosmetic palettes, and several amulets.[44] Gold jewelry from tombs included diadems, beads, rings, disks, and pendants. The *tholos* tomb at Kamilari (Fig. 4.9), built in MM IB, contained similar personal possessions, such as seals, jewelry, pins, and weapons.[45] The deceased were also given liquid in cups and jugs and perhaps cosmetics in stone vases, as in Egypt. Annexes were added later to *tholos* tombs to hold offerings from the continuing visits. Many jugs and cups found in the annexes suggest that group visits to the grave involved offering liquid (wine or water) to the ancestors. Cups were found turned upside down in the annex (Figs. 4.9 a, b, d, and 4.10) and walled court immediately to the north so their liquid contents could go down to the underworld. Clay models left at the grave show dancers (Fig. 4.11), relatives making offerings to the dead (Fig. 4.12), and kneading bread.

The Emergence of the State

The first Minoan political states appear at this time. These regional states were marked by at least three levels of administrative hierarchy, a permanent,

4.10 Offerings in court outside Kamilari tomb.
SAA. ASAtene 39/40 (1961–2), fig. 106

4.11 Model of dancers, from Kamilari tomb.
SAA. ASAtene 39/40 (1961–2), 140, fig.174a-b

centralized, and institutionalized political authority with sovereign coercive power. Archaeologically, this transformation is visible in the construction of monumental palaces and regional peak sanctuaries. Over the last forty years much of Minoan scholarship has focused on explaining how this happened.

The debate on the causes of Minoan state formation began with the publication in 1972 of Colin Renfrew's *The Emergence of Civilisation*. Renfrew rejected Arthur Evans' claims in *The Palace of Minos* that the Minoans imitated the more developed societies of the Near East. In Evans' diffusionist view, the Minoans simply accepted Near Eastern concepts and practices. Instead, Renfrew suggested a model of strictly internal growth. He envisioned Aegean culture as a self-contained system made up of internal subsystems, and that it was the interaction of these five subsystems – subsistence, technology, social, symbolic, and trade – that created social change. Following Renfrew's systemic model, many scholars explain changes within

4.12 Model of offerings being made to ancestors, from Kamilari tomb. SAA. ASAtene 39/40 (1961–2), fig. 170a

Aegean culture as an internal process, often looking for local "agents" who initiated the changes. These studies see Minoan cultural development as a long-drawn-out, incremental process stretching back into the Neolithic period[46]

A second, more realistic approach to the emergence of the Minoan states draws upon the world system model, advocated by Andrew and Susan Sherratt, which posits that large-scale cultural transformations in society result from the flow of materials, customs, and ideologies between cores (large urban areas with an active economy). Less developed, peripheral areas supplied the large core areas with materials, and with time were transformed in this interactive process. Local imitations, however, did not keep their original significance, but were usually transformed to meet native needs. Initial stages of this process took place in Mesopotamia and Egypt, and by the end of the third millennium BC Crete became integrated into this network.[47] For this reason, Aegean studies using this second approach see the rise of Minoan palace states as a relatively sudden revolution.[48] An important anthropological study, Mary Helms' *Ulysses' Sail: An Ethnographic Odyssey of Power, Knowledge and Geographical Distance*, published in 1988, has collected ethnographic parallels that support this second approach. The author gives ethnographic examples from across the world, including from the Mediterranean and Europe, that traditional societies view distant places as being magical and powerful. Those who have knowledge of these places acquired prestige and political power. For Minoan Crete, one thinks immediately of the Throne Room in the palace at Knossos, where the throne is flanked by exotic palm trees and majestic griffins, a Near Eastern half-eagle, half-lion beast of great strength. These figures act as attributes to the ruler seated on the throne, giving the ruler their power. To take a second example, the first Cretan palaces appropriate *ashlar* masonry, a royal funerary architectural form from Egypt. In this case the Cretans borrowed a foreign technique but changed its meaning entirely. Many other similar examples exist. Using this second approach, let us turn to consider the first palaces on Crete.

The First Palace States

The first palaces represented an architectural *institutionalization* of certain traditional religious ceremonies celebrated by the community. The concept of a monumental center was certainly derived from the Near East. *Ashlar masonry*, derived from Egyptian royal buildings, was used to signal the building's high religious status. The central and western courts of the Minoan palaces served as meeting places for community ceremonies that involved feasting and drinking held periodically during the year. Minoan palaces, however, are not temples in the Near Eastern sense since no votive offerings were made there.

What sort of ceremonies were carried out in the palaces? Minoan palaces are oriented north–south with eastward-facing ceremonial rooms (throne rooms and verandas) and a low single story of the east wing (making the rise of the sun on the eastern horizon visible). This suggests that some of the gatherings were related to the rising of the sun and moon at certain times of the year (Chapter 7). Unlike the fortress-like palaces of the Near East, the west courts of Minoan palaces were easily accessed by city streets. Minoan palaces have a theatrical aspect to them: their benched courts were meant to hold and observe large ceremonial gatherings. Another distinctive feature of Minoan palaces is an internal benched space that we call a banquet hall, where a small elite group met periodically to take part in meals and cult ceremonies. This privileged group possibly acted as a council for the palace official and was probably politically powerful.

There is little consensus about the nature of the main Minoan official resident in the palaces. At no time during the Minoan period is there clear evidence that this official had the massive centralized political powers we normally associate with a king. Rulers in the Near East, Egypt, Anatolia, and Syria, for example at Acemhoyuk, Kultepe, Ebla, Alalakh, Qatna, and Ugarit, possessed monumental palaces *and* urban temples.[49] This practice is missing on

Crete. In Crete there is also no clear sign of divine royal iconography, as is prevalent throughout Egypt and the Near East. There are, for example, no known royal tombs, no royal attributes like the crown, crook, or flail of Egyptian kings, and no Minoan parallels for a royal statue like that, for example, of King Idrimi of Alalakh. The Minoans were the first people in the Eastern Mediterranean to develop a culture and artistic tradition outside of an authoritarian political structure. The official resident in the Minoan palaces therefore seems initially to have been primarily a ceremonial figure, whose main role was to supervise communal religious activities. By the end of the Protopalatial period, however, certain objects such as the Phaistos seal (Fig. 4.13) from the palace depicting a royal military victory derived from Egyptian iconography, and unique weapons such as the ceremonial leopard ax (Fig. 4.14) and a huge dress sword from the Malia palace, suggest there was a military aspect to the official. Seals depicting a robed figure next to a griffin, or holding an ax or hammer, may also refer to a king or a priest.[50] Finally, at the very end of the Minoan era, one seal from Late Minoan IB Chania depicts an official standing in front of a city in an Egyptian pose used for nobles (not royalty) supervising their estate.[51] At the same time, the tomb of the high priest Menchepereseneb of Amun at Thebes during the reign of Tutmosis III (1479–1424 BC) also mentions a ruler of Crete, identified as a king like other Near Eastern rulers.[52]

We do not know how the first Minoan "rulers" came to power. Our evidence is meager but ethnographic parallels from other early societies may suggest a possible scenario. Kinship groups commonly trace their group back to a single ancestor, who either came from another land or was associated with a sacred place where they first lived.[53] In traditional societies leaders are regarded as directly related to the group's first ancestors, hence they are "living ancestors" relative to the populace as a whole. In the Near East, kings were regarded as ancestors going back to a divinity. For this reason, the palaces were often placed above the tomb of the royal ancestors, as at Ugarit, Ebla, and Qatna. Worship of these ancestors was controlled by the palace. Such a

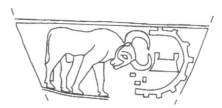

4.13 Phaistos sealing and its Egyptian prototype (Namer Palette) depicting the victorious Pharoah. *CMS* II 5, 268.
Plan author

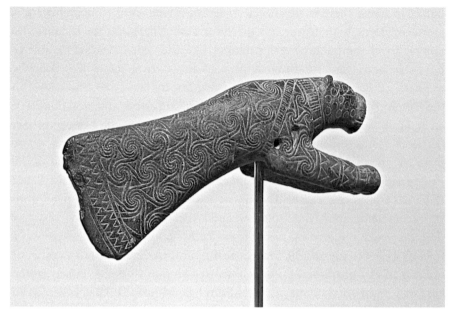

4.14 Leopard ax from palace at Malia. HM 2109. HMC/TAP.
Photo by Mark Williams

practice at Knossos would explain the enigmatic underground chamber (called a *hypogaeum* by Evans) under the south porch of the palace at Knossos.[54] The Knossian *hypogaeum* dates to MM IA just before the first palace, which is what one would expect if the palace were the result of the creation of a royal genealogy and a shared communal kinship structure. Hence, Homer *(Iliad,* xiii, 450; *Odyssey,* xi, 322) and Hesiod *(Theogony,* 948) identify Minos as the first king of Crete and the son of Zeus.

Phaistos

The only Protopalatial palace known in extensive detail is Phaistos (MM IIB) (Fig. 4.15), so we focus on it here.[55] At the beginning of MM IB a monumental structure, consisting of north and south wings, a central court, and a west court, was built at Phaistos on three terraces of a prominent ridge. No precedent exists in earlier Crete for a construction of this form and size. The palace was a huge, architecturally pretentious structure meant to stand out among the other buildings of the Phaistos town. Strictly oriented on north–south, east–west axes, the palace was situated on a location visible from afar, overlooking and dominating the Mesara Plain (Fig. 1.3). The central court is aligned north–south in line with the Kamares Cave to the north. The western façade was constructed in *ashlar orthostate* masonry facing out on to the west court and its raised walkways (Fig. 4.16). The blocks were quarried and moved into position by gangs of masons who marked each block with their sign, the so-called *masons' marks,* an Egyptian quarry technique. Three paved courts at

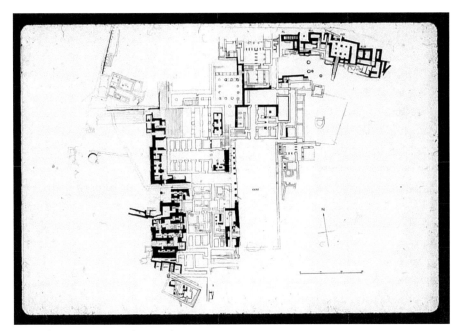

4.15 Plan, MM IB–II palace at Phaisto.
Levi (1961), fig. 1. SAA

4.16 View of west court and façade of MM IB–II palace at Phaistos.
Photo by the author

different levels lined the west façade of the palace. On the middle west court, a line of nine benches allowed an audience of 300–400 to sit and watch large-scale ceremonies held in the court. Raised walkways, probably for processions, led to the main entrance. Two stone aniconic stelae, called *baetyls,* marked the south edge of the court. Large stone basins, *kaloures,* were probably pits to hold trees. A paved ramp connected the lower and middle west courts. The south-west wing of the palace had three stories with an entrance to the lowermost west court. Inside the palace the central court was flanked along its west side by a row of columns creating an east-facing veranda.

Opening out on to the upper west court was a religious suite of five rooms (V–X) with areas for food preparation (grinding of grain) and consumption of food (burned animal bones and Kamares-style vases), as well as storage of liquids. The rooms had benches, storage jars, tables, lamps, two clay hearths, and an open hearth.[56] Cult objects found in these rooms included a stone *kernos*, sea pebbles, miniature vases, a triton shell, oyster and fossil shells, the foot of a figurine, an *agrimi* horn, three *ryhta* in the shape of a bull, three offering tables, a bronze double ax, and vases inscribed with a double ax. Room VIII was the main cult room. It had offering tables, stone libation bowls, a triton shell, stone palette and pestle, and low plaster benches. This complex of rooms was a meeting place for the preparation of food, eating and drinking, and cult ceremonies by a small group. In function, this area may presage the banquet halls found in the Late Minoan palaces. North and west of the west court, another complex (CV, CVII) also was provided with long benches for meetings, perhaps as a council chamber.

The lower wing of the palace had rooms (LIX, LX, LXIV) and annexes (LXI, LXIII, LXV) connected to large-scale communal feasting activities that took place in the lower west court. These rooms contained *pithoi*, one that produced the remains of grapes, and many cups and jugs to dispense wine. A deposit of over 700 vases found in Room IL contained many cups and jugs, a bull *rhyton,* cooking pots, and animal bones including an *agrimi* skull. A second series of rooms included a residence and signs of crafts-work, such as loom-weights and a potter's wheel. The upper floor produced loomweights, a lost-wax metallurgical mold of a human hand, a Linear A tablet, and administrative sealings. These rooms indicate that the first palace at Phaistos possessed a domestic suite and workrooms, as did the later palaces.

The fiery MM IIB destruction of the palace at Phaistos preserved its administrative clay documents, mainly Linear A tablets and sealings. These finds provide us with a window into the administrative functioning of the MM IIB palace.[57] The Linear A tablets were used to record the incoming com-modities and their redistribution as rations or goods. Tablets mention individ-uals who may have been palace staff and rations for groups of individuals (one numbering 102 and another eleven people). A deposit from under Room

25 yielded over 6,500 clay sealings (clay lumps stamped with a seal), plus Linear A tablets and inscribed *roundels*. These tablets mention at least 108 men, and quantities of vases, wine, grain, and figs. Sealings were impressed on clay lumps used mainly to seal storeroom doors as well as jars and baskets that were constantly being opened and resealed. This is a basic system imported from the Near East, although the Minoan system introduced different details.[58] Sealings show that certain doors or compartments were repeatedly opened and resealed without evidence (counter-stamping) of official supervision, unlike the Near Eastern temple practice which was closely supervised. Interpreted literally, the sealing system seems to record the activities of various cooperative groups that supported the palace's ceremonial functions.[59] Some 327 seal owners are represented in the MM II palace sealings. Most of the seals only appear a few times, but a small group of some ten owners who stamped their seals many times were probably officials working in the palace. Most of the seal owners probably lived in the town of Phaistos or the surrounding region and stamped their seals when they personally deposited or withdrew goods from the palace. Several of the seal motifs are paralleled from sites elsewhere in the western Mesara, suggesting a regional participation by sites, such as Kamilari (near Phaistos), Agia Triada, Moni Odigitria, and Platanos, in the functions of the Phaistos palace.

The territory of the MM II Phaistian state included the western Mesara Plain from Platanos to the coast (Fig. 5.5).[60] Burials for the town were made in chamber tombs on the hillside immediately north of the palace. To the northwest, Monasteraki, the central settlement in the Amari Valley, uses a seal system closely tied to Phaistos[61] and may have been politically allied with Phaistos. The Phaistos palace was also linked to a nearby harbor complex at Kommos on the coast. In MM IIB a broad artificial terrace was built at Kommos to support a large rectangular structure (Building AA) facing out to sea. Flanked by a paved road, Building AA possessed a *stoa* looking out to a court that served an administrative function as well as a storage/repair facility for ships. Foreign vases from the Cyclades and elsewhere confirm Kommos' function as a port.[62] Crushed murex shells (for making purple dye) and crucible fragments, along with imported pottery from Aegina, point to overseas trade in textiles and metal.

Malia

The palatial settlement of Malia was located on the north coast of the island (Fig. 4.1) to the east of Knossos.[63] The town was also reorganized during this period with a system of streets with raised walkways.[64] Immediately north of the MM IB–II palace, a rectangular open area was faced with seats on three sides and a portico on the fourth, west side. Streets connected the space to the palace, sea, and town. Its location and what may be small shops lining it resemble a marketplace. A large building, labeled the "Hypostyle Crypt" by the excavators, with plastered benches and a storeroom of jars next to the open area, may have been a meeting place, perhaps for a town council. In this period most of the houses known in Malia were small and without a consistent plan. A fort near the village of Mochos, at the border of the plain and the mountainous area of Lasithi to the south, suggests that Lasithi was politically independent of Malia. If this is true, it did not prevent the two areas from trading with each other, since a burial cave at Agios Charalambos in the Lasithi Plain contained seals and pottery imported from the coast.[65]

At Malia, two large *ashlar* masonry residences, Houses A and B, were also built in Quartier Mu west of the palace in MM II (Fig. 4.17).[66] These houses

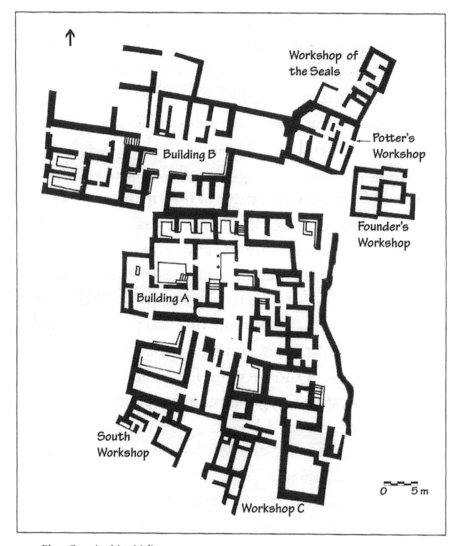

4.17 Plan, Quartier Mu, Malia.
McEnroe (2010), 64, fig. 6.15

illustrate what an upper–class Protopalatial Minoan household looked like and how it functioned. Fronting on a paved court to the west, Building A had a row of storage magazines along the north, a central light well (open to the sky, to let light into the building), a Minoan hall with pier and door partitions to the east, and a sunken lustral basin to the west. The lustral basin and room (I 12) west of it may have had a religious function. A large extension added to the south created space for magazines and benched meeting rooms. Clay figurines, sealings, tablets, and inscribed medallions, found fallen from the second floor, indicate a domestic shrine and administrative activity there. On the ground floor, the storage rooms 5, 13, and 14 also produced inscribed medallions and tablets. To the west, House B was entered by a paved causeway from the south. The house also had a central hall, light well, and storage magazines on the ground floor. The upper floor produced figurines and inscribed so-called Chamaizi vases from a domestic shrine. Clay sealings, crescents, and *noduli* from the upper floor indicate administrative activity. Outside House B were found two large stone anchors.

Houses A and B produced over 300 stone vases and much fine Kamares ware. One tablet from House A records a list of 7,000 items, probably sheep. If true, this would mean the household owned large flocks of sheep, which were valuable for the production of textiles, used for trade. Also, this would imply a manorial-type system with many rural families caring for flocks that belonged to a seigniorial household. Both houses produced hundreds of loomweights, for the weaving of textiles. Some of their larger vases were imported from the Mirabello area of east Crete and the Mesara to the south. Five small workshop/ residences attached around the edges of Houses A and B look as they were socially dependent on the wealthy households of Houses A and B. They manufactured stone seals and vases, pottery, and metal vases and tools (made of copper imported from the Black Sea area of Anatolia). The potter's work-shop produced brightly painted Kamares ware and relief-decorated vases with Egyptian motifs. The seal workshop produced some 130 prism-shaped seals mostly made of soft steatite. The wealth of Houses A and B seems to have come from the commercial production of these items – stone vases and seals, metal vases and tools, pottery, and especially textiles, for internal and overseas export.

Petras

In east Crete, Petras became the palatial urban center of the valley overlooking the Bay of Siteia with its peak sanctuary on a high hill to the south at Prinias (Fig. 4.1).[67] In the MM IIA period (1800 BC) the inhabitants leveled a hilltop overlooking the bay to create a plateau on which they constructed a small local version of a Minoan palace, with storerooms on the ground floor and a residence and archives above (Fig. 4.18). This *ashlar* building had an entrance

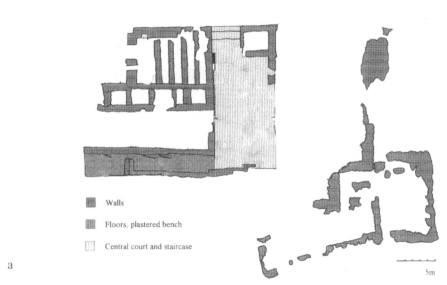

Walls

Floors, plastered bench

Central court and staircase

a

4.18 Plan, MM II palace at Petras.
Tsipopoulou (1999), pl. 89

and a stairway on the west side. A corridor ran along its south side, and three flagstone-paved rooms connected to the court. The building looked out onto a small paved court to the east, entered from the north by a monumental staircase flanked by a guard room and bounded on the west by a bastion. A massive *cyclopean* fortification wall with towers ringed the palace and separated it from the settlement below. Material from an archive, including hieroglyphic documents and sealings, fell from the upper floor of the building when it was destroyed in MM IIB.[68] Some of the sealings seem to have been used to seal cupboards, boxes and other containers in the archive. Scribes in the archives kept track of incoming materials and disbursements. Pottery found at Petras indicates that communal feasting and public ceremonies were held there and that the site enjoyed commercial connections with other places in central and eastern Crete.[69]

THE END OF THE PROTOPALATIAL PERIOD

The end of the Protopalatial period in 1700 BC is marked by a distinct horizon of destructions on many Cretan sites. The first palaces at Knossos and Phaistos were violently destroyed. Some of these destructions have been attributed to earthquakes, which is possible, but the presence of fire at these sites and the subsequent occupation of refuge sites, such as Katalimata, at this time also suggest that armed conflict between regional states may have played a role.

NOTES

1 J. Wright, "Early Mycenaean Greece," in C. Shelmerdine, ed., *The Aegean Bronze Age*, Cambridge: Cambridge University Press, 2008, 230–57.

2 M. Tsipopoulou, ed., *Petras, Siteia – 25 Years of Excavations and Studies*, Monographs of the Danish Institute at Athens, vol. 16, Athens: Danish Institute at Athens, 2012.

3 C. Davaras, "The Oval House at Chamaizi Reconsidered," *Athens Annals of Archaeology* 5 (1972) 283–88.

4 A. Zois, *Vasiliki I*, Athens: Archaeological Society at Athens, 1976. V. Watrous, "Review of Aegean Prehistory III: Crete from the Earliest Prehistory through the Protopalatial Period," in T. Cullen, ed., *Aegean Prehistory: A Review*, *AJA* Supplement I, 2001, 183.

5 T. Whitelaw, "The Urbanization of Prehistoric Crete: Settlement Perspectives and Minoan State Formation," in I. Schoep, P. Tomkins, and J. Driessen, eds., *Back to the Beginning*, Oxford: Oxbow, 2012, 114–76.

6 S. Todaro, "Craft Production and the Social Practices at Prepalatial Phaistos,"in Schoep, *Back to the Beginning*, 195–235.

7 M. Wiener summarizes the evidence for overseas contacts in this period, "Contacts: Crete, Egypt and the Near East, circa 2000 B.C.,' in J. Aruz et al., eds., *Cultures in Contact: From Mesopotamia to the Mediterranean in the Second Millennium B.C.*, New York: Metropolitan Museum of Art, 2013, 34–46. See also Watrous, "Review of Aegean Prehistory III, especially 196–8. The first images on Cretan seals of sailing ships also appear at this time.

8 V. Watrous, "Late Bronze Age Kommos: Imported Pottery as Evidence of Foreign Contacts," *Scripta Mediterraneana* 6 (1985) 12.

9 A. Karetsou, *ΚΡΗΤΗ-ΑΙΓΥΠΤΟΣ. Πολιτισμικοι δεσμοι τριων χιλιετιων*, Athens: Kapon Editions, 2000, nos. 12, 13c, 14, 15a–d, 16a–d, 17, 18, 19a–c, 20, 25a–c, 25e–j. See also P. Yule, "Early and Middle Minoan Foreign Relations: The Evidence from Seals," *SIMA* 25 (1987) 161–75. J. Aruz, *Marks of Distinction: Seals and Cultural Exchange between the Aegean and the Orient*, CMS Beiheft 7, Mainz: Verlag von Zabern, 2008, 57–61.

10 I. Pini, "Eine fruhkretissche Siegelwerkstatt?" *Pepragmena tou ST' Diethnous Kritologikou Synedriou* 6 (1990) A2, 115–27. O. Krzyszkowska, *Aegean Seals: An Introduction*, British Institute of Classical Studies Supplement 85, London: University of London, 2005, 72–4.

11 Yule, "Early and Middle Minoan Foreign Relations." Aruz, *Marks of Distinction*. Karetsou, *ΚΡΗΤΗ-ΑΙΓΥΠΤΟΣ*. Some examples of EM I–MM I Egyptian imports appear in catalogue numbers 1–25 with excellent photographs. See also F. Woudhuizen, "The Bee Sign (Evans no. 86): An Instance of Egyptian Influence on Cretan Hieroglyphic," *Kadmos* 36 (1997) 97–110.

12 M. Helms, *Ulysses' Sail: An Ethnographic Odyssey of Power, Knowledge, and Geographic Distance*, Princeton: Princeton University Press, 1988. Citing Helms' work in her recent review of Middle Minoan Crete (I. Schoep, "Looking Beyond the Palaces," *AJA* 110 [2006] 37–64, especially 57), Schoep states that, "In the construction of social power, it seems that links with the symbolically charged worlds of the East (Levant and/or Egypt) played a major role."

13 J. Soles, "The Prepalatial Cemeteries at Mochlos and Gournia, and the House Tombs of Bronze Age Crete," *Hesperia* Supplement 24, 1992, 51–62.

14 G. Cadogan, "Myrtos-Pyrgos," in W. Myers, E. Myers, and G. Cadogan, eds., *The Aerial Atlas of Ancient Crete*, Berkeley: University of California, 1992, 282–5.

15 The evidence for this process is summarized in Watrous, "Late Bronze Age Kommos," 188–9.

16 Soles, "The Prepalatial Cemeteries," 160–71. J. McEnroe, *Architecture of Minoan Crete*, Austin: University of Texas, 2010, 39–40.

17 E. Hadzidaki, and P. Betancourt, "A Minoan Shipwreck off Pseira Island, East Crete: Preliminary Report," *Eulimine* 4 (2005–6) 79–96. E. Hadjidaki, *The Minoan Shipwreck at Pseira, Crete*, Philadelphia: INSTAP Press, 2019.

18 D. Matsas, "Minoan Long Distance Trade: A View from the Northern Aegean," in R. Laffineur and W. D. Niemeier, eds., *Politeia I: Society and State in the Aegean Bronze Age*, Aegeaum 12, Liege: University of Liege, 1995, 235–47.

19 N. Coldstream, and G. Huxley, eds., *Kythera*, Park Ridge, NJ: Noyes Press, 1973.

20 P. Betancourt, "Middle Minoan Objects in the Near East," in E Cline and D. Harris-Cline, eds., *The Aegean and the Orient in the Second Millennium*, Aegaeum 18, Liege: University of Liege, 1998, 5–11.

21 B. Kemp and R. Merrillees, *Minoan Pottery in Second Millennium Egypt*, Mainz: Verlag Philipp von Zabern, 1980, 176–219.

22 K. Foster, "Mari and the Minoans," *Groniek* 217 (2018) 343–62.

23 J. Weingarten, "The Silver Kantharos from Gournia Reconsidered," in R. Koehl, ed., *Studies in Aegean Art and Culture*, Philadelphia: Instap Academic Press, 2016, 1–10.

24 J. Weingarten, "The Transformation of Egyptian Taweret into the Minoan Genius: A Study in Cultural Transmission in the Middle Bronze Age," *Astroms* (1991) 4 and pl. 4 (*CMS* II. 1 283). Aruz, *Marks of Distinction*, fig. 195.

25 P. Yule, *Early Cretan Seals: A Study of Chronology*, Mainz: Verlag Philipp von Zabern, 1981, 192–7. Imported NE seals include two cylinder seals of lapis lazuli, one recarved in Crete, two north Syrian cylinder seals (from Mochlos and Tylissos), and a lapis lazuli cylinder seal from Archanes.

26 V. Karageorghis et al., *Kypriaka in Crete*, Philadelphia: Instap Academic Press, 2014.

27 J. Aruz, "Syrian Seals and the Evidence of Cultural Interaction," in I. Pini and J.-C. Poursat, eds., *Corpus der Minoischen und Mykenischen Siegel, Sceaux Minoens at Myceniens, Beiheft V*, Berlin: Gebr. Mann Verlag, 1995, 1–22.

28 J.-C. Poursat and M. Loubet, "Metalurgie et contacts exterieurs a Malia (Crete) au Minoen Moyen II: Remargues sur une serie d'analyses isotopiques du plomb," in R. Laffineur and E. Greco, eds., *EMPORIA, I*, Aegaeum 25, Liege: University of Liege, 2005, 117–21.

29 M. Shaw, "Ceiling Patterns from the Tomb of Hepzefa," *AJA* 74 (1970) 25–30.

30 J. Weingarten, "Three Upheavals in Minoan Sealing Administration: Evidence for Radical Change," in T. Palaima, ed., *Aegean Seals, Sealings and Administration*, Aegaeum 5, Liege: University of Liege, 1990, 105–20.

31 P. Betancourt, "Egyptian Connections at Hagios Charalambos," in R. Laffineur and E. Greco, eds., *EMPORIA, II: Aegeans in the Central and Eastern Mediterranean*, Aegaeum 25, Liege: University of Liege, 2005, 449–54. P. Betancourt, *Hagios Charalambos: A Minoan Burial Cave in Crete*, Philadelphia: Instap Academic Press, 2014, 69–72. Six sistra were found in Agios Charalambos Cave. Other examples come from Krasi, Trapeza Cave, Agia Triada, and Mochlos.

32 Aruz, *Marks of Distinction*, lists some twelve examples in her Protopalatial chapter, 76–82.

33 Weingarten, "The Silver Kantharos from Gournia Reconsidered."

34 P. Yule, "Early and Middle Minoan Foreign Relations: The Evidence from Seals," *SIMA* 25 (1987) 161–75.

35 For Knossos, Phaistos, and Malia in this period, see Whitelaw, "The Urbanization of Prehistoric Crete."

36 V. Watrous, D. Hadzi-Vallanou, and H. Blitzer, *The Plain of Phaistos*, Monumenta Archaeologica 23, Los Angeles: Cotsen Institute of Archaeology, University of California Press, 2004, 253–83.

37 S. Chryssoulaki, "Minoan Roads and Guard Houses – War Regained," in R. Laffineur, ed., *POLEMOS: Le Contexte Guerrier en Egee a l'age du Bronze*, Aegaeum 19, Liege: University of Liege, 1999, 75–85.

38 S. Beckmann, *Domesticating Mountains in Middle Bronze Age Crete: Minoan Agricultural Landscaping in the Agios Nikolaos Region*, PhD thesis, University of Crete (Rethymnon), vols. I–II, 2012. A website for the park exists: (www.kroustas-park.gr).

39 P. Betancourt, C. Davaras, and R. Hope Simpson, eds., *The Archaeological Survey of Pseira Island, II*, Philadelphia: Instap Academic Press, 2005, 251–2.

40   See the recent summary by H. Thomas, "Cretan Hieroglyphic and Linear A," in E. Cline, ed., *The Oxford Handbook of the Bronze Age Aegean*, Oxford: Oxford University Press, 2012, 340–55 with earlier bibliography. Also, J. Younger and P. Rehak, "Review of Aegean Prehistory VII: Neopalatial, Final Palatial and Postpalatial Crete," in T. Cullen, ed., *Aegean Prehistory: A Review*, AJA Supplement 1, 2001, 422–6. J. Younger and P. Rehak, "Minoan Culture: Religion, Burial Customs, and Administration," in C. Shelmerdine, ed., *The Aegean Bronze Age*, Cambridge: Cambridge University Press, 2008, 165–85.

41   A list of studies follows. Lycian: M. Finkelberg, "The Language of Linear A: Greek, Semitic, or Anatolian?", in Robert Drews (ed.), *Greater Anatolia and the Ind-Hittite Language Family, Journal of Indo-European Studies*, Monograph 38 (2001). Greek-like: G. Nagy, "Observations on the Sign-Grouping and Vocabulary of Linear A," *AJA* 69 (1965) 295–330. Hurrian: P. van Soesbergen, *Minoan Linear A. Volume I, Hurrians and Hurrian in Minoan Crete. Part 1, Text*, Amsterdam: Brave New Books, 2016. Indo-European/Sanskrit: H. La Marle, *Linéaire A, la première écriture syllabique de Crète*, 4 vols., Paris: Geuthner, 1997–9, 2006; H. La Marle, *Introduction au linéaire A*, Paris: Geuthner, 2002; H. La Marle, *L'aventure de l'alphabet: les écritures cursives et linéaires du Proche-Orient et de l'Europe du sud-est à l'Âge du Bronze*, Paris: Geuthner, 2002; H. La Marle, *Les racines du crétois ancien et leur morphologie: communication à l'Académie des Inscriptions et Belles Lettres*, 2007. Indo-European: G. Owens, "The Structure of the Minoan Language," *Journal of Indo-European Studies* 27 (1999) 15–56.

42   The so called Parading Lions-Spiral and Border/Leaf groups. O. Krzyszkowska, *Aegean Seals*, 66–89. See J. Weingarten, "Minoan Seals and Sealings," in E. Cline, ed., *The Oxford Handbook of the Bronze Age Aegean*, Oxford: Oxford University Press, 2012, 317–39 with bibliography.

43   B. Burke, "Textiles," in Cline, *The Oxford Handbook of the Bronze Age Aegean*, 430–5.

44   S. Xanthoudides, *The Vaulted Tombs of the Mesara*, Liverpool: University of Liverpool , 1924, 88–125.

45   D. Levi, "La Tomba a Tholos di Kamilari presso a Festos," *Annuario della Scuola Archeologica di Atene* 23–4 (1961–2) 7–148.

46   J. Driessen, "Recent Developments in the Archaeology of Minoan Crete," *Pharos* 20 (2014) 75–115. Y. Hamilakis, ed., *Labyrinth Revisited: Rethinking Minoan Archaeology*, Oxford: Oxbow Books, 2002.

47   For the world system model, see A. and S. Sherratt, "From Luxuries to Commodities: the Nature of Mediterranean Bronze Age Trading Systems," in N. Gale, ed., *Bronze Age Trade in the Mediterranean*, SIMA 90 (1991) 351–86.

48   J. Cherry, "Evolution, Revolution and the Origins of Complex Society in Minoan Crete," in O. Krzyszkowska and L. Nixon, eds., *Minoan Society*, Bristol: Bristol Classical Press, 1983, 33–45. V. Watrous, "The Role of the Near East in the Rise of the Cretan Palaces," in R. Hagg and N. Marinatos, eds., *The Function of the Minoan Palaces*, Stockholm: Astroms Forlag, 1987, 65–70. C. Broodbank *An Island Archaeology of the Early Cyclades*, Cambridge: Cambridge University Press, 2000, 350–61.

49   A. Burke, "Introduction to the Levant during the Middle Bronze Age," in M. Steiner and A. Killebrew, eds., *The Oxford Handbook to the Archaeology of the Levant*, Oxford: Oxford University Press, 2014, 403–13. N. Laneri and M. Schwartz, "Southeastern Eastern Anatolia in the Middle Bronze Age," in S. Steadman and G. McMahon, eds., *The Oxford Handbook of Ancient Anatolia*, Oxford: Oxford University Press, 2011, 337–60.

50   C. Boulotis, "From Mythical Minos to the Search for Cretan Kingship," in M. Andreadaki-Vlasaki, G. Rethemiotakis, and N. Dimopoulou-Rethemiotaki, eds., *From the Land of the Labyrinth, II*, New York: Onassis Foundation, 2008, 44–55.

51   The so-called Master Impression, see E. Hallager, "The Master Impression: A Clay Sealing from the Greek-Swedish Excavations at Kastelli, Khania," SIMA 69, 1985.

52   J. Vercoutter, *L'Egypte et le monde egeen prehellenique*, Cairo: L'insitut francais de archae-ologie orientale, 1956, 64.

53 M. Helms, *Access to Origins: Affines, Ancestors and Aristocrats*, Austin: University of Texas, 1998, 38–9; 73–120.

54 A. Evans, *The Palace of Minos at Knossos, I*, New York: Biblo and Tannen 1964, 103–7.

55 L. Pernier, *Il Palazzo Minoico di festos, I*, Rome: La Libreria dello Stato, 1935. D. Levi, *Festos e la civilta minoica, I–II*, Incunabula 9, Rome: Edizioni dell' Ateneo, 1976, 1988. D. Levi, "The Recent Excavations at Phaistos," *SIMA* 11 (1961). English summary in Watrous, "Late Bronze Age Kommos," 201–3. McEnroe, *Architecture of Minoan Crete*, 44–50. P. Militello, "Emerging Authority: A Functional Analysis," in Schoep et al., *Back to the Beginning*, 236–72. S. Todaro, "The Phaistos Hills before the Palace: A Contextual Reappraisal," *Praehistorica Mediterranean* 5. Monza, Italy: Polimetrica, 2013.

56 G. Gesell, "Town, Palace, and House Cult in Minoan Crete," *SIMA* 67 (1985), 120–4.

57 E. Fiandra, "A che cosa serviano le cretule di Festos," in *Pepragmena tou B'Diethnous Kritologikou Synedriou*, Athens: Italian School of Archaeology at Athens, 1968, 383–97 and E. Fiandra, "Ancora a propsito delle cretule di Festos," *Bollettino del arte* 60 (1975) 1–25.

58 J. Weingarten, "The Sealing Structures of Minoan Crete: MM II Phaistos to the Destruction of the Palace of Knossos," *Oxford Journal of Archaeology* 5 (1986) 1–25 and Weingarten, "Three Upheavals in Minoan Sealing Administration," 105–20. For the similar looking seal deposit from Karahoyuk in Anatolia, see J. Weingarten, "Two Sealing Studies in the Middle Bronze Age. I: Karahoyuk I: Phaistos," in P. Feroli et al., eds., *Archives before Writing*, Turin: Ministero per I Beni Culturali e Ambientali, 1994, 261–95.

59 M. Relaki, "The Social Arenas of Tradition: Investigating Collective and Individual Social Strategies in the Prepalatial and Protopalatial Mesara, in Schoep et al., *Back to the Beginning*, 290–324.

60 Watrous et al., *The Plain of Phaistos*, 277–91.

61 A. Kanta and A. Tzigounaki, "The Protopalatial Multiple Sealing System: New Evidence from Monasteraki," in M. Perna, ed., *Administrative Documents in the Aegean and their Near Eastern Counterparts*, Torino: Paravia Scriptorium, 1999, 193–210.

62 J. Shaw and M. Shaw, eds., *Kommos V. The Monumental Minoan Buildings at Kommos*, Princeton: Princeton University Press, 2006. A. van de Moortel, "Kommos and Its East Mediterranean Connections in the Protopalatial Period," in P. Betancourt, M. Nelson, and H. Williams, eds., *Krinoi kai Limenes: Studies in Honor of Joseph and Maria Shaw*, Philadelphia: Instap Academic Press, 2007, 177–84.

63 H. van Effenterre, *Le palais de Malia et la cite Minoenne, I–II*, Incunabula Graeca 76, Rome: Edizioni dell'Ateneo, 1980. T. Whitelaw, "The Urbanization of Prehistoric Crete," 122–7.

64 For the Malia state: J.-C. Poursat, "Malia: Palace, State, City," in O. Krzyskowska, ed., *Cretan Offerings: Studies in Honour of Peter Warren*, BSA Studies 18 (2010), 259–68.

65 P. Betancourt, "Lasithi and the Malia–Lasithi State," in Betancourt et al., *Krinoi kai Limenes*, 209–20.

66 J.-C. Poursat, Fouilles executees a Malia. Le Quartier Mu, I–IV, (*Etudes Cretoises* 22, 26, 32–34), Paris: De Boccard, 1978–2005, J.-C. Poursat, *Guide de Malia, Le Quartier Mu*, Paris: De Boccard, 1992, and J.-C. Poursat, "The Emergence of Elite Groups at Protopalatial Malia: A Biography of Quartier Mu," in Schoep et al., *Back to the Beginning*, 177–83.

67 M. Tsipopoulou, "Before, During, After: The Architectural Phases of the Palatial Building at Petras, Siteia," in P. Betancourt et al., *Meletemata Studies in Aegean Archaeology Presented to Malcolm H. Wiener as He Enters his 65th Year*, Aegaeum 20, III, Liege: University of Liege, 1999, 848–56, and M. Tsipopoulou, "The Central Court of the Palace of Petras," in Betancourt et al., *Krinoi kai Limenes*, 749–60, and Tsipopoulou, *Petras, Siteia*.

68 M. Tsipopoulou and E. Hallager, *The Hieroglyphic Archive at Petras, Siteia*, Danish Institute at Athens Monograph 9, Aarhaus: Narayana Press, 2010.

69 D. Haggis, "The Lakkos Pottery and Middle Minoan IB Petras," in Tsipopoulou, *Petras, Siteia*, 191–201.

FIVE

THE MATURITY OF MINOAN CRETE

The Second Palace Period, 1700–1450 BC
(Middle Minoan III–Late Minoan IB)

MINOAN SOCIETY REACHED ITS MOST DEVELOPED FORM DURING THIS period, culminating in Late Minoan IA (LM IA), as is apparent in its social and political organization, level of literacy, and settlement sizes. The end of the preceding period was marked by major destructions at Knossos, Phaistos, Malia, Gournia, and many other sites[1] (Fig. 4.1). At Knossos, Phaistos, and elsewhere the palaces were rebuilt. In LM IA many Cretan towns reach their greatest size. They were the largest settlements in the Aegean. Knossos becomes a dominant kingdom on Crete and some sites, for example Galatas, Phaistos, and Agia Triada, came under its political control. Many local peak sanctuaries on the island cease in this period when their area comes under Knossian control.

Late in LM IA the Theran eruption produced severe earthquakes, clouds of ash, tephra, and seaborne pumice carried to central and eastern Crete. The physical phenomenon – earthquake, tsunami, and ash fall – and their subsequent environmental effects were quite severe.[2] The Theran ash fall, whose layer has been estimated to be 5–15 cm, contained high levels of silicate and fluoride that would have killed animals and crops, poisoned wells, and produced famine and severe social stress. Based on the direction of the winds (northwest–southeast) the eruption has been estimated to have taken place in early summer: therefore, fields of unharvested wheat, olives, and grapes would have been destroyed. The loss of a year's harvest would have produced a food crisis. The tsunami certainly hit the north coast of Crete and damaged Minoan ships at harbor and coastal sites. Extensive earthquake damage has also been noted on LM IA sites. In the succeeding LM IB period it is clear that the population of Crete had dropped. Unaffected by the Thera catastrophe, the mainland Greeks moved into this vacuum, expanding their economic contacts with the Aegean islands.

We will begin by considering several basic features of Neopalatial Minoan society, that is, its social and political organization, the evidence for literacy, the people themselves and their daily life, and finally the main archaeological sites, that is, Knossos, Malia, Agia Triada and Kommos, Galatas, Zakros, Gournia, Nirou Chani, Vathypetro, Myrtos Pyrgos, and Chalinomouri.

MINOAN SOCIETY

Social Organization

Much of the Late Minoan population was urban. LM I Knossos (Fig. 5.1) has been estimated by Whitelaw as having a population of over 40,000 people.[3] Other major settlements were also quite large, bigger than present-day villages, depending on the size of their supporting region (catchment). Some, e.g. Knossos, Zakros, Petras, Palaikastro, were situated on or near the coast at the mouth of a valley and by a river. Large settlements possessed a palace, an open area for commerce (agora), paved streets, and a wide range of houses. For example, Gournia, at about 4–5 ha in size, with a minimum population of 800–900 persons, possessed a small palace, agora, a system of cobbled streets and houses of varying sizes. Smaller settlements possessed what we call a "villa" at its center, e.g. Vathypetro and Nirou Chani. These villas functioned as miniature versions of palaces – as ceremonial and administrative centers – for their smaller regional communities. The landscape was also densely settled with hamlets of varying sizes (e.g. 2–6 houses), single farmsteads, and in the mountains, shepherds' compounds (see below. These sites were interconnected by an extensive network of trade.[4]

The architecture in and around a large town such as Knossos allows us to tentatively recognize the political/social hierarchy of Minoan Crete:

A. *Nobility.* (1) ruler/high priest, resident in the palace; (2) a small select group of nobles (perhaps a royal council) who dined in the palace and lived in mansions (Little Palace, South House [Fig. 5.2], Unexplored Mansion, Royal Villa, etc.) next to the palace, as at Knossos; (3) local officials/ governors/priests who lived in "villas" in outlying settlements, such as Archanes, Nirou Chani, and Vathypetro.

B. *Upper class.* Probably merchants who resided in large *ashlar* houses found in towns such as Palaikastro, Malia, and Mochlos.

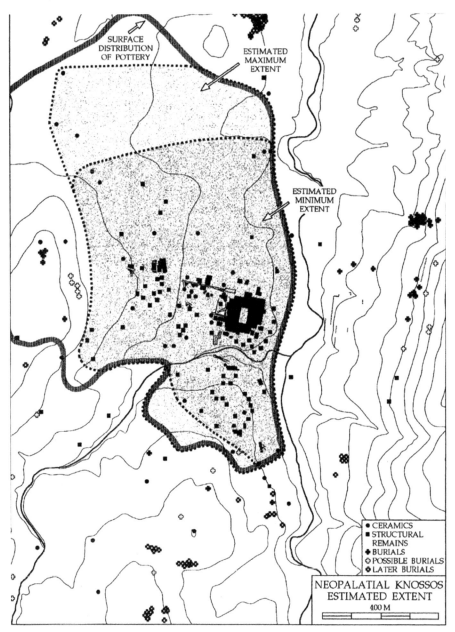

5.1 Plan of urban Knossos.
Evely et al. (1994), 96, fig. 2

    C. *Middle class*. Artisans (bronzeworkers, potters, seal carvers, masons), who lived in spacious rubble houses in towns and villages like Malia (Quartier Mu) and Gournia.

    D. *Lower class*. Farmers and shepherds who inhabited small rubble houses (e.g. Chelinomouri, Gournia, Ag, Bc) and huts (Fig. 5.4).

    E. *Slaves/serfs*. Occupying service quarters, as in Agia Triada Villa A and small one- or two-room rural farms.

5.2 South House adjacent to palace at Knossos.
Photo by the author

Burials at Knossos show the similar social hierarchy. Aristocratic tombs can also be recognized, that is, the large Temple Tomb whose plan imitates an Egyptian elite XVIII Dynasty tomb[5] and lower-class chamber tombs east of the palace along the Mavro Spilio ridge (Fig. 5.1).

Elite Minoan houses are characterized by their size and *ashlar* masonry. They possess specific types of rooms: (a) Minoan hall, (b) light well, (c) lustral basin, (d) pillar crypt, (e) pier and door partition, (f) storage/industrial wing, and (g) stairway.[6] Most Minoan houses were smaller, with a basic set of some seven rooms; these constitute 70 percent of all excavated Neopalatial houses on Crete. At a basic level, houses contained an entrance vestibule, storage areas for food and animals, workspaces for food preparation and other industries, a social center (living room), and stairs leading up to a second-floor residence.

Minoan settlements also reveal differing levels of prosperity. Houses at Palaikastro (Fig. 5.3) have an average size of 215 square meters, while those at Gournia are 80 square meters in size. Palaikastro seems to have become wealthy through sea trade, while Gournia (Fig. 5.4) was a town of artisans and shopkeepers. Within the town of Gournia some neighborhoods are made up of sizable houses (Ah, Da, De with 5–10 rooms) flanked by miniature houses along the margins (Ag, Ba, Bb, Bc, Db, Dc, with 2–4 rooms) It is tempting to see the latter as residences of a lower middle class, perhaps farmers. A similar pattern can be seen in the burials. Gournia possessed two cemeteries; a complex of stone

5.3 Plan of Palaikastro.
Cline (2010), 573, fig. 43.1

tombs built in the form a miniature house (Fig. 4.4) which produced rich finds
including a silver vase (Fig. 4.6). In another location nearby, (Sphoungaras), only
simple jar and pit burials were made. Artifacts at Gournia suggest some of the
main economic professions in the town: bronzeworkers, masons, potters, textile
weavers, and stone carvers (including seals).[7] A comparison of the houses at
Gournia with those on the rocky, waterless island of Pseira, for example, reveals
another social level: the Pseira houses are for the most part much smaller than
those at Gournia, and so probably belonged mainly to farmers, shepherds, and
seamen as opposed to artisans.[8]

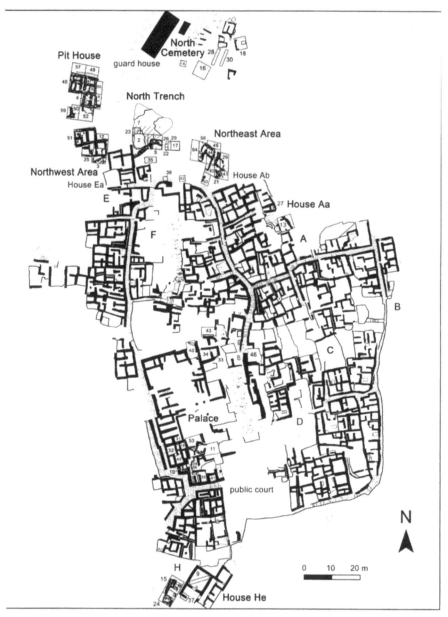

5.4 Plan of Gournia.
Plan J. McEnroe and M. Buell

One of the most important indications we possess about the nature of Minoan society comes from its literacy (see below) and seal imagery (Chapter 8). Both are so widely distributed and diverse that they imply the Minoans were culturally a middle-class society, not like Egypt or the Near East where literacy and art were largely confined to the small royal and noble sector of society.

5.5 Map of core territories of well-known Late Minoan states.
Map by Arielle Channin

Political Organization

At the beginning of the second millennium BC (MM IB) Minoan society
formed itself into large and small states (Fig. 5.5). Crete's mountainous topography of separate plains and valleys encouraged such an organization. This
political pattern was normal for much of Crete's history.[9] In the eighth century
BC, for example, Homer (*Odyssey*, xix, 172–4) speaks of ninety cities (poleis)
on the island. Larger states, such as Knossos, Phaistos, and Malia, possessed an
urban center, rural sanctuary (cave or peak sanctuary), and ideally a harbor.
Minoan state territories would have ranged in size and changed over time with
the formation of alliances and conquests, as did Classical Cretan states. Some of
these Minoan states – Knossos, Phaistos, Kydonia – were in fact also states later
in the Classical period.

Outside the larger Minoan states rural regions were headed by a local "villa"
(elite mansion) such as at Myrtos/Pyrgos and Nirou Chani (see below).
Miniature versions of the palaces, these "villas" produce evidence for an
administrative and religious function within their local area. It is possible that
communities (e.g. Vathypetro, Nirou Chani) near the large palace state of
Knossos may have had religious, familial, and/or political links with Knossos,
but the exact nature of these links remains unclear. The French excavators of
Malia believe that by LM IB their town, for example, had become a Knossian
dependency, either vassal or satellite. Other towns further from Knossos
remained politically independent.

Minoan states were competitive with one another. In Arthur Evans' ideal-
ized view, Minoan society was by nature peace loving. Subsequent archaeological exploration, for example at Gournia, Malia, and Palaikastro, has
revealed that Minoan states were protected by fortification walls and towers.
At Gournia recent work has revealed that a MM–LM I fortification system of
walls and a tower ran along the open coastline where the town was most
vulnerable.[10] Site destructions and abandonments during the Minoan period
also indicate that these states were at times actively hostile to one another.

A survey of the region of Zakros has described a series of isolated MM II–LM I buildings along natural routes. These small structures were built on defensive locations with a commanding view of the area, suggesting that they are forts guarding the routes into the local center.[11] Moreover, from the Early Minoan period onwards, Minoan graves were filled with weapons – spearheads, arrowheads, swords, and daggers, indicating that such weapons were the normal possession of men (Chapters 3 and 4). The legend of a Minoan thalassocracy (sea empire) within the Aegean (Chapter 6) is also a memory of Cretan militarism.

Literacy

Inscribed tablets and other objects (described in Chapter 4) have been found across the entire island – literacy appears to have been widespread in Minoan society.[12] A recent excavation within an urban section of the prosperous LM I town of Chania found that almost all the houses excavated were literate, using Linear A tablets. The widespread distribution of sealings on Crete points to a similar pattern of literate interconnections. Stamped sealings made by the same ring found at Knossos, Agia Triada, Sklavokambos, Zakros, and Thera indicate the scope of Knossian involvement, economic if not political. Distinctive sealings from sites show that trade connections existed between palace centers on Crete. The distribution of nodules and lookalike seals are also a record of literate agents who traveled among sites on Crete. For example, sealings indicate that the owner of a Knossian bull jumper ring sent documents (or carried tokens) to Agia Triada, Zakros, Sklavokambos, and Gournia; a second agent from Zakros went to Agia Triada, Sklavokambos, and Knossos.[13] With the rise in population and prosperity in Neopalatial Crete, the number of middle-class seal owners also increased.

THE MINOAN PEOPLE AND DAILY ACTIVITIES

What about the Minoan people themselves? DNA studies have linked the Minoan population to the early farmers of western Anatolia as well as to the Near East. A recent study has also linked the DNA of Cretans to the populations of Eastern Europe and the Middle East.[14] Physical anthropology tells us the average height for males was 167 cm. For women it was 154 cm. The average life expectancy for men during the Minoan Palatial Period was thirty-five years, for women twenty-eight years.[15] The lower rate for women is probably linked to the hazards of childbirth.

What did the Minoans eat? Their diet included wheat, barley, legumes, dried fruits such as figs, nuts, olives and olive oil, grapes, flax (used for oil, as well as to make clothes, ropes, and nets), pulses (dried seeds of plants), cheeses, eggs, milk, honey, and wine. Animal husbandry was important: livestock consisted of sheep and goats, as well as pigs and cattle. Fishing produced diverse seafood: shellfish, snails, mullet, sea bass, sole, mackerel, octopus, tunny, lobster, crab, sea perch, and wrasse.[16] Men hunted birds, deer, and boar. Some of these activities are depicted on seals (see Chapter 8). Women gathered wild plants such as *horta* (still gathered today). Herbs and spices, whose pre-Greek names indicate their prehistoric use, included thyme, sage, marjoram, and mint. The natural landscape of the island provided a rich harvest. Plants recently identified from Neopalatial Gournia are: olive, caper, fig, pear, carob, juniper, lentisk, poplar, oak, buckthorn, and pine.[17] Aromatic oils and herbal medicines were an important Minoan export.

In Minoan society it is clear that women played elevated roles. This might be expected since the dominant deities in Minoan religion were female (Chapter 7). Fierce male figures like the Near Eastern Teshub, Baal, and Reshep, as well as the later Greek Zeus and Poseidon, are conspicuous by their absence in Minoan art. Mortal women also figure conspicuously in Minoan art, as dancers and worshippers, and in processions and communal gatherings. Female figures, identified as priestesses, are prominent in religious scenes.[18] It has been suggested by some scholars that the throne in the palace at Knossos was occupied by a priestess. Within the household, middle-class women made clothes for the family and valuable textiles for export.[19] Wool was spun, and woven on vertical wooden looms. Women wore elaborate long skirts and above, on formal occasions, a bodice-like a dirndl. Facial cosmetics were common. Figurines and frescoes show that Minoan clothing and textiles were intricately decorated with various designs and motifs drawn from nature. Women's dresses were decorated with spirals, panels, curved lines and flowers, rosettes, and birds. Clothing was important in Minoan society – it defined one's social status. Both men and women often wore their hair long. Jewelry for both sexes was elaborate and diverse: hairpins, earrings, bracelets, anklets, and necklaces of beads; common materials were gold, silver, amethyst, rock crystal, cornelian, and faience.[20]

Men had their own ideal role in society. The standard dress for men was a short kilt, folded underneath like a pair of shorts. The male torso was left open. Public athletic games, such as bull leaping, gave young males the opportunity to display courage, skill, and physical ability. Seals and ritual vases depict these events – in bull leaping, boxing, running, hunting wild animals, and fighting in war.[21] Spectators (Grandstand Fresco) and an architectural background (Boxer Rhyton) to these scenes suggest that these ceremonies were theatrical in nature, prefiguring later Greek examples such as the Olympic Games. Minoan males were brought up to be able to protect society. Grave finds indicate that weapons were a basic possession for males. Many of the weapons

5.6 Dancers and central woman playing a lyre,
Palaikastro.
SM. HMC/TAP. BSA

found in LH I Mycenaean graves, for example the shaft graves at Mycenae and elsewhere, are Cretan types or of Minoan manufacture.

The Minoans enjoyed communal activities throughout the year, at the palaces, sanctuaries, courts, and in houses. They sang and played music at these gatherings: ritual ceremonies, banquets, dances (Fig. 5.6), athletic contests, processions (Harvester Vase, Fig. 8.15), and funerals (Fig. 7.29), many of which were accompanied by music. Scenes of cult activities and votives from shrines depict dancers, which imply music and probably song. We can recognize several Minoan musical instruments – lyres, flutes, triton and reed trumpets, and rattles (*sistra*)[22] – and Minoan music would have included hymns, songs, and poetry (Chapter 8), as they did later during the Greek historical period.

MINOAN SETTLEMENTS

Towns

We turn now to the large Minoan settlements on Crete – the best preserved are Knossos, Malia, Agia Triada, Palaikastro, and Zakros. Each section below provides a short physical introduction to the site, its buildings, and their functions.

Knossos

The Minoan settlement at Knossos was situated in a broad valley flanked on the east by the Kaireatos River.[23] On the hill slope east of the river was the cemetery of Mavro Spilio (Fig. 5.1). Approaching the palace from the south, a traveler would come upon Evans' so-called Caravanserai on the south slope of the Gypsades hill. One entrance of the Caravanserai held a stone bath where one could wash one's feet. East of this was a pavilion that led inside to a paved court, painted with a fresco frieze running around three sides of the walls.[24] Continuing toward the palace, the visitor crossed the Vlychia stream on a massive bridge (Fig. 5.7) supported by four piers and corbelled arches.

At the center of the town was the palace (Fig. 5.8), the largest on Crete. Over a hectare in size, it possessed a central court, flanked around its sides by sets of rooms with different functions. The religious practices of the palace are discussed in Chapter 7. Approaching the impressive *ashlar* western façade of the

5.7 Monumental elevated walkway ("viaduct") leading from the south to the Knossos palace. Evans (1927), 97, fig. 46

palace, one reached a wide paved court supplied with raised walkways and trees. Following a walkway, the visitor entered the palace stepping into a porch with frescoes of a running bull, and then passing into a long corridor. Following the corridor one continued into an open propylon and upstairs to the second floor of the palace. At the northwest corner of the palace, a paved city street approaching it ended in a benched area where an audience could view a procession coming up the street. From there a causeway led past a sunken lustral basin for visitors to clean themselves and into a large pillared hall, which in turn opened to the south to a corridor that led to the central court, flanked by a veranda overhead painted with a charging bull.

At the west side of the central court was an antechamber leading into the frescoed Throne Room (Fig. 5.9) and lustral chamber. The Throne Room had benches around its sides and a stone throne, flanked in LM II/III by a wall fresco depicting fantastic beasts – hawk-headed lions (griffins) – set in an exotic landscape of palm trees and papyri. South of the Throne Room, a wide exterior staircase led from the court to the second floor. Further south, within the west wing, was a complex of some eight small rooms used to store religious objects. West of these rooms, running along the entire west façade of the palace, was a long row of twenty-one storerooms that held large storage jars

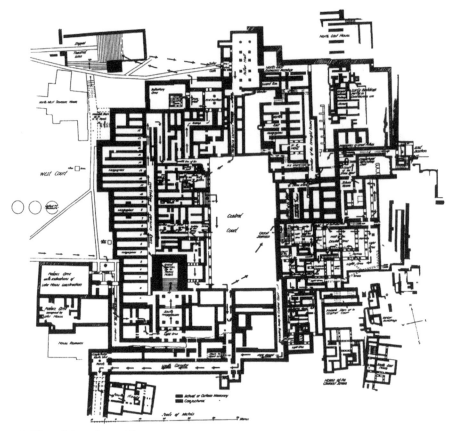

5.8 Plan of the palace at Knossos.
Marinatos (1993), 41, fig. 34

5.9 Reconstruction of the Throne Room, palace at Knossos.
Marinatos (1993), fig. 80

(*pithoi*) filled with agricultural produce. It has been estimated that these storerooms could have held over 400 *pithoi* holding some 231,000 liters of food. The rooms on the second floor were probably used for receptions, cult ceremonies, and administrative purposes.

The area east and north of the central court seems to have held workshops for metal, pottery, and stone objects. Further south a grand staircase led down two stories to two residential suites. The larger suite, which Evans called the King's Megaron, consists of two main rooms, lit at one end by a light well and opening out through a porch on to an open terrace, probably a garden. The smaller, adjacent suite of rooms, called the Queen's Megaron, had a well-lit main room with a porch and light wells as well as a bathroom and toilet connected to drains.

Malia

Excavation at Malia on the north coast of the island (Fig. 5.5) gives us an idea of the overall extent of a Minoan town and its cemetery, estimated to have reached a size of 40–60 hectares by the MM II period.[25] Burials and a fortification wall ran along the coast. Blocks of houses around the palace were connected by a system of streets (Fig. 5.10). The LM I palace held storage wings on the east and west of the central court, a throne room ("Loggia"), a second-floor banquet hall, residential quarters, ivory and stone vase workshops, eight circular grain silos on its southwest corner, and a shrine room (Room XVIII:1; see Chapter 7).

Phaistos, Agia Triada, and Kommos

In the southern Mesara Plain, the sites of Phaistos, Agia Triada, and Kommos (Fig. 5.5) were at different times functionally linked, as center and port. They will be considered together. The Neopalatial town of Phaistos was roughly 40–50 hectares in size with an estimated population of over 3,000 people.[26] In MM III the palace at Phaistos was remodeled: storage and work areas went out of use or were reused for industrial functions. Later in MM III the Phaistos palace was destroyed by earthquake and partially left in ruins until LM IB when it was rebuilt. The new palace possessed a monumental west façade (67), a storage wing (26), a central court (40), three residential suites (50, 63, and 77–9), a northeast court with potters' workshops and a potter's kiln (90). Finds from the LM IB palace point to a public ceremonial role, but not an administrative one.

Elegant new buildings constructed at Agia Triada (Fig. 5.11) in LM I suggest that the ruling authority was transferred there from Phaistos. Extensive Linear A tablets from Agia Triada give us an idea of its role as a

5.10 Plan, central part of Malia town.
Krzyszkowska (2010), fig. 25.1

regional center. The site was dominated by the Royal Villa (two houses, called here Villas A and B) around two sides of an upper court (Piazzale dei Sacelli).[27] The Royal Villa, remodeled in LM IB, shows Knossian features in its architecture and frescoes. Several sealings were made by gold rings linked to Knossos.

Villa A forms the west and northwest border of the upper court. It consists of three groups of rooms: servants' quarters (rooms south of rooms 3 and 4), a residential complex (rooms 3, 4, 11, 12, 13, 51, 55), and a north storage wing (rooms 7, 8, 17, 57–9, 61). The servants' sector held living quarters, a large kitchen (45) with built-in mortars, a pantry (15) with stacks of domestic vases, and a storage room (16) with *pithoi* and bronze tools. The main residence held a suite with a cubicle (4a, a bedroom), a hall with an inner room (4), a lightwell (49), and two outer halls (12 and 3). Food was consumed there. This suite, with a bench in Room 4 capable of sitting seventeen persons, looks like a formal hall to receive visitors. To the north of the main suite is another set of rooms: a

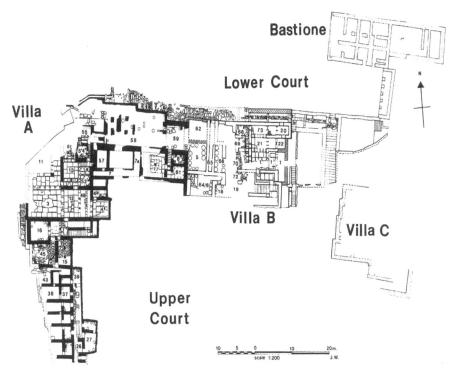

5.11 Plan of LM I Agia Triada.
Watrous (1984), 124, ill. 1. Plan author

bedroom (14) with a fresco (Chapter 8), a possible bathroom (52), and Room
13. A stairway from Room 14 leads to a light well (54), a staircase to the upper
floor, and to Room 55. Rooms 54 and 55 had an archival and administrative
function. On the south wall of Room 54 was painted a list of numerical
fractions in geometrical progression (1, 1.5, 2.25, 3.37, etc.) that could be used
to figure out 95 percent of a given total, a sign of the building's administrative
function. Finds (bronze tools, elegant carved stone and painted clay vases,
Linear A tablets and sealings, loomweights, figurines, and miniature double
axes), fallen from the upper floor indicate that this upper story was used as
storage for valuables, an archive/scribal area, and weaving, and had a domestic
shrine. The north storage wing held the well-known nineteen copper ingots
from Cyprus and rooms with *pithoi*. Villa B possessed store rooms (18, 66, and
64/6) with *pithoi*, and a possible service quarter (69, 70, 72, 19) that produced
bronze tools and Linear A tablets.

North of Villas A and B was a lower open court (Rampa del Mare) running
from a stoa on the east westwards toward the sea. Next to the stoa was a large
building (Bastione) that looks like a storage warehouse with a residence on the
upper floor. This sector of Agia Triada seems to have been concerned with
commerce. Six stone bases for double axes from the upper floor of Villa A may

have been displayed in the upper court as signs of the religious nature of the spot.

Two archives (from the Royal Villa and a house, Casa del Lebete, in the village to the north) produced 147 Linear A tablets, some 1,000 *cretulae*, and a smaller number of sealings and *roundels* that provide a detailed glimpse into the functions of the Agia Triada complex.[28] At least sixteen different scribal hands have been recognized at Agia Triada. These Linear A tablets record the production and shipment (using the ideogram of a ship) of textiles, olive oil, olives, figs, wine, and grain. The main subject of the tablets was agricultural products (barley, wheat, figs, olive oil, and wine) and lists of men as well as wool, cloth, bulls, sheep, goats (by gender), and vases.[29] Commodity lists are often recorded as totals or deficits indicating quota assessments by the administration. On other tablets commodities are simply recorded, perhaps as taxation from land directly owned by the local authority. A total of about 2,788 people are recorded, although overlaps are possible. Groups of men are probably workers, including bronze smiths, who were provided with food rations of wheat, figs, and wine.

One exceptional tablet (HT 102) lists 1,060 units of wheat, which, using Linear B values, would amount to 101,760 liters or about the capacity of 180 *pithoi*. Oil occurs frequently on the tablets. An oil tablet (HT 2) record that Kiretana, a place name, contributed 101 units (2,828 liters) of oil that would fill 4–5 *pithoi*. Livestock cited are sheep, goat, and pigs. Some seventy-seven sheep occur on the tablets. One tablet (HT 30.45.5) mentions a hundred oxen, perhaps in relation to plowing or transportation of produce. Wool and textiles occur on a tablet (HT 24) from the southwest part of the Royal Villa where loomweights were found, suggesting the production of textiles there. Tablets HT 31 and 39 list vases – conical cups, *pithoi*, and cookpots. The territory controlled by Agia Triada may have been local, but one *pithos* is inscribed with the name *su-ki-ri-ta*, which is probably the Minoan site of Sybrita in the Amari valley to the north.

These tablets, however, do not give us a complete picture of the local Linear A administration. Local and long-distance trade is not described in the documents. Written receipts, indicated by surviving roundels from nonadministrative individuals taking goods, were not preserved.[30] Flat-based *nodules*, sealed records written on perishable parchment or leather, are also missing. Hanging *nodules*, found at the site originally would have been tied to small valuable objects (bags, chests, etc.) or to written documents, point to other missing objects.

A short distance to the west of Phaistos and Agia Triada, the coastal site of Kommos served as the region's harbor facility and port town in the MM III–LM IA period.[31] The monumental harbor complex, Building T (Fig. 5.12), at the site is separated from the town to the north by a paved road that led to

5.12 Reconstruction of Building T at the harbor complex of Kommos.
Shaw and Shaw (2006), frontispiece

Phaistos. Building T had a huge orthostate *ashlar* wall facing the road. A central pebble-paved court (39 × 28 m) had fresco-painted rooms and a stoa on the north and south sides facing on to the court. Rooms in the stoa included space 42, which may have been a pantry, and the frescoed Room 19, a dining room; Room 25 held storage jars. Along the east side of the court were eight long galleries (4 m wide) probably used to house and repair ships during the winter months when sailing was impossible. The complex was open to the sea on the west. On its northwest corner a massive threshold led into an administrative office. As a port, Kommos received pottery imported from mainland Greece, Anatolia, Egypt, Cyclades, the Levant, and Cyprus.[32]

After a late LM IA destruction, Kommos lost its character as an important port. The main complex (J/T) was converted into a collection of separate industrial areas. The north stoa became a metalworking area, and a large pottery kiln was built in the central court.

Galatas

The settlement of Galatas is located in the Pediada, the elevated spine of central Crete. The settlement, about 25 hectares in size with an estimated population of *c*.3,000, sits on a dominant hill (Galatiani Kephala) overlooking a well-watered valley to its west. A small palatial state in the Neopalatial period,

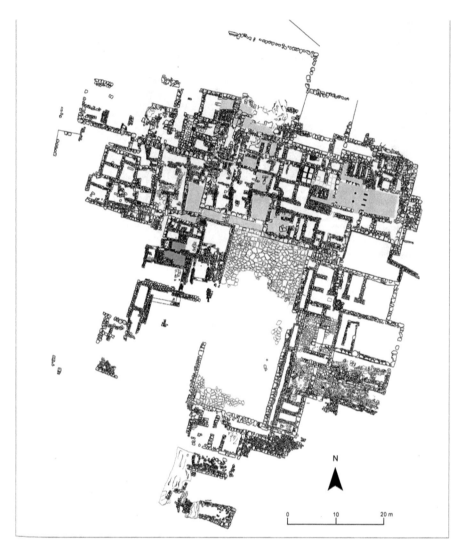

N

0   10   20 m

5.13 Plan of palace at Galatas.
Watrous et al. (2017), fig. 13

the settlement possessed a palace that was relatively recently excavated by
George Rethemiotakis.[33]

A palace (Fig. 5.13) was constructed at Galatas in MM IIIA. It was connected
to the town by a road that encircled the building with open walkways leading
directly to its entrances. Built of fine *ashlar* masonry the exterior walls enclosed
four wings surrounding an open paved central court. On its west, the building
possessed a second paved court. The interior façade of the west wing takes the
form of a stoa that shelters the entrance to the north wing. The east wing
possessed a hearth, kitchen area, storage magazines, groups of pithoi, and
dining rooms. Built of especially monumental and fine masonry, the two-
story north wing advertised its status as a center of power: it possessed a

residential Minoan hall, light well, and small *stoa*. Both the east and north wings were used for banquets. The poorly preserved west wing held a hearth, a paved veranda facing the court, and some magazines. The south wing was for religious ceremonies: it consisted of a self-contained building with a massive tripartite wall facing south as a background to a theatrical-like court with a *baetyl* set on a stone platform. Immediately north of the palace was a court with an altar and stone-lined pit for libations. In early LM IA the palace was destroyed and only partly rebuilt. Feasting continued but on a limited scale. Finally, in later LM IA, an earthquake destroyed the entire building. In the town of Galatas six houses, variously spanning the MM IB–LM IIIA period, have been excavated.

Palaikastro

In far eastern Crete, the plan of Palaikastro provides a picture of a prosperous, literate Minoan town.[34] The settlement sits on a natural bay and harbor sheltered from the north winds by the hill of Kastro (Fig. 1.5). After an earthquake destruction in MM IIIA, the town (Fig. 5.3) was rebuilt and expanded, perhaps to a size of 30 hectares. A main street ran through the town with three smaller streets branching off it at right angles. Flanked by *ashlar* houses, the paved streets were broad and provided with drains. Houses were organized in blocks, each block having one large house with elite *ashlar* masonry and an open central colonnaded court. Floors were often paved with brightly colored slabs and painted plaster. Houses in the town produced evidence for the production of textiles, pottery, and metal and ivory objects. A house shrine is described in Chapter 7.

The town was destroyed in later LM IA by the Theran eruption, and then again by fire in LM IB. The rebuilt site was finally abandoned after 1300 BC.

Zakros

At the far east of the island (Fig. 5.5), the town of Zakros sat in a small coastal bay with a protected harbor, facing due east across the sea to Syria.[35] The LM IA town resembled Thera in its wealth gained from seafaring. One day many years ago I came to Zakros. The north wind (*melemi*) had been blowing fiercely for days. I sat at the one tavern on the beach. At the next table were four seamen from two fishing boats from the Cyclades. They had come two days previously to the protected bay at Zakros to seek shelter from the wind. They had been drinking for two days: they were incoherent, but very happy. It struck me that similar events must also have taken place in Bronze Age Zakros.

A visitor to Zakros landing at the harbor in antiquity would have entered the town by a cobbled street (Harbor Road) from the sea. The town of Zakros consisted of stone-paved streets and blocks each with 2–4 houses. Houses at Zakros were built of large rough limestone blocks, and are square in plan, with a simple hall, storage, and industrial rooms and upstairs living quarters, much different from the elegant *ashlar* residences at nearby Palaikastro. In LM IA, the houses at Zakros have produced some signs of prosperity, for example a gold-covered bull rhyton, a faience jug, many stone vases, wine presses, loom-weights, and storage pithoi. Building E (Oblique Building), for example, had a wine press and seven pithoi. The Tower Building produced a rhyton carved with dolphins in relief. On the Harbor Road, the House of the Niches produced evidence (molds and crucibles) of metal production. House A near the palace held a wine press; Room 7 contained many metal objects, a Marine-style *rhyton* and 500 local sealings used by the palace bureaucracy, and a Linear A tablet and roundel. South of the Harbor Road, House Zita held a faience workshop.

The small palace (Fig. 5.14) at Zakros is especially valuable today because it was not reoccupied after its LM IB destruction, so when excavated its rooms produced all of their original finds undisturbed, giving us a vivid picture of the functions of a Minoan palace. A visitor would have entered the palace through a corridor (LXIX) that opens out on to the cobbled northeast court (LXIII) provided with underground drains to prevent flooding. In LM IB it served as a work area for making stone vases. At its southwest corner a narrow passage led into the central court. Faced with *ashlar* masonry on its west side, the central court divided the east and west wings of the palace and had a small altar at its north end. On its north side a raised porch (XXXIV) overlooked the court. The east wing of the palace was residential: it consisted of two suites (XXXVI, XXXVII) with light wells. A veranda facing the central court ran along its west side providing privacy. On its south side it was crowned with horns of consecration. To the east the residence opened out on to a private walled garden (LXII) with a pool, similar to those found on wealthy estates in Egypt.

The west wing was the largest and most important complex of the palace. Running along the west side of the central court were large rooms (XXVIII, XXIX) and a light well. Their floors were painted with panels at the center imitating stone slabs. Around the edges of the rooms we can reconstruct wooden couches for feasting (described in Chapter 7) like that of a Classical period symposium. Light was provided by windows and the open light well.

Immediately west and accessible to the four rooms was a sunken lustral basin (XXIV) and a small shrine room (XXIII). The first room had steps leading down to the floor. A ledge on its south wall probably held vases. An elegant stone *rhyton* (for perfumed oil?) found in a level above the floor may have been used there. The second room had a small niche supplied with a shelf that functioned as an altar to hold statuettes of the gods. A bench facing the altar held *rhyta* and pedestaled cups for libations. A pantry (XIII) next to this shrine

5.14 Plan of palace at Kato Zakros.
Marinatos (1993), 44, fig. 37

room had wooden shelves holding painted cups, jugs, a bridge-spouted jar, and
decorated stirrup jars. South of the pantry was an archives room (XVI) with
shelves on its south wall for holding sealed boxes where Linear A inscribed
tablets were stored. Only thirteen tablets, accounts with lists, survived. A small
open court ran along the west façade of the palace. A workshop (XVII–XXI) for
dyeing textiles was a later addition to the southwest corner of the palace.

The rooms of the northwest sector of the palace functioned for the storage,
preparation, and consumption of food. Six rooms at the north end of the west
wing were storerooms (III–VIII) with forty-six *pithoi* and many smaller pots.
One *pithos* had the Linear A sign for wine inscribed on it. A space beneath the
stairway held two bronze saws. To the east at the northwest corner of the central
court a large six-columned room (XXXII), where cooking pots and many
animal bones were found, was a kitchen. Two adjacent rooms (L, LI) to the
east with a hearth, cooking pots, and a mortar were service rooms. A staircase to
the east led upstairs to a large banquet hall where meals were served.

At the south end of the central court was a separate two-story wing of seven rooms (XLII–XLVIII). One room (XLII) contained storage vessels, cooking pots, and clay kitchen utensils. Most of the rooms held evidence of workshop activity, a porphyry block, bronze sheets, vases, fragments, and cores of ivory, rock crystal, and faience, stone, and bronze tools. These rooms were workshops for making stone vases, perfumes, or incense, faience objects (shells and a figurine), and bronze vases for elites and export. Residential rooms on the second floor produced fine pottery, stone weights, and evidence of food preparation and weaving.

Many objects were found fallen from the second floor of the west wing, including two large saws, more than 500 fine ware vases painted in the Marine style and with reeds, palms, lilies, flowers, spirals, garlands, and festoons. Shapes included amphoras, jugs, bridge-spouted jars, hole-mouth jars, *rhyta*, a fruit stand, and cups. There were also stone vases, a double ax, a few tools, and loomweights. Room XV produced many amphoras, cups, jugs, three tripod offering tables, six bronze ingots, three large elephant tusks, and incense burners. From upstairs two swords with gold rivets, a bronze cauldron, and bronze sheets were found. Objects fallen into the lustral basin included more than thirty braziers, small stone vases, a saw, and stone and metal tools. A saw, axes, picks, needles, pins, chisels, knives, and drills were found in the upper levels of Room XII. Rooms XXV–VII yielded faience and ivory inlays, and a stone *rhyton*. The storeroom produced stone vases and a silver jug. Fallen into XXVIII–9 were a bull's head *rhyton*, another *rhyton* with a scene of a peak sanctuary (Fig. 7.5), two saws, chisels, knives, two ostrich eggs, wooden boxes, a *rhyton*, a sealing depicting a woman kneeling before a *baetyl*, and a stone cup. The upper floor seems to have been a storage space for fine ware vases, cult paraphernalia, tools, and valuable raw materials.

Zakros suffered destructions in LM IA (Theran eruption) and in LM IB (by fire). After the Thera eruption the town lost much of its prosperity. In LM IB many houses were abandoned and industrial production was concentrated in the palace. The town had a limited reoccupation in LM III.

Gournia

The town of Gournia sits on a low ridge (Fig. 5.15) looking down on the Bay of Mirabello. It was excavated between 1901 and 1904 by the American archaeologist Harriet Boyd.

Because the entire center of the town has been revealed by excavation, a visitor to the site can see what a Late Bronze Age town actually looked like. Some sixty houses line a circuit of cobbled streets (Fig. 5.4), running around the ridge, enclosing a large town square and a central administrative building, the so-called "palace."[36] The physical arrangement between the structures

5.15 View of Gournia from the east.
Photo Janet Spiller

reflects the basic social organization of the town. The full town may have had a
population of *c.*800 people. Gournia was a town of shopkeepers and artisans.
They produced manufactured goods, mainly metal tools and weapons and clay
vases (Figs. 5.16 and 5.17) that were sold to locals in return for agricultural
produce and exported abroad. From the finds in the excavated houses, seventeen households have been identified as metalworking shops and eighteen as
pottery workshops. Sixteen pottery kilns have been identified in the recent
excavations of the site. The town traded coarse and fine ware pottery, known
as Mirabello ware, to a wide variety of places in Crete and the Aegean. Wine
also was an important export (Fig. 5.18).[37] In turn, Gournia was able to import
tin (via Syria), copper and obsidian (from Cyprus), lead and gold, and silver
(from Anatolia).

   The Neopalatial palace was built with storerooms (3–9, 11, 23), a bathroom
(28), and a hall (20) opening through a porch to an open court (21). Fresco
fragments of a swallow and figure of eight shield probably came from the
second floor. Finds from the palace – a bronze figurine, an amulet, a saw,
lamps, a stone *rhyton*, an ax, a bronze jug, clay jugs, a cup, a wine press, sixteen
pithoi, a Linear A tablet listing a distribution of items, sealstones, sealings and
nodules, a piece of a tin ingot, a Knossian sealing, a roundel with Linear A,
some seventy pieces of scrap metal, and masses of cups – are evidence of the
palace's role as a community center for administration, manufacture, and cult

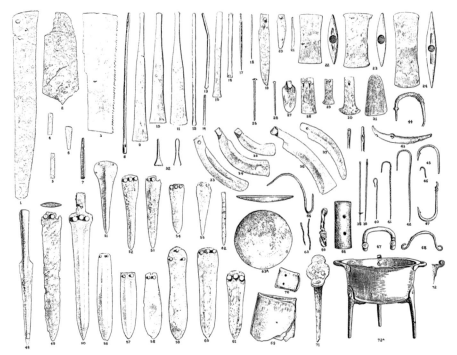

5.16 Metal objects produced at Gournia.
Boyd-Hawes et al. (2014), pl. IV

5.17 Pottery produced at Gournia.
Boyd-Hawes et al. (2014), pl. VII

5.18 Vat found in situ in House D for pressing grapes to make wine. Hole below spout would
have held a jar.
Boyd-Hawes et al. (2014), 27, fig. 11

ceremonies. In LM IB an *ashlar* wing was added along the south of the
building. One room (13) was filled with the remains of cult offerings whose
date and pumice seems a response to the Thera eruption. Recent excavation
has found masses of conical cups in the central court, indicating that groups
met there on ceremonial occasions.

Many of the houses in the town are preserved up to a height of 1.8 m. Built
of light gray limestone blocks set in orderly courses the foundations of these
houses line the streets, Houses varied in size and shape, and usually possessed
6–10 small rooms on the ground floor. Finds from these rooms tell us they
were used for the storage of produce, cooking, and as pens for small animals
(goats and sheep). Staircases led to an upper floor where the occupants lived
and worked. Walls were often plastered with reddish clay. House Ck is typical
(Fig. 5.19). One enters this house from the street by three steps up to a door
threshold leading into a central space (1) framed by two side rooms (2 and 3)
and two staircases. In total the house had six rooms or spaces on the ground
floor. The walls of these rooms are of stone and still visible today; the walls
upper floor were of mudbrick and no longer preserved. The back of the house
had three narrow parallel rooms (4–6) facing out on to a corridor: this area
would have been used for the storage (in *pithoi*) and preparation of food
(grinding grains and legumes, cutting meat) and cooking over a hearth. The
two staircases led to an upper, residential floor with bedrooms and a space for
communal activities (meals and worship). At the front of the house the two
rooms are provided with a *gourna*, a large stone trough set into the floor, used
for animals (e.g. goat, sheep) and kept in the house at nighttime for safety.

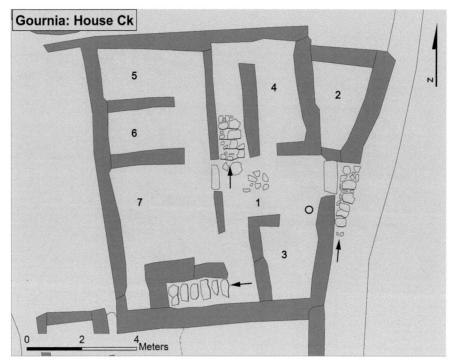

5.19 House Ck.
Plan by M. Buell

Gournia had two cemeteries, one on the ridge immediately north of the town and another further north in the valley (see Chapter 4). A cobbled street ran from the town down to the coast where a large two-galleried shipshed provided covered shelter for ships during the winter (Fig. 5.20). The promontory on the shore functioned as a wharf: it was cut with steps leading down to the water's edge and had rope holes for mooring ships. The coast was protected by fortification walls.

As a local center of production of metal, stone, and ceramic, Gournia traded with the many regional villages, hamlets, and farms surrounding it (Fig. 5.21).

VILLAGE-SIZED SETTLEMENTS

Most village-sized settlements are only known through excavation of their main building, misleadingly named "villas." They are interesting nevertheless because they provide insight into the role of the leading local household within a rural settlement.

Nirou Chani

A Neopalatial village existed at Nirou Chani on the coast east of Amnissos (Fig. 5.22).[38] Nirou Chani, shows us what the residence of a leader of a

5.20 The shoreline at Gournia, with fortification wall and shipshed (Shore House). Settlement visible at left.
Reconstruction J. McEnroe

parochial region outside the palaces was like and suggests the cultic functions of his office. A massive wall on the adjacent shoreline may have been part of a harbor installation. The magnificent *ashlar* "villa" possessing gypsum dados and wall frescoes had a civic and religious function. The main hall (2) of this large *ashlar* building faced through a pier and door partition directly out on to a paved open courtyard, suggesting the building's official status. At the south edge of the court was a large stepped altar and stone *horns of consecration*. On the north side of the building were storage magazines (24, 25) with *pithoi*. Storerooms 17 and 18 contained stacks of 40–50 clay offering tables, an indication of the building's cultic function. Staircases in rooms 10 and 10a led to the upper floor. In the center of the building a small private room (12) with a bench faced on to a light well (13). Corridor 4 led back to Room 7 that held a vase containing pigment, cups with pumice, and four gigantic ceremonial double axes, meant to be used outside in the courtyard. Room 14 had four stone lamps. Spaces 26–30 were bins filled with carbonized beans and chickpeas.

Vathypetro

Vathypetro was a village-sized settlement in a small valley 3 km south of Archanes.[39] The central mansion ("villa") was an impressive *ashlar* two-story

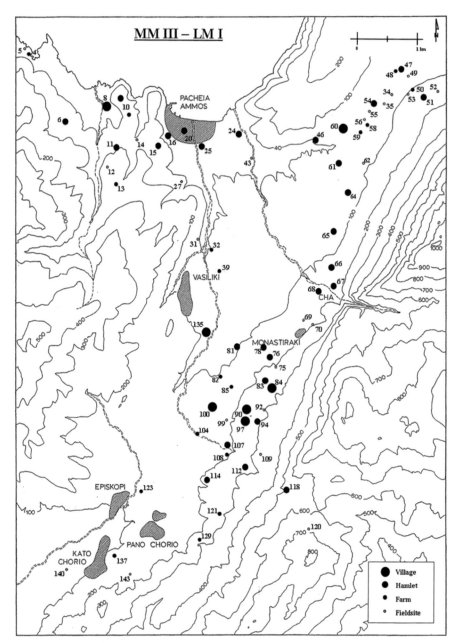

5.21 Regional settlements around Gournia.
Plan author

residence (Fig. 5.23) within the settlement, situated to have a magnificent view
of the Cretan landscape to the south. The site is worth a visit for that reason
alone. The main hall faces eastward through a columned portico out on to a
court with a built tripartite shrine with a central niche flanked by two stands
(Fig. 5.24). The alignment of the northern niche is oriented so the sun would

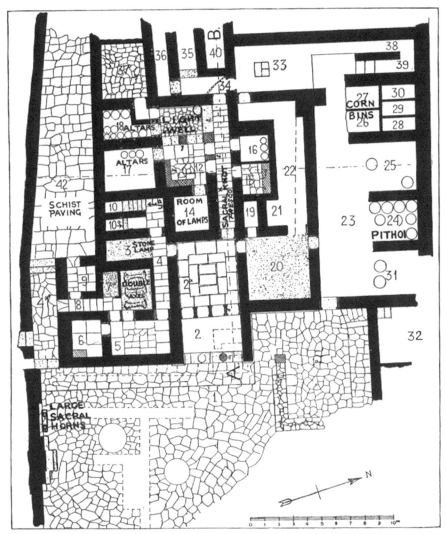

5.22 Plan of Nirou Chani.
Graham (1962), fig. 31

have risen above it on the spring and autumn equinox.[40] A stone horns of consecration was found in the court in front of the tripartite shrine. Entered from the west, the building had a paved road that led to a court (35) and columned storeroom (40). Like the palaces, the villa has evidence of ample storage for attached workers, wealth (gold leaf), administration (three sealstones), and cult ceremony (including a bronze figurine). The building possessed a Minoan hall, frescoed walls, large storerooms with *pithoi*, a lustral basin (17), and a light well. Second-floor rooms looked out to the west and south for their views.

The villa was destroyed in LM IA. Later, in the LM IB period, the architecture of the villa was much modified. Vathypetro seems to have lost

5.23 Plan, Vathypetro "villa."
Driessen and Macdonald (1997), fig. 7.39

5.24 Tripartite shrine in courtyard at Vathypetro.
Photo by the author

its LM IA political/ritual function and was converted into an industrial site. In this period there is much preserved evidence of kitchen work, of pottery production (kiln), a wine press, oil pressing, and agricultural storage. A later Minoan wine-pressing installation is visible next to the villa.

MYRTOS/PYRGOS

The site is located on the top of a high conical hill just east of the village of Myrtos on the south coast. Myrtos/Pyrgos provides an excellent example of a rural "villa," the residence of the local ruler.[41] The main building sits on the very peak of the hill facing directly south out on to the Libyan Sea below. (Fig. 5.25). Behind it were a cistern and ossuary (a chamber for human bones). Below it to the north were the rubble-built houses of the village. Two stories high, the villa fronts on to a gray flagstone courtyard that runs along the very edge of the cliff. A stone staircase led up from the town to the courtyard and villa. On the east side of the court was a covered veranda that provided shade. A line of specially selected reddish purple stones form a border to its entrance.

The west section of the façade has a veranda with two columns and a pillar. An entrance corridor from the façade led into the villa, past a light well and

5.25 Reconstruction of house at Myrtos/Pyrgos.
Evely (1999) 173

bench, and up a staircase to the second floor whose white gypsum wall contrasts with the purple stone floor. At the rear of the building, Room 1 was a pantry full of domestic vases. The second floor would have possessed living rooms, a veranda, and an administrative space that produced clay sealings and Linear A tablets, one mentioning ninety units of wine. A domestic shrine above Room 12 produced two triton shells, four tubular stands, and a model triton of pink faience. The two-story east wing of the house held storerooms (8 and 9) on the ground floor with *pithoi* and jars holding barley and oil; the second floor produced two Cycladic jugs. From the back of the second floor one looks up the Myrtos River valley to the Dictaean mountain range in the distance.

FARMS

The countryside of Minoan Crete was dotted with hamlets and farmhouses. A visitor walking along rural roads and paths would have passed by fields and terraces holding crops and vineyards. Ravines and streambeds often had a dam to prevent erosion and create a standing water source. Groups of small clay beehives, found on archaeological surveys, were a common feature in fields and on slopes. Minoan farms harvested the crops described above. Small gardens near houses were planted with fruits and vegetables. The mountains were intensively settled with small seasonal pastoral sites, field walls, and paths.[42] Sites (Fig. 4.8) there consist of one or two stone huts surrounded with enclosure walls that acted as pens for sheep and goats. The shepherds there produced wool, meat, cheese, and honey. Loomweights are missing on these sites, so, as today (Chapter 1), the animals must have been driven down to the lowland villages where they were sheared, and where women wove the wool.

The excavated LM IB farmhouse of Chalinomouri near Mochlos provides us with an example of a Minoan farm.[43] The one-story house had six rooms with earth floors. Walls were of large rough stones at the base and mudbrick above; the roof was of schist slabs laid on beams of olive, oak, pine, and maple. A yard with a bench and an oven were used for cooking food (sheep/goat and pig bones were found) and making bread. One of the bones found there had been gnawed by a dog. Another yard sat on a terrace on the west side of the house. It was also used for cooking and held a pottery kiln later converted into an oven. Terrace walls may have acted as corrals to pen animals.

Inside the farmhouse Room 6 was used for food preparation, cooking, eating, and weaving. It had a hearth and a stone platform with four benches. A basin with a drain used to press grapes for wine sat on the platform. The area produced cooking and other domestic vases, olive stones, bones of sheep/goat, pig, fish, deer, limpet shells, and loomweights. Room 3 was also used to prepare food, eat, and work. It had two stone benches, and several stone floor slabs (work surfaces) by the benches. The room contained traces of cooking fires on the floor, many limpet shells, some animal bones, cooking pots and dishes, a scored basin, jars, an amphora, and a *rhyton*. A stone drill guide is evidence of stone vase production. Room 2, closed with a wooden door, was for storage. It produced *pithoi*, jars (eight buried in the floor), grain and nuts, pieces of emery, quartz granules, a stone drill, and a stone pounder. Room 1 had a pivot for a wooden door (it may have been a bedroom). A stand, triton shell, and bowl probably belonged to a small domestic shrine. Rooms 4 and 5 were storage rooms.

Chelinomouri held remains of farming: cereals, almonds, grapes, olives, and figs as well as of hunting (deer and hare bones), and fishing (bones). The farm possessed herds of sheep or goats, and pigs, which provided a main source of meat, milk, cheese, and wool. The small size of the storage facilities resembles a farmer's normal surplus – enough for a hedge against a bad year. There are no signs that the farm was producing a surplus of any kind required by an external authority: the family seems to have been economically independent. The family at Chelinomouri could have sold their animals and part-time crafts, such as stone vases, and perhaps textiles, to buy needed goods, such as pottery from Mochlos and metal tools from Gournia

THE END OF THE SECOND PALACE PERIOD

The massive eruption of Thera late in LM IA brought the era of Minoan prosperity to an end. Following that, some 150 years later in LM IB the mainland Greeks invaded Crete, destroying many sites across the island and bringing the Second Palace Period to an end.

NOTES

1   J. Driessen and C. Macdonald, *The Troubled Island*, Aegaeum 17, Liege: University of Liege, 1997, 11–118.
2   R. Blong, "The Possible Effects of Santorini Tephra Fall on Minoan Crete," in C. Doumas, ed., *Thera and the Aegean World, II*, Athens: The Thera Foundation, 1980, 217–26. In *The Troubled Island*, 85–105, Macdonald and Driessen discuss the effects of the Santorini earthquake/eruption and abandonment of sites, and list around forty sites with LM IA earthquake destruction – see 37–8, fig. 4.2. The changed economic status of houses is discussed at 52–4.
3   T. Whitelaw, "Recognizing Polities in Prehistoric Crete," M. Relaki and Y. Papadatos, eds., *From the Foundation to the Legacy of Minoan Society*, Sheffield Studies in Aegean Archaeology, Oxford: Oxbow Books, 2018, 210–55.
4   J. Weingarten, "Late Bronze Age Trade within Crete," in N. Gale, ed., *Bronze Age Trade in the Mediterranean*, SIMA 40 (1991) 303–24. For example, the owner of a Knossian bull jumper ring sent documents or carried tokens to Agia Triada, Zakros, Sklavokambos, and Gournia.
5   W. Graham, *The Palaces of Crete*, Princeton: Princeton University Press, 1962. J. McEnroe, "A Typology of Minoan Neopalatial Houses," *AJA* 86 (1982) 3–17, and more recently,

J. McEnroe, *Architecture of Minoan Crete*, Austin: University of Texas, 2010, 93–116. See also, C. Palyvou, *Daidalos at Work*, Philadelphia: INSTAP Academic Press, 2018.

6   A. Evans, *The Palace of Minos, IV*, New York: Biblo and Tannen, 1964, 965–70; 973–83; 990–9.

7   The bronze vessels and tools are illustrated in H. Boyd-Hawes et al., *Gournia, Vasiliki and Other Prehistoric Sites on the Isthmus of Hierapetra, Crete*, Philadelphia: INSTAP Academic Press, 2014 (reprint), 33–4, pl. IV. See also the Minoan bronze vases, in L. Marangou, ed., *Minoan and Greek Civilization from the Mitsotakis Collection*, Athens: Goulandris Foundation, 1992, 228, fig. 13. A summary of economic activities at Gournia appears in V. Watrous and A. Heimroth, "Household Industries of Late Minoan IB Gournia and the Socioeconomic Status of the Town," in *ΣΤΕΓΑ: The Archaeology of Houses and Households in Ancient Crete, Hesperia* Supplement 44 (2011) 199–212.

8   J. McEnroe, *Pseira V: The Architecture of Pseira*, Philadelphia: Instap Academic Press, 2001.

9   For the Classical period, forty-two autonomous cities are known to have minted their own coins. See J.-N. Svoronos, *Numismatique de la Crete Ancienne*, Bonn: Rudolf Habelt, 1972. M. Guarducci's *Inscriptiones Creticae*, vols. 1–4, Rome: Libreria dello Stato, 1935–50, lists sixty-four literate settlements in Crete that produced Greek inscriptions.

10   V. Watrous, "The Harbor Complex at Gournia," *AJA* 116 (2012) 521–42.

11   S. Chryssoulaki, "Minoan Roads and Guard Houses – War Regained,' in R. Laffineur, ed., *Polemos: Le Contexte Guerrier en Egee a l'age du Bronze*, Aegaeum 19, Liege: University of Liege 1999, 75–85.

12   L. Godart and J.-P. Olivier, *Recueil des inscriptions en Lineaire*, vols. I–5, *Etudes Cretoises* 21, Paris: Librairie Orientaliste Paul Geuthner, 1976–1985. E. Hallager, "The Minoan Roundel and Other Sealed Documents in the Neopalatial Linear A Administration, I–II" Aegaeum 14, Liege: University of Liege, 1996, 39–77. I. Schoep, "Context and Chronology of Linear A Administrative Documents," *Aegean Archaeology* 2 (1995) 29–64.

13   Weingarten (supra n 4), "Late Bronze Age Trade within Crete," 303–24.

14   L. Martinez et al., "Middle Eastern and European DNAS Lineages Characterize Populations from Eastern crete," *American Journal of Physical Anthropology* 137 (2008) 213–23. Reported in *Nature*, August 2017.

15   P. McGeorge, "Health and Diet in Minoan Times," in R. Jones and H. Catling, eds., *New Aspects of Archaeological Science in Greece*, BSA Occasional Paper 3 (1988) 47–54; P. McGeorge, "Morbidity and Medical Practice in Minoan Crete," in M. Andreadaki-Vlazaki, G. Rethemiotakis, and N. Dimopoulou-Rethemiotaki, eds., *From the Land of the Labyrinth, Minoan Crete, II*, New York: Onassis Foundation, 2008, 118–27.

16   M. Andreadaki-Vlazaki, "Resources for Life: From Food to Aromatics," in Andreadaki-Vlazaki et al., *From the Land of the Labyrinth*, 110–17.

17   E. Margaritis, personal communication.

18   N. Marinatos, *Minoan Religion: Ritual, Image and Symbol*, Columbia: University of South Carolina Press, 1993, 127–46.

19   E. Barber, *Prehistoric Textiles*, Princeton: Princeton University Press, 1991, 311–30. B.R., Jones, *Ariadne's Threads: The Construction and Significance of Clothes in the Aegean Bronze Age*, Aegaeum 38, Liege: Peeters, 2015. See also the articles in M.-L. Nosch and R. Laffineur, eds., *Kosmos: Jewellery, Adornment and Textiles in the Aegean Bronze Age*, Aegeaum 33, Liege: Peeters, 2012.

20   For Minoan jewelry see Nosch and Laffineur, *Kosmos*, 345–799.

21   N. Marinatos, "The Ideals of Manhood in Minoan Crete," in L. Morgan, ed., *Aegean Wall Painting, BSA Studies* 13 (2005) 149–58.

22   J. Younger, *Music in the Aegean Bronze Age*, Jonsered: Astroms Forlag, 1998.

23   A. Evans, *The Palace of Minos, II*, vol. 1, New York: Biblio and Tannen, 1964, 93–140.

24   Maria Shaw, "The Painted Pavilion of the 'Caravanserai' at Knoss," in L. Morgan, ed., *Aegean Wall Painting: A Tribute to Mark Cameron*, 2005, 91–112. Evans, *The Palace of Minos, II*, vol. 1, 109–16 and color frontispiece.

25   J.-C. Poursat, "Malia: Palace, State, City," in O. Krzyszkowska, ed., *Cretan Offerings, BSA* Studies 18 (2010) 259–68. J. Driessen, "Malia," in E. Cline, ed., *The Oxford Handbook of The Aegean Bronze Age*, Oxford: Oxford University Press, 2010, 556–70.

26   V. Watrous, D. Hadzi-Vallianou, and H. Blitzer, *The Plain of Phaistos*, Monumenta Archaeologica 23, Los Angeles: Cotsen Institute of Archaeology, University of California Press, 2004, 277–98.

27   V. Watrous, "Ayia Triada: A New Perspective on the Minoan Villa," *AJA* 88 (1984) 123–35, and V. La Rosa, "La Villa Royale de Haghia Triada," in R. Hagg, ed., *The Function of the Minoan Villa*, Stockholm: Astroms Forlag, 1997, 79–89.

28   R. Palmer, "Linear A Commodities: A Comparison of Resources," in R. Laffineur and W.-D. Niemeier, eds., *Politeia: Society and State in the Aegean Bronze Age*, Aegeum 12, Liege: University of Liege, 1995, 133–56.

29   I. Schoep, "The Administration of Neopalatial Crete," *Minos* Supplement 17 (2002) 175–99.

30   E. Hallager, *The Minoan Roundel and Other Sealed Documents in the Neopalatial Linear A Administration, I–II*, Aegaeum 14, Liege: University of Liege, 1996, 39–77. For the port of Knossos, see N. Dimopoulou, "The Neopalatial Cemetery of the Knossian Harbor Town at Poros: Mortuary Behavior and Social Ranking," in *Eliten in der Bronzezeit*, Mainz: Verlag der Romisch-Germanisches Zentral Museums and Rudolf Halbet Verlag, 1999, 27–36.

31   J. Shaw and M. Shaw, *Kommos V: The Monumental Minoan Buildings at Kommos*, Princeton: Princeton University Press, 2006.

32   V. Watrous, *Kommos III: The Late Bronze Age Pottery*, Princeton: Princeton University Press, 1992, and J. Rutter, *House X at Kommos, II, The Pottery*, Philadelphia: Instap Academic Press, 2017.

33   V. Watrous, G. Rethemiotakis et al., *The Galatas Survey*, Philadelphia: Instap Academic Press, 2017. For the palace, see Rethemiotakis' summary, 51–4.

34   J. Driessen, A. MacGillivray, and H. Sackett, eds., "Excavations at Palaikastro in East Crete 1902–2002, A Centenary Exhibit," *BSA* (2002) 5–6. See *Archaeological Reports* (62) for 2015–16, 11–12. for recent work at the site.

35   N. Platon, *Zakros: The Discovery of a Lost Palace of Ancient Crete*, New York: Charles Scribner's Sons, 1971. L. Platon, "Kato Zakros," in E. Cline, ed., *The Bronze Age Aegean*, Oxford: Oxford University Press, 2010, 509–17.

36   Boyd-Hawes et al., *Gournia, Vasiliki and Other Prehistoric Sites*. V. Watrous et al., "Excavations at Gournia, 2010–2012," *Hesperia* 84 (2015) 397–465. V. Watrous and A. Heimroth, "Household Industries of Late Minoan IB Gournia and the Socioeconomic Status of the Town," in *ΣΤΕΓΑ: The Archaeology of Houses and Households in Ancient Crete*, *Hesperia* Supplement 44 (2011), 199–212. M. Buell and J. McEnroe, "Community Building/Building Community at Gournia," in Q. Letesson and C. Knappett, eds., *Minoan Architecture and Urbanism*, Oxford: Oxford University Press, 2017, 204–27.

37   In her annual report to the Gournia Project, the palaeobotanist Dr. Evi Margarites has reported that seeds of grapes are especially numerous in the Gournia floral material. The Minoan terraces along the coast north of the town may well have been vineyards. Some of the coarse ware exported pottery may also have contained wine.

38   Xanthoudides' excavation of Nirou Chani is usefully discussed in Driessen and Macdonald, *The Troubled Island*, 178–80.

39   Marinatos' excavations between 1949 and 1956 are summarized in W. Myers, E. Myers, and G. Cadogan, *The Aerial Atlas of Ancient Crete*, Berkeley: University of California Press, 1992, 282–5, and Driessen and Macdonald, *The Troubled Island*, 176–8. See also I. Driessen and I. Sakellarakis, "The Vathypetro Complex: Some Observations on Its Architectural History and Function," in R. Hagg, ed., *The Function of the Minoan Villa*, Stockholm: Astroms Forlag, 1997, 63–78.

40 Observed by Dr. Clark Reynolds and reported in Driessen and Sakellarakis, *The Troubled Island*.

41 G. Cadogan, "Pyrgos, Crete, 1970–1977," *Archaeological Reports* 24 (1977–8) 70–84.

42 S. Beckmann, *Domesticating Mountains in Middle Bronze Age Crete: Minoan Agricultural Landscaping in the Agios Nikolaos Region, Volumes I–II*, PhD thesis, University of Rethymnon, 2012.

43 J. Soles, *Mochlos IA, Period III. Neopalatial Settlement on the Coast: The Artisans' Quarter and the Farmhouse at Chalinomouri*. Philadelphia: Instap Press, 2013, 103–34. See also a farm at Malia, described briefly by O. Pelon, "Maison D'Hagia Varvara et Architecture Domestique a Mallia," *BCH* 90 (1966) 552–85.

SIX

MINOAN OVERSEAS CONNECTIONS DURING THE SECOND PALACE PERIOD (1700–1450 BC)

Minos was the oldest of those who we know possessed a navy and he dominated most of what is now called the Greek Sea. He ruled the Cycladic islands and was the first to colonize most, after he drove out the Carians and established his own sons in them as sovereigns.

Thucydides, I. 4. 1

In the Second Palace (Neopalatial) Period Cretan society became powerful (see epigraph), wealthy, and cosmopolitan. This chapter discusses three topics that made this development possible: maritime trade, cultural influences, and artistic interconnections.

MINOAN INTERCONNECTIONS IN THE AEGEAN: THE THALASSOCRACY OF MINOS?

During the Neopalatial period (1700–1420 BC) Minoan overseas trade and cultural expansion in the Aegean increased greatly.[1] Cretan ships brought trade goods and cultural items across the entire Aegean and further east, to Egypt, Anatolia, and the Levant. Within the Aegean, Minoan pottery and objects have been found at Telos, Kasos, Karpathos, Kos, Kalymnos, Samos, Ios, Miletos, Iasos, Didyma, Lemnos, Cesme (Baglarasi), and Troy, to name a few. More than pottery was exported from Crete. Religious ideas spread: Minoan peak sanctuaries were established on many Aegean sites, for example Kythera, Rhodes, and Kea. Other possible peak sanctuaries include Mikri

Vigla on Naxos in Melos, Karpathos, Telos, Kythnos, Aegina, Miletos, and Iasos.[2] On Rhodes a peak sanctuary on Mount Phileremos (for Trianta) from LM IA to LM IIIA–B.[3] Cretan interactions may have been backed by force: Minoan society at this time possessed a military side to it. "Warrior burials" are known at Poros, the harbor of Knossos, in Cretan tombs, and the Archalochori Cave which produced masses of bronze swords and daggers.[4]

At this time, Cretan interaction with Aegean settlements varied from site to site. Let us to look at some specific examples. Nearest of the Cycladic islands to Crete (Fig. 6.1), Thera seem to have avidly assimilated Minoan culture. At the beginning of the Late Bronze Age, Minoan cultural features become pervasive in the Akrotiri settlement on Thera. Minoan clay and stone vases first start to arrive in significant numbers as early as MM III.[5] Drinking, pouring, and storage vases begin to arrive in large numbers in MM IIIA, suggesting perhaps a new Minoan table practice. The architecture at Akrotiri was a mixture of a few local features and many borrowed from Crete, such as *ashlar* masonry, pier and door partitions, indented external facades, the use of columns, and lustral basins. The buildings at Thera were reorganized to include new open areas probably related to new (Minoan) practices. Most importantly, the scenes/themes of Theran wall paintings reveal a cultural ideology that closely resembles that of Minoan Crete. For example, scenes of visitations to a peak

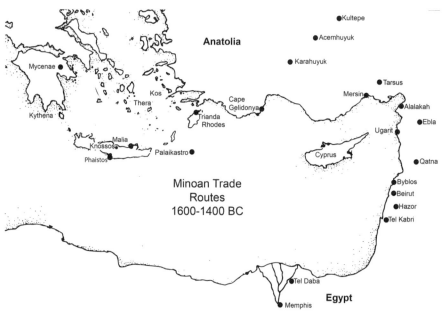

6.1 Map of the eastern Mediterranean.
Plan by Leslie Smith

sanctuary on Thera (probably located on top of Mount Profitis Ilias) point to adaption of a Minoan religious practice. Theran household shrines are also furnished with Minoan cult items, such as offering tables, animal *rhyta*, conical cups, shells, horns of consecration, and lustral basins.

The Therans also absorbed Minoan administrative and commercial practices: Linear A was written on local tablets and vases and stamped sealings began to be used. The wheel for making pottery and the Minoan system of textiles production (with disk-shaped loomweights for an upright loom) were adopted. These innovations may have made the Therans more competitive in Aegean trade. It is important to remember, however, that the local Cycladic nature of pottery found in Theran houses indicates that the Theran population consisted of local islanders, not Cretans.

The island of Kythera (Fig. 6.1) provides a different scenario of Cretan interaction. Minoan pottery began to reach Kythera in EM II. Based on the pottery found there, the main settlement at Kastri was a Minoan colony from MM I to LM IB. Burials there are typically Minoan.[6] The Minoan settlement at Kastri established a peak sanctuary(MM IB–LM) at Agios Georgios.[7] Excavation on the sanctuary produced typical Minoan ritual offerings: a miniature clay horns of consecration, murex shells, figurines (many in bronze) of animals, worshippers, jewelry, cups, *rhyta*, jugs, stone vases, libation tables, a lamp, and a ladle inscribed *da-ma-te* (to Demeter?) with Linear A, and figurines of worshippers and animals (bird, bull, scorpion). These objects have parallels at Mount Jouktas and other peak sanctuaries on Crete. Adorant figurines raise their right hand to their forehead, hands on or crossed on breast as on Crete. Votive offerings include cut-outs of a torso, hand, or feet as on Crete. Bronze objects included weapons, a bronze double ax, and ingot fragments. Lakonian stones such as basalt and porphyry were types found imported to Crete.

Miletos (Fig. 6.1) on the Anatolian coast also appears to have been colonized by Cretans. Minoan pottery here began to reach Middle Bronze Age Miletos (III), but by Miletos IV (LM I) almost all (95 percent) of the pottery is of Minoan character: the pottery consists of Cretan shapes, for example conical cups, bowls, *amphoras*, and fireboxes (holders for spits), indicating that the settlement had been colonized by Cretans. The Minoan weight system and writing (Linear A) was introduced at the same time.[8] Evidence for Minoan religious practice also appears: Minoan-type offering tables and three major storage buildings were built around a courtyard with altars, recalling the palatial organization of a Minoan palace. This picture of Minoans settled at Miletos is corroborated by the later Greek historian Ephoros of Kyme who records the tradition that Miletos was founded by Sarpedon, a brother of King Minos, who brought settlers from Crete.[9]

Another possible type of Minoan–Aegean interaction is suggested by sites that exhibit signs of destruction followed by the subsequent construction of a large Minoan-type house in the center of the settlement. These have been interpreted as "Minoan govern colonies."[10] Agia Eirene on Kea, or Phylakopi on Melos, are possible examples. The offshore island of Kea, for example, was crucial for Minoan connections to important metal sources in nearby Attica, which may explain its tumultuous history. Kea was a metal-working center: cupellation of silver and copper working from Lavrion were found across the entire site. At the beginning of period V (MM II/III), the fortification wall at Agia Irini on Kea was strengthened, but the settlement and wall were violently destroyed by fire soon after.[11] New buildings of period V were laid on earlier remains. Imported Minoan pottery (and a drop off in mainland pottery) point to increased relations with Crete. Linear A, the Minoan system of measurement, Minoan-type vases, and Minoan miniature frescoes were introduced to the town in period V. Monumental House A, built in Late Cycladic I, was the most important house in the town, and possessed Minoan features such as a light well and bathrooms. Next to House A, the Middle Cycladic temple acquired Minoan cult paraphernalia (statuettes and votives) in early LM IA. A rural shrine, established in MC III/LC I at Troullos above the town, resembles a Minoan peak sanctuary: it produced stone libation bowls, a bronze figurine, Minoan offering tables, and a ladle.[12] In Late Cycladic I Agia Irini seems to have been a Minoan colony that was forcibly established.

Later Greek tradition strengthens this interpretation. For Kea the native Kean Bacchylides (I. 113–23) wrote:

> On the third day warlike Minos came, bringing fifty ships with gleaming sterns and a company of Cretans. By the grace of Zeus who grants glory, he took the low-girded maiden Dexithea, and left half of his contingent-soldiers. He allotted the craggy land to them and sailed to the lovely city of Knossos. After nine months the fair-haired maiden Dexithea bore Euxanthos to rule over the celebrated island of Keos.

On the Minoan route to Kea and Attica, the site of Phylakopi on the island of Melos also experienced violence at this time. It was destroyed at the end of phase II (MM III). Following that, in phase III (LM IA–B) a fortification wall was constructed, much Minoan pottery was imported, and a large mansion was built that used Linear A. These events may also suggest a forceful Cretan acquisition of the island.

Minoan influence on other Aegean sites, however, took other forms. Some sites produce selective aspects of Minoan culture (imported Minoan pottery, writing, measurement, weaving, local ceramic imitations, cooking habits, and

burial practices) while others only have imported Minoan pottery. In the first
instance, Minoan customs may have been attractive to local elites who were
motivated to acquire and display fashionable possessions. Some fresco scenes,
for example, found in Cycladic houses have close parallels with Cretan
scenes, and may have been displayed as a sign of the owner's elite knowledge
in the way that upper-class Roman houses c.100 BC–100 AD were decorated
with scenes taken from Greek literature. In other cases, Minoan practices
may have been attractive because they were technologically and commer-
cially beneficial to locals. Imitation of Minoan ceramic style, for example,
may have made their sale of local pottery more competitive. Minoan loomweights, that is, the adoption of Minoan weaving technology (vertical
looms), could have helped increased textile specialization and export. Some
Aegean islanders probably welcomed their alliance and the Minoan cultural
and economic benefits.

What was the impetus for Minoan expansion? Most agree that Minoan
trade across the Aegean was primarily driven by the Cretan need for
metals.[13] The island of Crete is metal-poor, yet massive amounts of metal
are known from Cretan sites at this time. Several of the islands, from
Melos to Keos (Fig. 1.2), that produced much Minoan pottery form a
route (dubbed the "Western String") that leads from Crete along the
western side of the Cyclades to Lavrion in Attica, a source of silver and
lead for the Minoans. A parallel "Eastern String" of heavily Minoanized
sites on Kasos, Karpathos, Rhodes, Kos, Samos, Knidos, and Iasos led to
Miletos on the Anatolian coast that was connected with the Assyrian
centers like Kultepe and Acemhoyuk where Near Eastern products were
available. Minoans also set up a trading post in the northern Aegean on
Samothrace as a stepping stone to the metal-rich region of Mount
Pangeion to the north.[14] With the acquisition of metal from these sources,
Crete became the primary Aegean center for the production of finished
metal objects, such as weapons, tools, and vases for Cycladic and
Mycenaean sites.

INTERNATIONAL RELATIONS: EGYPT AND THE LEVANT

At this time Crete also entered the larger economic network of the eastern
Mediterranean.[15] Minoan vases were exported to Anatolia, Cyprus, Egypt,
and the Levant (Fig. 6.1). In the Levant, Late Minoan IB vases (Fig. 6.2)
have been found near Megiddo, Kamid-el-Loz, Gezer, Lachish, and
Alalakh[16] Relations with Cyprus were particularly close. So many
Minoan vases have been found at the Cypriote site of Tomba tou
Skourou that it has been interpreted as a Minoan emporium, motivated

6.2 Middle Minoan vases exported to the Near East.
Smith (1966), fig. 20

by Minoan interest in Cypriote copper. In turn, the Cypriotes fashioned a local script derived from Linear A. Masses of Minoan pottery was exported to Egypt.[17] The amounts of Cypriote, Anatolian, Levantine, and Egyptian pottery imported to Crete are equally impressive. Cypriote pottery has been found at Zakros, Kommos, Malia, Gournia, and Pseira.[18] Canaanite jars reached Zakros, Kommos, Pyrgos/Myrtos, and Pseira. At Kommos on the south coast storage jars from the Levantine coast, containing oil and resin, and from Egypt begin to arrive in LM IB.[19]

Cretan international connections are also apparent in the many Near Eastern objects found on Crete. Egyptian objects imported to Crete are numerous: faience and stone vases at Knossos, Agia Triada, Phaistos, Zakros, Palaikastro, and Pyrgos, an amulet at Pyrgos, a scarab at Knossos, a seal (Amenophis III) at Chania, and an ivory figurine at Malia.[20] An Egyptian alabaster vase from Knossos with the cartouche of Khyan may have been a gift from the Hyksos pharaoh of Avaris. Levantine imports to Crete in this period include a seal at Poros and at Tylissos.[21] Egyptian stones – jasper, hematite, cornelian, and amethyst – were imported as raw materials for Cretan jewelry. More than 130 Minoan seals found on Crete have been identified as having been made from Near Eastern stones.[22] Egyptian stone vases were brought to Crete, at Knossos (Isopata Tomb), Malia, Zakros, and Agia Triada, and were often reworked to local tastes. Copper ingots and elephant tusks found in the Zakros palace vividly illustrate Cretan interest in the Near East. A tablet from

6.3 Minoan tribute bearers from Keftiu, Tomb of Senmut, Egypt.
Evans (1927), fig. 470

6.4 Minoan designs on tomb fresco from Malkata, Thebes.
Karetsou et al. (2001), 294, number 289a 3. MMA 11.215.451. MMA

6.5 Bull leaping on fresco from Tell Da'ba, Egypt.
Aruz (2013), 193, fig. 8

Mari mentions a Cretan purchasing tin at Ugarit.[23] These objects indicate that the Cretan interest in the Near East was primarily as a source of raw materials such as tin, bronze, semi-precious stones, and ivory.

Aside from pottery, what did the Minoans export in return for these goods? The Egyptians knew the Cretans as the Keftiu, inhabitants of "islands in the middle of the sea" or "of the islands in the middle of the Great green (sea)." Processions of Keftiu on Egyptian wall paintings (Fig. 6.3) depict them arriving at the royal court in Thebes carrying bolts of cloth and elaborate metal vases.[24] Keftiu are also shown bringing objects from Syria such as elephant tusks, silver or gold, and lapis. The annals of Tutmosis III mention ships of the Keftiu loaded with poles, masts, and trees headed for Egypt.[25] The Syrian King Zimri-Lim sent a gift of Kaphtorite (Cretan) cloth to Hammurabi.[26] Minoan production of decorated textiles, as revealed in many purple dye workshops on Crete, was certainly important. Decorated Cretan textiles were traded to Egypt, since several Egyptian tombs are painted with Minoan textile designs.[27] A Mari tablet mentions a Kaptarite inlaid metal weapon. Cretan imports mentioned in Egyptian texts include oil, probably wine, medicinal plants, textiles, vases, and luxury items.[28]

Minoan artists also traveled to Egypt and Syria on commission to make fresco paintings for royal patrons.[29] Minoan frescoes were prized by Eastern rulers as a means to display their international status. A myth of Ugarit

6.5 (cont.)

mentions that the goddess Anat sends a messenger to Kaphtor (Crete) to bring back the god of handicrafts, Kothar wa-Khasis, to build and decorate a palace for Baal. Minoan artists painted or helped local artists paint royal palaces in the Near East, at Tell Daba (Avaris) in Egypt, and Alalakh and Tel Kabri in the Levant.[30] At Malkata, the palace of Amenhotep III has frescoes done in the local dry plaster technique depicting Minoan motifs – a field of spirals and bucrania, and fragments of marbling and a rocky landscape (Fig. 6.4). At Tell Da'aba on the Nile delta there are two fresco scenes directly derived from Minoan art; bull leapers and grapplers in a rocky landscape as well as a Minoan labyrinth-like frieze with a half-rosette and triglyph dado (Fig. 6.5).[31] At the palace at Alalakh wall dados in true Minoan (wet) fresco technique imitate stone veining (as at Knossos), clumps of white reeds against a red background, and a row of trees with green leaves and twigs on a red ground. At Tel Kabri the palace floor was painted in Minoan fashion with red lines defining squares of imitation alabaster and sprays of iris blossoms. Other fragments come from scenes depicting the sea, swallows, boats, and city architecture similar to the Theran Fleet fresco.

This artistic exchange of imagery worked both ways. Near Eastern motifs are also found in Minoan art. Sealings depict: a dragon (Agia Triada), a lion-headed eagle (Zakros and Agia Triada), a goat-man, and griffins flanking a central papyrus (Agia Triada).[32] Minoan male figures wearing robes and carrying a Syrian ax are a motif used by rulers and elites in the Near East.[33] The Egyptian papyrus also appears on Cretan seals and beads.

NOTES

1   Much has been written on this subject, see R. Hagg and N. Marinatos, eds., *The Minoan Thalassocracy*, Stockholm: Astroms Forlag, 1984; C. Macdonald, E. Hallager, and W.-D. Niemeier, eds., *The Minoans in the Central, Eastern and Northern Aegean – New Evidence*, Athens: Monographs of the Danish Institute at Athens, vol. 8, 2009. For Italy, see B. P. Hallager, "Crete and Italy in the Late Bronze III Period," *AJA* 89 (1985) 293, and E. Cline, *Sailing the Wine-Dark Sea: International Trade and the Late Bronze Age Aegean*, BAR International Series 591 (1994) 78.

2   W.-D. Niemeier, "The End of the Minoan Thalassocracy," in R. Hagg and N. Marinatos, eds., *The Minoan Thalassocracy*, Aegaeum 32, Liege: University of Liege, 1984, 205–15. N. Gale, ed., "Bronze Age Trade in the Mediterranean," *SIMA* 90 (1991) 327–34. Macdonald et al., *The Minoans*. For the types of Minoan ships, M. Wedde, "Aegean Bronze Age Ship Imagery," in R. Laffineur and L. Basch, eds., *Thalassa: L'Egee Prehistorique et la Mer*, Aegaeum 7, Liege: University of Liege, 1991, 73–94.

3   T. Marketou, "Ialysos and Its Neighboring Areas in the MBA and LB I Periods: A Chance for Peace," in Macdonald et al., *The Minoans*, 73–97.

4   N. Di Cairo: Hellenic mopoulou, "The Neopalatial Cemetery of the Knossian Harbor-Town at Poros: Mortuary Behavior and Social Ranking," in *Eliten in der Bronzezeit*, Mainz: Verlag der Romisch-Germanisches Zentral Museums and Rudolf Halbet Verlag, 1999, 27–36.

5   I. Nikolapoulou "'Beware Cretans Bearing Gifts': Tracing the Origins of Minoan Influence at Akrotiri, Thera," in Macdonald et al., *The Minoans*, 31–40.

6   J. Coldstream and G. Huxley, *Kythera*, Park Ridge, NJ: Noyes Press, 1973. C. Broodbank and E. Kiriatzi, "The First "Minoans" of Kythers Revisited: Technology, Demograohy and Landscape in the Prepalatial Aegean," AJA 111 (2007) 241–74.

7   Y. Sakellarakis, "Minoan Religious Influence in the Aegean: The Case of Kythera," *BSA* 91 (1996) 81–99. G. Sakellarakis, *Κυθερα: Ο Αγιος Γεωργος στον βουνο*, Athens: Ammos, 2013, 3–166. Γ. Σακελλαράκης, "Βιβλιοθήκη της εν Αθήναις Αρχαιολογικής Εταιρείας αρ. 287," in *Κύθηρα Ο Άγιος Γεώργιος στο Βουνό Μινωική Λατρεία-Νεότεροι Χρόνο*. Αθήνα: Η εν Αθήναις Αρχαιολογική Εταιρεία.

8   W.-D. Niemeier, "Minoanisation versus Minoan Thalassocracy –An Introduction," in Macdonald et al., *The Minoans*, 11–30, and P. Warren, "Final Summing Up," in Macdonald et al., *The Minoans*, 263–5.

9   Recorded in Herodotus, I, 173. Strabo, XIV, 1.6.

10 K. Branigan, "Minoan Colonialism," *BSA* 76 (1981) 23–33. See also C. Broodbank, "Minoanization," *Proceedings of the Prehistoric Society* 50 (2004) 46–91.

11 J. Davis, "Cultural Innovation and the Minoan Thalassocracy at Ayia Irini," in R. Hagg and N. Marinatos, eds., *The Minoan Thalassocracy*, Liege: The University of Liege, 1984, 159–66; J. Davis, *Keos V, Ayia Irini: Period V*, Mainz: Philipp von Zabern, 1986, 101–7.

12 J. Caskey, "Investigations in Keos: Part 1" *Hesperia* 40 (1971) 392–5.

13 M. Wiener, "The Isles of Crete? The Minoan Thalassocracy Revisited," in D. Hardy et al., eds., *Thera and the Aegean World, III*, London: The Thera Foundation, 1990, 128–61. M. Wiener, "Aegean Warfare at the Beginning of the Late Bronze Age in Image and Reality," in E. Aram-Stern et al., eds. *Metaphysis: Ritual, Myth and Symbolism in the Aegean Bronze Age*, Aegaeum 39, Liege: Peeters, 2016, 139–48.

14 D. Matsas, "Minoan Long Distance Trade: A View from the Northern Aegean," in R. Laffineur and W.-D. Niemeier, eds., *Politeia I*, Aegaeum 12, Liege: University of Liege, 1995, 235–48. Samothrace: stone vases, administrative documents, balance weights, and sealings with Linear A and hieroglyphic script suggest a Minoan trading post.

15 S. Hood, "A Minoan Empire in the Aegean in the 16th and 15th Centuries BC?" in Hagg and Marinatos, *The Minoan Thalassocracy*, 33–8; S. Hiller, "Pax Minoica versus Minoan

Thalassocracy: Military Aspects of Minoan Culture," in Hagg and Marinatos, *The Minoan Thalassocracy*, 27–31. For the palaces' role in Minoan foreign trade, see M. Wiener, "The Nature and Control of Minoan Foreign Trade," in N. Gale, ed., *Bronze Age Trade in the Mediterranean*, SIMA 40, Jonsered: Paul Astrom, 1991, 325–50. A. Karetsou, M. Andreadaki-Vlazaki, and N. Papadakis, eds., Κρητη-Αιγυπτος (catalog), Herakleion: Archaeological Museum of Herakleion, 2000.

16 J. Aruz, *Marks of Distinction: Seals and Cultural Exchange between the Aegean and the Orient ca 2600–1360 BC*, CMS Beiheft 7, Mainz: Verlag von Zabern, 2008, 160–1.

17 B. Kemp and R. Merrillees, *Minoan Pottery in Second Millennium Egypt*, Mainz: Verlag Philipp von Zabern, 1980.

18 Cline, *Sailing the Wine-Dark Sea*, 268. On Cretan–Egyptian relations generally, see J. Vercoutter, *L'Egypte et le monde egeen prehellenique*, Cairo: L'insitut francais de archaeologie orientale, 1956, and Y. Duhoux, *Des Minoens en Egypte?* Louvain: University of Louvain Press, 2003.

19 P. Day et al., "A World of Goods: Transport Jars and Commodity Exchange at the Late Bronze Age Harbor of Kommos, Crete," *Hesperia* 80 (2011) 511–58.

20 For Egyptian scarabs overseas, see V. Boschloos, "Traded, Copied and Kept: The Ubiquitous Appeal of Scarabs," in P. Creaseman and R. Wilkinson, eds., *Pharaoh's Land Beyond*, Oxford: Oxford University Press, 2017, 149–66. Aruz, *Marks of Distinction*, catalogue number 27, fig. 310. For an ivory figurine at Malia see Cline, *Sailing the Wine-Dark Sea*, 259.

21 Cline, *Sailing the Wine-Dark Sea*, 263. A catalogue of Egyptian objects imported to Crete appeared in 2000 as part of an exhibition in the Heraklion Archaeological Museum, A. Karetsou and M. Andreadaki- Vlasaki, ΚΡΗΤΗ-ΑΙΓΥΠΤΟΣ. Πολιτισμικοι δεσμοι τριων χιλιετιων (essays). Athens: Kapon Editions. A second volume of essays was part of the same exhibition, A. Karetsou, ed., *Crete–Egypt: Political Connections over Three Millennia*, Athens: Kapon Editions, 2000. See also J. Phillips, *Aegyptiaka on the Island of Crete in Their Chronological Context: A Critical Review*, vols. 1–2, Vienna: Austrian Academy of Science 18 (2008), and Wiener, "The Nature and Control of Minoan Foreign Trade," 325–50.

22 P. Yule, *Early Cretan Seals: A Study of Chronology*, Mainz: Verlag Philipp von Zabern, 1981, 199.

23 J. Muhly, "Copper and Tin: The Distribution of Mineral Resources and the Nature of the Metals Trade in the Bronze Age," *Transactions of the Connecticut Academy of Art and Sciences* 43 (1973) 293–4.

24 P. Rehak, "Aegean Natives in the Theban Tomb Paintings: The Keftiu Revisited," in E Cline and D. Harris-Cline, eds., *The Aegean and the Orient in the Second Millennium*, Aegaeum 18, Liege: University of Liege, 1998, 39–52.

25 Wiener (supra n 13), "The Isles of Crete?" 329.

26 E. Barber, *Prehistoric Textiles*, Princeton: Princeton University Press, 1991, 312–57.

27 M. Shaw, "Ceiling Patterns from the Tomb of Hepzefa," *AJA* 74 (1970) 25–30.

28 Cline, *Sailing the Wine-Dark Sea*, 31–42; 108–20.

29 W.-D. Niemeier, "Minoan Artisans traveling Overseas: The Alalakh Frescoes and the Painted Plaster Floor at Tel Kabri," in R. Laffineur and L. Basch, eds., *Thalassa: L'Egee Prehistorique et la Mer*, Aegaeum 7, Liege: University of Liege, 1991, 189–20.

30 W.-D. and B. Niemeier, "Minoan Frescoes in the Eastern Mediterranean," in Cline and Harris-Cline, *The Aegean and the Orient*, 69–98, and M. Bietak, "The Setting of the Minoan Wall Paintings at Avaris," in L. Morgan, ed., *Aegean Wall Painting: A Tribute to Mark Cameron*, BSA Studies 13 (2005) 83–90.

31 M. Bietak, "Connections between Egypt and the Minoan World: New Results from Tell el-Dab'a," in W. Davies and L. Schofield, eds., *Egypt, the Aegean and the Levant*, London:

British Museum Press, 1995, 19–28. Rehak, "Aegean Natives in the Theban Tomb Paintings," 78–82.

32 R. Laffineur, "From West to East: The Aegean and Egypt in the Early Late Bronze Age," Cline and Harris-Cline, *The Aegean and the Orient*, 58–68; W.-D. Niemeier and B. Niemeier, "Minoan Frescoes in the Eastern Mediterranean, " in Cline and Harris Cline, *The Aegean and the Orient*, 69–98.

33 Aruz (supra n 13), *Marks of Distinction*, fig. 355.

SEVEN

MINOAN RELIGION DURING THE FIRST AND SECOND PALACE PERIOD

A RCHAEOLOGICAL ARTIFACTS ASSOCIATED WITH THE CRETAN CULT during the MM IB–LM IB period come from different levels of society: community/state functions in the palaces and sanctuaries, domestic ritual in household shrines and burials, and personal beliefs, seen on amulets. We will consider each level in turn.

COMMUNITY/STATE CULT

Palaces

A generation ago, cult ceremonies carried out in the first palaces were regarded as an innovation beginning when the first palaces were constructed. More recent excavation at Knossos and Phaistos has shown that large communal ceremonies were carried out there much earlier, during the Early Minoan period, well before the palaces were built.[1] Several EM II wells at Knossos have produced substantial amounts of pottery indicating that large-scale communal eating and drinking took place on the site at that time. At Phaistos, two areas under the later central and western courts of the palace were used by sizable groups for community ritual. The first palaces therefore represent a social *institutionalization* of a pre-existing cult.

The establishment of regional nature (rural) sanctuaries located in high places was contemporary or possibly a little earlier than the palaces. In

Minoan society these sanctuaries and the palaces served complementary roles, that is, popular cult and state religion, respectively. It is possible that one led to the other. Archaeology provides no evidence for worship at mountain sanctuaries before MM I, indicating that the deities worshiped there may have been new (see below). At this time (MM IA, 2100–1900 BC), after a period of isolation in the late third millennium, Crete reestablished international connections with the Near East just before the construction of the first palaces.[2] New concepts must have been absorbed. Cretan tombs, for example at Mochlos and Archanes, are filled with imported motifs on ivory, scarabs, and jewelry from Egypt, Syria, and Anatolia. Minoan pottery was traded to Cyprus and Syria. As a result of the climatic disaster of the period c.2200–2000 BC the Minoans may have sought help from deities they had learned about in Egypt and the Near East. Minoan deities often have Eastern attributes (see below); they were believed to descend to meet mankind at mountain peak sanctuaries. Similarly, Egyptian and Eastern gods were believed to reside or meet on mountaintops. In the Canaanite Levant, for example, worship took place on a mountaintop at a "High Place" called a *bamah*.

Certain elite individuals may then have achieved their positions as chief palace officials by successfully claiming descent from the god(s) worshiped at the local nature sanctuary (Chapter 4). For example, Zeus was worshiped on the sanctuary at Mount Jouktas near Knossos, and King Minos of Knossos was regarded as the son of Zeus (*Iliad*, 13, 450).

Minoan palaces, with their large open spaces, operated as central meeting places for the community to celebrate ceremonies in honor of the gods. Most of the palaces share certain basic features – a large central court, a west court provided with rows of seats ("theatrical areas"), raised processional pathways open to the town, storage rooms for food, a throne room, and a banquet room for eating and drinking. Palaces have a common north–south orientation of the central court with the cult rooms in the west wing facing east toward the rising and setting of the sun and moon.

Evidence from the palaces help us to understand palatial cult activities, which we will consider site by site.

Knossos

At Knossos, evidence for cult practices comes mainly from objects found in the Temple Repositories, from wall paintings, and from the Throne Room.

Evans believed that a complex of rooms (Chapter 5) in the west wing of the palace south of the Throne Room had religious functions. These rooms had an exterior shrine-like façade of three sections ("Tripartite Shrine") facing on to the central court.[3] Cult objects in the adjacent "Temple Repositories" buried in these rooms give us some idea of religious practices carried out within the

7.1 Shrine finds from temple repositories in Knossos palace.
Evans (1925), fig. 377

palace. This deposit consisted of many diverse finds: objects of clay were MM III vases (a *pithos* and many clay jugs) and clay plaques depicting crabs and seashells. Faience objects included three goddess figurines (Fig. 7.1) holding snakes, panels with plaques depicting scenes of wild goats and cows nursing their young, sprays of lilies, crocuses, as well as jugs, beads, bowls, chalices and faience, inlay fragments of marine life (argonauts, flying fish, and cockle shells), saffron flowers, and a pomegranate. The deposit also produced many seashells painted different colors, small stone offering tables, mace heads, a clay Linear A tablet, more than 150 sealings, deer horns, and wheat. Judging from the objects, the associated shrine seems to have belonged to fertility deities who cared for wild animals, sea creatures, and plant life, like the later Greek Artemis, Aphrodite, and Athena. The actual performance when these cult objects were brought out probably took place in the central court in front of the Tripartite Shrine.

At Knossos, wall paintings in the palace provide additional information about the cult there. The palace frescoes were meant to depict actual ceremonies held within the building.[4] Entering the palace from the west court, a visitor walked down a corridor whose walls were painted with a LM II/III procession of men and women bearing gifts to a goddess. The Throne Room (Fig. 5.9) shows griffins and palm trees and a frieze of altars flanking the throne. Fantastic beasts, the griffins protect the throne and its occupant, and proclaim their divine status. On the upper floor of the west wing a fresco, known as the Camp Stool fresco, depicted seated men drinking wine in front of a female figure, a goddess, shown at a larger scale. This scene shows a ceremonial

7.2 Reconstruction of Sacred Grove fresco, palace at Knossos.
Marinatos (1993), 59, fig. 49

banquet dedicated to a goddess that must have actually taken place in the room. From the north wing of the palace, the Sacred Grove fresco (Fig. 7.2) shows a scene of two groups, men and women, taking place in the west court with its two olive trees in a ceremony of some sort. Probably part of this scene is another group of armed men saluting a male figure holding a spear. The north wing of the palace produced another fresco, the Grandstand fresco that depicts a crowd of women and men spectators, set in the palace, watching a large public ceremony of some sort.

From the area of the staircase connecting the ground floor of the domestic quarter with the central court comes a scene of men in procession ascending stairs. From north of the quarters the famous panel shows a bull-leaping scene (Fig. 7.3) of an acrobatic ceremony in which a man somersaults over the back of a bull. This ceremony must have taken place in the central court of the palace. An upper room in this area had a floor, probably a shrine, with a marine scene painted with dolphins and sea sponges.[5] From the north entrance of the palace a visitor walking toward the central court would have been confronted by a large bull charging across a landscape. A similar scene also appeared at the western entrance to the palace.

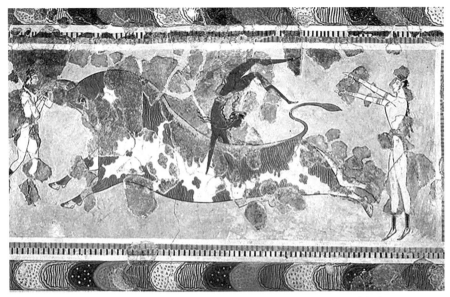

7.3 Reproduction of Bull-Leaping fresco, palace at Knossos. HM 14. HMC/TAP.

In the Throne Room four benches supplied seating for a small select group of individuals. An attached lustral basin may have been for ceremonial purification. A second room to the west held a raised ledge, probably a shrine. The anteroom had four doors oriented in such a way that they offered a view of the rising of the sun at the midwinter and summer solstices. At the midwinter solstice the sunbeam shines directly on the throne itself (Fig. 7.4), suggesting that the room was the setting for a festival at that time.[6] The solar cycle seems to have played an important role in Minoan religion. The wavy shape of the back of the throne has been interpreted as a reference to a mountaintop shrine, as the same shape appears on the peak sanctuary *rhyton* from Zakros (Fig. 7.5), implying an association between the person seated on the throne and the deity of the peak sanctuary.

Malia

The palace at Malia possessed several unique cult features. Approaching the palace entrance from the south, a visitor could enter a three-room complex (Fig. 7.6) of the MM III period that possessed an incurved Minoan stone altar (incised with a star and cross), flanked by two storage rooms. Around the altar were a low bench, a wooden statue of a deity whose clay feet were preserved, four clay stands for burning incense, various types of seashells, and other vases.[7] Entering the central court, one came upon a platform with an elegantly carved stone kernos (Fig. 7.7) with thirty-four cupules for offerings. The foundations for a stand in the central court were probably for a low altar.

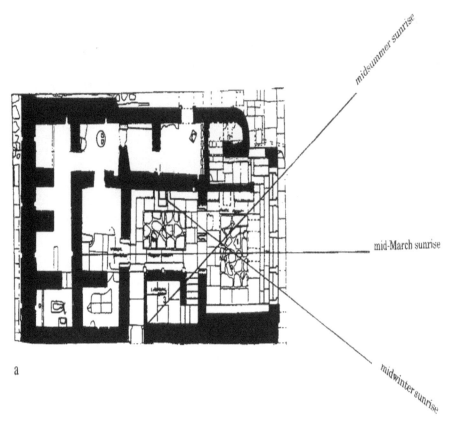

midsummer sunrise

mid-March sunrise

midwinter sunrise

a

7.4 Midwinter sunrise in Throne Room, palace at Knossos.
Goodison (2001), pl. XXIIa

Zakros

Because the palace at Zakros (Fig. 5.14) was not disturbed after its LM IB
destruction, its rooms produced their original contents, which are particularly
informative about the use of the building.[8] As described in Chapter 5, an
important complex of rooms in the west wing was used for cult dining. The
adjacent sunken lustral basin would have been used for cleansing before
gathering. Next to it was a small shrine room (XXIII) built with bench and
wall ledge on the south for small figures of the gods. The storeroom (XXVI)
held objects used by the participants in the adjacent dining rooms. These
include a multitude of *rhyta* for pouring and other cult paraphernalia.
Faience objects included cups, and *rhyta* in the shape of a nautilus shell
(Fig. 7.8), a sheep head, and a lion's head. One stone *rhyton* from the light
well of XXVIII has a relief scene depicting a peak sanctuary (Fig. 7.5) which
allows us to reconstruct the shrine (Fig. 7.9). Another *rhyton* in the shape of a
bull's head was found in the light well next to the ceremonial hall (XXVIII).

7.5 Scene of Minoan peak sanctuary, *rhyton*, Zakros palace.
Marinatos (1993), 120, fig. 85

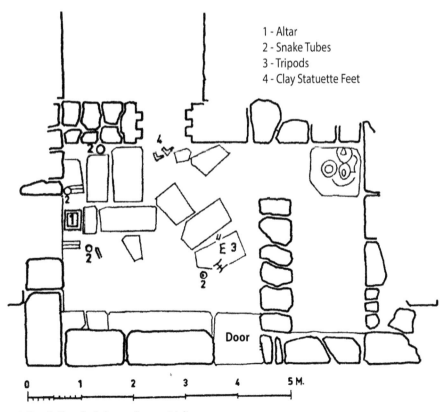

1 - Altar
2 - Snake Tubes
3 - Tripods
4 - Clay Statuette Feet

7.6 South Bench shrine, palace at Malia.
Van Effenterre (1980), fig. 602. Plan redrawn by Arielle Channin

7.7 Kernos, Malia palace.
Photo by the author

7.8 Nautilus *rhyton*, palace at Zakros. HM 311.
HMC/TAP.
Photo by the author

The contents of this complex indicate elite groups of people gathered there to eat and drink, to make offerings and libations, and to burn incense. If the marine, sheep, lion, and bull motifs on the objects are understood as divine attributes, then probably at least two different deities – one of the sea and another of wild animals – were honored there. In the southernmost room (XXIX) the excavators found ten wine *amphoras* and eight jugs stored in the corners and along the wall. Groups met in this complex to drink wine. Three rooms connected directly with these rooms. One, a storeroom (XXVII), held fifteen storage jars of various sizes and other vases. Another room (XXV) was fitted with eighteen clay bins along the walls containing a unique collection of cult objects: sixteen stone conical *rhyta* carved out of alabaster, marble, and porphyry, six ovoid *rhyta* of basalt and rock crystal, an ostrich egg-shaped alabaster jug, an imported Egyptian vase converted into a bridge-spouted jar, and several chalices, one carved out of obsidian from the island of Giali. Other ceremonial objects included two large

7.9 Reconstruction of a peak sanctuary.
Gesell (1985), 176, fig. 27

bronze double axes, three stone maceheads, three stone lamps, and the remains (metal hinges) of wooden boxes and their ivory inlays in the shape of a butterfly. A *rhyta* made of faience had the shape of a bull's head, a nautilus (Fig. 7.8), and a lioness. These objects would have been used in the ceremonies held in the adjoining large rooms (XXVIII, XXIX).

Gournia

Recent excavations at the town at Gournia have provided evidence for cult practices in the palace and central court.[9] A dramatic example comes from the area of the upright stone *baetyl* (Fig. 7.10) at the southwest corner of the palace.

7.10 Stone *baetyl* at Gournia.
Photo by the author

Following the Theran eruption, cult dedications were left in hundreds of conical cups
(found in Room 13) including Theran
pumice. In the central and west court masses
of conical cups indicate groups of people
gathered there for ceremonies that involved
drinking. At the northwest corner of the court
a large stone slab with a natural perforation
(for liquid run-off?) has been interpreted as an
altar for sacrifices. The portico next to this slab
faces east toward the Thryphti mountain
range where an LM I peak sanctuary has
recently been found.[10] The orientation of
the court suggests that gatherings were held
there periodically to observe and celebrate the
rise of the sun, moon, and constellations
during the course of the year.

SANCTUARIES

Peak Sanctuaries

The first peak sanctuaries appear on Crete in *c.*2000 BC, probably in response
to the disastrous heat/drought climatic phase that began *c.*2200 BC.[11] Large
groups of people within a region began to collect periodically during the year
at a prominent peak or mountain cave to take part in a range of religious
rituals, some of which were intended to procure rain from the gods. This
practice implies an important restructuring of Minoan society. On site, libations were poured into the ground for chthonic gods and left to evaporate for
celestial gods.[12]

How did this worship on mountains begin? I will offer a speculative explanation. Offerings – libation jugs, cups, figurines, and stone vases – recovered
from Middle Minoan peak sanctuaries have an obvious predecessor: the
dedications left to ancestors at Early Minoan tombs. This may suggest that
the later peak sanctuary cult was in some way derived from Early Minoan
ancestor worship. Peak sanctuaries appear to have been chosen for two reasons.
First, they were prominent and visible (Fig. 7.11) from the surrounding
settlements in the region. Ceremonies conducted on the peak were a collective
activity of the region, meant for display. Second, the mountaintops were also
the sites of the earliest local inhabitation. Both Mount Jouktas and the
Amnissos Cave, for example, were settlement sites during the Late Neolithic
and Early Minoan period. Hence local settlers may have viewed these sites as

7.11 View of peak sanctuary on Mount Kophinas.
Photo by the author

the original home and burial place of their ancestors. In traditional societies, kinship groups commonly trace their group back to an ancestor who was associated with the mountains, caves, or lakes where they first lived.[13] This may have been the case in Minoan Crete since peak sanctuaries were often the places where the original (Neolithic–Early Minoan) settlers within a region lived (Chapter 3) Regional communities may have come to believe in a shared kinship structure which allowed them to unite in worship at a single place held to be sacred, perhaps associated with one or more divine ancestors. These early ancestors would have been believed to have been direct descendants of the gods, a common belief in later Greek mythology (Hesiod, *Works and Days*, 109–11). The "ruler" residing in the palace would probably have claimed descent from the god who was worshiped at the peak sanctuary. Zeus, for example, was worshiped on Mount Jouktas, and King Minos of Knossos was viewed as his son (*Iliad* XIII, 449).

Well over fifty peak sanctuaries have now been identified on Crete.[14] Since the landscape of Crete consists largely of valleys bounded by mountains, peak sanctuaries are often found on the highest mountain in each of these valleys, near to (2–3 hours' walk away) and visible from the Minoan settlements. Approaching the sanctuaries was a physical ordeal – as the wounded girl in the Xeste 3 fresco at Thera shows – and may well have produced an intense physical and emotional experience

The distribution of peak sanctuaries is most numerous in east Crete where practically every valley had its own sanctuary, but are relatively rare in west Crete. East Crete is dramatically drier than west Crete, which suggests an important connection with rain and crop fertility. Their eastern location on the island also points to their probable source: the Near East. Worship at peak sanctuaries can also be compared to the traditional annual (July 23) pilgrimage still made today to the hilltop chapels of Profitis Elias where worshippers pray for rain for their crops and animals.

Archaeologically, most peak sanctuaries consist mainly of a scatter of votives left on a hilltop. Larger sanctuaries have open spaces or a complex of rooms where people gathered to make offerings, sacrifice animals, and cook and eat meals together. Large bonfires were lit, perhaps at night, so the fumes would bear the smell of the sacrificed animals up into the sky where the gods lived. The well-published finds from the MM IB–LM IA sanctuary at Vrysinas above (south of) Rethymnon are instructive about the use of a peak sanctuary.[15] Vases were mostly for cooking (cooking pots and dishes) drinking (conical cups, jugs, *amphoras*), and serving food (trays, plates). Many animal figurines (mostly bovids) were model offerings. Large numbers of worshippers came to the shrine to eat and drink in communal groups: excavation at Vrysinas produced 6,000 human and more than 4,000 animal figurines and over 8,000 conical cups. Analyses of the clay vases has shown that worshippers came from different locations within an area of roughly 20 square km around Rethymnon. Various possible ceremonies have been suggested by the excavator Iris Tzachili: seasonal meetings, communal feasts following sacrifices, gatherings of kinship groups, male and female initiation, and marriage, marked by prayer, singing, hymns, and dancing.

Votives left at the sanctuaries tell us what the worshippers' concerns were – requests or thanks for divine help with healing, the fertility of women, flocks and crops, successful childbirth, male and female initiation, and possibly artisan activity. Such a diversity indicates that a variety of deities were worshiped on peak sanctuaries. Many peak sanctuaries continued into MM III, but by LM I far fewer were functioning. Only a few, for example Jouktas, Gonies, Kophinas (Fig. 7.11), Petsophas, Troastalos, and Vrysinas – have produced LM I finds. This abandonment has been linked to the population loss after the Theran eruption, although political causes may also have had a role. Mount Jouktas is exceptional for its continuation into LM III, which must be linked to the growth of Knossian political power in that period. Cessation of community worship at a sanctuary may have been the result of loss of political independence. Worship at peak sanctuaries also spread from Crete to other parts of the Aegean; examples are known at Kythera, Kea, Rhodes, and Epidauros.[16]

Peak sanctuaries are depicted in Minoan art. A stone *rhyton* from the palace at Zakros (Fig. 7.5) has a scene of a mountain shrine. The structure consists of a

small court with steps leading up a three-part
façade whose roof is crowned with horns of
consecration. Birds and wild goats sit on the
roof, indicating its rural location. The façade
has a central niche. In the court is an altar and
offering tables, one holding what looks like a
bundle of flowers. A second scene on a stone
vase from Gypsades shows a worshipper on a
mountaintop, placing offerings in a basket
before a tripartite façade surmounted by horns
of consecration. Worshippers are depicted on
Minoan art in a mountainous landscape or
other places that include individuals making
an offering to a deity seated under a tree
(Fig. 7.12), pulling the branches of a tree,
hugging a *baetyl*, and dancing in front of a
small tree shrine (Fig. 7.13), or greeting a
deity who is appearing before a shrine
(Fig. 7.14). A seal shows a deity in the form
of an avatar (bird) appearing before a worshipper at a *baetyl* (Fig. 7.15). Scenes and
votive models of worshippers are often
shown dancing. Such a practice, known in
Eastern religions, brings participants into an
ecstatic state where one enters into commu-
nion with the deity who speaks to the
worshipper.[17]

Four peak sanctuaries are described
below.

7.12 Worshippers approaching a goddess
under a tree.
CMS 1, 17.

7.13 Cult scene on gold ring from Archanes.
Marinatos (2010), 96, fig. 7.6a

Petsophas

Petsophas, the first peak sanctuary excavated
(in 1902) on Crete sits on a mountain imme-
diately south and overlooking the Minoan town of Palaikastro.[18] The sanctuary dates to MM I–LM I. Several small terraced platforms and rooms, one with
a plastered floor and bench, were built on the summit and found covered with
votives and ash (Fig. 7.16). Male figurines of young men with scalp-locks
wearing kilts, boots, and daggers usually had their arms crossed across their
chest (Fig. 7.17). Much less common, female figurines were depicted wearing
jewelry, skirts, and bodices, with their hair wrapped high above their head in a
cloth or fillet. They stretch their arms out in a gesture of supplication or laid
across their breasts. Two figurines of children were found. Animal figurines

7.14 Worshipper in front of a shrine welcomes young god descending from sky.
Evans (1925), 160, fig. 115

7.15 Cult scene, ring from Sellopoulo, Knossos.
Marinatos (2010), 89, fig. 7.2a

(Fig. 7.18) – oxen, birds, rams and sheep, pigs, hedgehogs, and weasels – were a common offering. In later Greek religion each of these animals was associated with a specific deity: Poseidon/Zeus, Aphrodite/Athena, Hermes, and Artemis, respectively. Votives also include conical cups, miniature vases, tools, inscribed stone libation tables, lamps, and stone vases, as well as figurine models of anatomical parts (limbs, and male and female torsos) (Fig. 7.19). Peak sanctuary figurines have a modern counterpart in the Greek Orthodox Church (Fig. 7.20). These are discussed in Chapter 2.

It has been suggested that Petsophas functioned as an astral observatory at certain times of the year.[19] From the peak one can see the setting of the sun behind the prominent peak of Modi to the north on the vernal and fall equinoxes. Every nineteen years the moon can also be seen to set behind Modi once every month for several months in succession. Some years the new crescent and the full moon will set below the peak on the equinoxes.

Mount Jouktas

The largest peak sanctuary on Crete is Mount Jouktas, near Knossos (Fig. 1.3). The shrine lies 13 km southwest of Knossos with a magnificent view to the north and west. First dug by Evans, Jouktas has had continuing excavations since 1974 (Fig. 7.21).[20] Worship there begins in MM IB. Worshippers prayed, ate meals together, and offered sacrifices of animals, libations, and clay figurines of themselves and animals. Finds included figurines of animals (oxen, goats, snakes, bulls, beetles, and birds) and of human limbs, clay locks of hair, a stone ladle, offering tables, *kernoi*, and other inscribed votives. Ash layers are a sign of bonfires. At the top of the shrine area an altar was surrounded by offering tables, figurines, and a group of over thirty bronze double axes. Clay figurines of humans are mostly male. A group of over sixty figurines, however, has been interpreted as women crouching in childbirth (Fig. 7.22). Next to the altar was a natural chasm in the bedrock, found filled with MM I–III offerings. The shrine was enlarged in MM II–III: below the altar a terrace of five large rooms produced evidence of storage and dining.

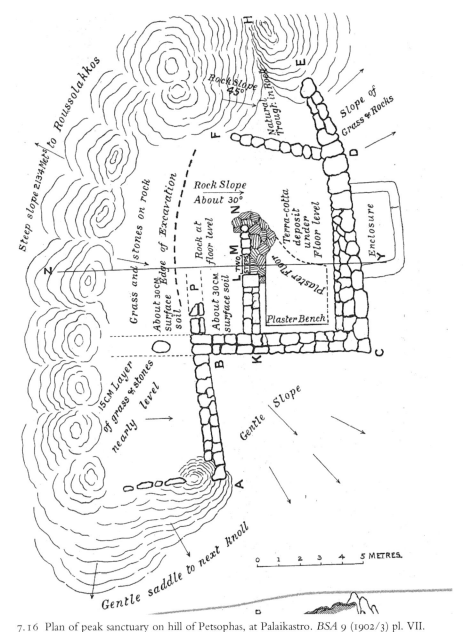

7.16 Plan of peak sanctuary on hill of Petsophas, at Palaikastro. *BSA* 9 (1902/3) pl. VII.

Running along the eastern edge of the rooms a long bench may have been for the placement and display of votives. An ancient road, still visible today, linked Jouktas to Knossos, via Anemospilia. Later Greek tradition identified the Jouktas peak as the tomb of Zeus. Today pilgrims ascend the mountain annually on August 6 to worship there at the chapel of Ephendis Christos (Christ the Lord).

7.17 Figurines from Petsophas peak sanctuary. HM 3409, HMC/TAP. 3422, 3418, 3425, 3441, 3405.
Photo by the author

7.18 Animal figurines from peak sanctuary at Petsophas. HMC/TAP. HM 3409, 3422, 3418, 3425, 3441, 3405, 3466.
Photo by the author

On the road from Knossos near to Mount Jouktas, an MM III shrine (Fig. 7.23) at Anemospilia, produced evidence, preserved in an earthquake collapse, of a human sacrifice.[21] A stairway at the west end of the antechamber led to an upper floor. The antechamber on the north produced a deep stone

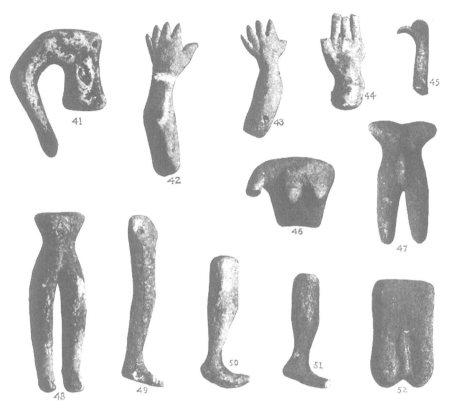

7.19 Votive figurines of limbs and torsos from Petsophas peak sanctuary. *BSA* 9 (1902/3), pl. III.

7.20 Modern votive plaques (*anathemata*) depicting a child, arm, eye, and ear, from the hilltop chapel of Efendis Christos, Crete.
Photo by the author

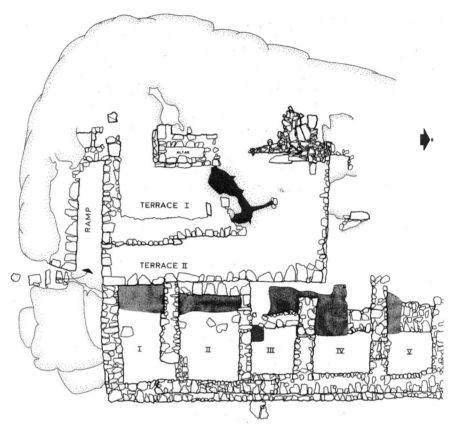

7.21 Plan of peak sanctuary on Mount Jouktas.
Karetsou (1981), 142, fig. 5

7.22 Figurines of women giving birth from peak sanctuary at Mount Jouktas.
Karetsou (1981), 142, fig. 5.149, fig. 16

7.23 Anemospilia shrine near Mount Jouktas.
National Geographic Magazine 159 (1981), fig. 1. National Geographic Society

basin for libations and signs of food preparation: pestles, cooking pots, *pithoi*, and the bones of pigs, goats, and bulls. Along the sides of the central room were many *pithoi* and smaller storage jars. On the rock-cut back bench were two clay feet of a life-size wooden cult statue beside which were placed a clay pail and a *rhyton* for offerings. In the east room, jars lined the walls and a three-stepped altar was located at the back. On the altar were placed sea pebbles and twenty-four vases, cups, a large bowl, jugs, and a stone offering table, used for offerings of food and liquid. The west room produced three skeletons: in the rear a man and woman were found, killed when the roof collapsed. Another skeleton of an eighteen-year-old boy was found on a raised dais in the center of the room. He was the sacrifice: his feet had been bound and he had been killed by a lance found next to him. An individual carrying a jar had fallen in the antechamber as he tried to escape the collapse. This rare form of sacrifice seems to have been carried out at the onset of a major earthquake in the hope of averting destruction.

Kato Syme

In south Crete, a sanctuary was established in MM II high in the mountains above the village of Kato Syme, near Viannos.[22] This sanctuary sits in a natural

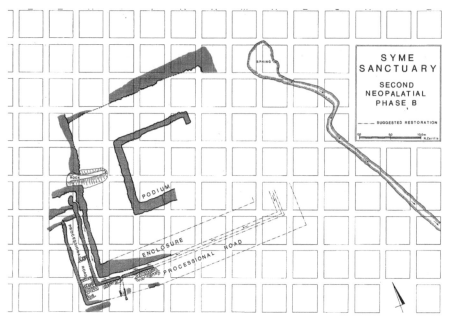

7.24 Plan of sanctuary at Kato Syme.
Preziosi and Hitchcock (1999), 141, fig. 88

amphitheater (1,130 m) on the south slope of Mount Dicte in a physical
location very reminiscent of Delphi. Building V, a large structure with column
bases and a stone- paved floor, was the earliest structure on the site. In MM II
it was replaced by Building U that had over twenty-two rooms with plastered
floors that produced conical cups and lamps. Its administrative function is
indicated by a Linear A tablet. The north wing of the building served for food
preparation and storage of cult objects. A door led out to a terraced area facing
an open space with offering tables and cups, used for sacrifices by worshippers,
and animal bones. Nearby was a workshop that produced stone vases. A paved
road led to the natural focus of the site: a large spring. After its destruction by
earthquake in MM IIB, an open-air sacrificial area, surrounded by a peribolos
wall, was constructed on its ruins (Fig. 7.24). In the Neopalatial period a large
podium (12 × 7 m) with its own temenos wall was used as an altar for burned
animal sacrifices. Worshippers used and dedicated vases, clay chalices, and
offering stands, as well as stone offering tables, seals, and male and animal
figurines. Sacrifices were made from LM I into the Archaic period. Clay animal
figurines and anatomical models are absent. In the Archaic period inscriptions
tell us that the sanctuary was dedicated to Hermes and Aphrodite.

Atsipades
Atsipades, a rural shrine established in the Protopalatial period, served the small
Agios Vasilios valley south of Rethymnon. The recent excavation of Atsipades

gives us the most detailed archaeological record of worship on a peak sanctuary.[23] Finds were limited to a small area on two terraces of the peak. Many of
the votives were found concentrated in the rock clefts on the west side of the
site below the upper terrace. On the upper terrace water-worn pebbles were
laid out to form a small space around an artificial earth platform. Set within this
platform was a circular hole lined with stones that seems to have supported
something, perhaps a wooden statue. The densest concentration of pottery
fragments were around this feature. Fragments of human and animal figurines
as well as libation vessels, rhyta, jars, and lamps were numerous around the
platform, indicating that libations were offered there. Other types of vases
were found spread across the lower terrace, suggesting that different activities,
such as feasting, took place there. In the open area of the lower terrace were
many human figurines but few of animals. The human figurines from
Atsipades usually assumed a posture of arms up and away from the torso.
This suggested to the excavators that the figurines were worshippers depicted
in a ritual that included a visionary and mystical experience. Male and female
figurines were concentrated in different areas, suggesting separate gender-
related rites.

CAVE SHRINES

Many caves on Crete used as occupation sites in the Neolithic–Early Minoan
period (Chapter 3) were subsequently converted into shrines in MM I.[24] Most
of known cave shrines are located in central Crete. Bronze weapons and
jewelry were a popular votives at these shrines. Unlike peak sanctuaries, they
continue through LM III at which time many small caves attracted worshippers. These cave shrines may have replaced local worship on peak sanctuaries.
Worshippers carried out their ceremonies inside the cave and then ascended
from darkness into the light of the outer world above, a transition basic to
ancient mystery religions. Passage from darkness into light/enlightenment is a
major theme in the Homeric *Hymn to Demeter* and Plato's *Allegory of the Cave*.

Psychro Cave

In the Lasithi Plain, the Neolithic settlement site in the Psychro Cave began to
be used as a sanctuary in MM I.[25] The cave possessed an upper and lower
chamber. At the bottom of the lower chamber was an impressive array of
stalagmites and stalactites behind a pool of water, which may have been used
for ritual cleansing/purification.

In the Neopalatial period a one-meter-high plaster and stone altar was built
on paving stones in the upper cave. Surrounding it were stone offering tables
and conical cups, a double axe fixed in a pyramidal base, braziers, and lamps or

incense burners. An ash level with animal bones attests to sacrifice and feasting there. Nearby a walled-off room held large storage vessels for food. Bronze votives were especially numerous: figurines of bulls, oxen, wild goat, sheep, deer, pigs, and wild boar. Many cups and jugs testify to libations and drinking. In the lower cave, metal votive blades and double axes were found stuck in between the stalagmites. Worshippers left votive male and female figurines of themselves in the poses of supplication or "saluting." First fruits from farmers were placed in small stands and in a *kernos* with many tiny cups. Over 200 weapons – full-size daggers and miniature models of swords and daggers – were dedicated, perhaps by young men as part of an initiation ceremony to manhood. Women offered personal possessions, for example rings, pins, beads, and seals, and clothing ornaments such as pins, fibulae, gold strips, and sprays. Hair pins and rings, combs and razors (over 250 examples) and more than a hundred tweezers dedicated at the cave may have been part of an initiation ceremony celebrated by young women. Finally, tools of various sorts – knives, needles, spindlewhorls, chisels, and sickles – were probably offered either by artisans or in thanks offerings for work accomplished. Models of anatomical parts, common on peak shrines, are missing.

The terrace outside the cave provided space for large groups of pilgrims. Votives suggest that the worshippers' supplications were diverse and held at different times of the year. Pilgrims gave thanks for a successful harvest, young women for marriage and safe childbirth, and young men for initiation into manhood. Votive figurines show dancing women, an activity that probably took place on the large outside terrace.

The Psychro Cave continued to function as a sanctuary during LM III and into the Geometric–Roman period. Many of the same types of votives – figurines (animal and human), personal possessions, weapons, jewelry, vases, and tools can be dated to LM IIIA and the Early Iron Age. In the eighth century BC, Hesiod (*Theogony*, 477–84) records the myth that Zeus was born in a cave on a mountain near Lyttos, a location that fits the Psychro Cave. Strabo (10.3.7; 10.3.11) also tells us that the *kouretes* (young men) danced, beat their drums, and clashed their spears on their shields after the birth of Zeus.

The Cave of Eileithyia at Amnissos

A Final Neolithic–EM I occupation site, this cave began to function as a shrine sacred to the goddess of childbirth, Eileithyia, in the MM I period. A large stone stalagmite (Fig. 7.25) had a small temenos wall built around it where offerings were placed during Middle Minoan–Late Minoan times. A Linear B tablet from Knossos recording an offering of a jar of honey to Eileithyia at Amnissos has been interpreted as referring to this shrine.[26] Odysseus mentions her shrine at Amnissos in *Odyssey* XIX. 198

7.25 Stalagmite figure in cave of Eileithyia, Amnissos.
Photo by Mark Williams

Kamares Cave

The Kamares Cave, located high on the south face of Mount Ida, looks out
over Phaistos and the western Mesara Plain below.[27] The earliest votives from
the cave date to the MM I period. Offerings continued into LM I and LM III.
Protopalatial pottery included bridge-spouted jars, cups, jugs for food, and
pithoi for storage of food. Small finds included a piece of pumice, a bone awl,
and needles. Inside the cave were found a stone built-hearth, high-quality
Kamares ware, Barbotine decorated jugs, cups, *pithoi*, and a vase filled with
grain, stored for periodic gatherings there. A burned level produced bones of
cattle and sheep/goat from communal meals. Worshippers also left animal
figurines, such as oxen and a pig, in place of actual sacrifices. Snow-covered in
winter, it may have only been visited in warmer parts of the year, perhaps for
seasonal festivals.

URBAN SHRINES

The Minoans also practiced their religion at small shrines in towns. Marine-
style vases and frescoes have been identified at such shrines after the LM IA
Theran eruption.[28] At Malia a small MM II shrine (Fig. 7.26) had a hall, storage
room with *pithoi*, lamps, a miniature stone *pithos*, and a cult room.[29] The room
had a bench along one side and a central clay hearth in the floor. The four jars,
a cooking pot, plate, cups, juglet, four portable clay offering tables, pedestaled

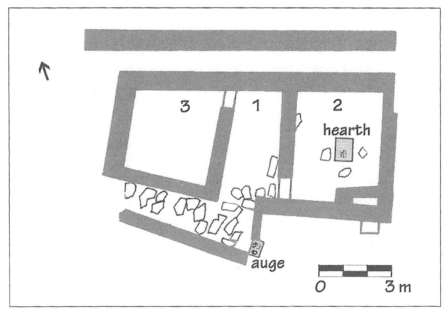

7.26 Plan of urban shrine at Malia.
McEnroe (2010)

(a)

Fig. 26. — Cornes de consécration (n° **6**) et figurines animales (n° **8** a et b) (1 : 1.

(b)   (c)

7.27 Finds from the Malia shrine.
BCH 90 (1966), figs. 20, 25, 26, 30, 45. EFA

lamp stand, a snake tube, a clay model of a triton shell, and two animal
figurines (Fig. 7.27) are the remains of the religious services there.

At Palaikastro an *ashlar*-built three-room complex in Building 5 faced out
on to a public court.[30] The anteroom had a red-painted paved floor, frescoed

(a)

(b)

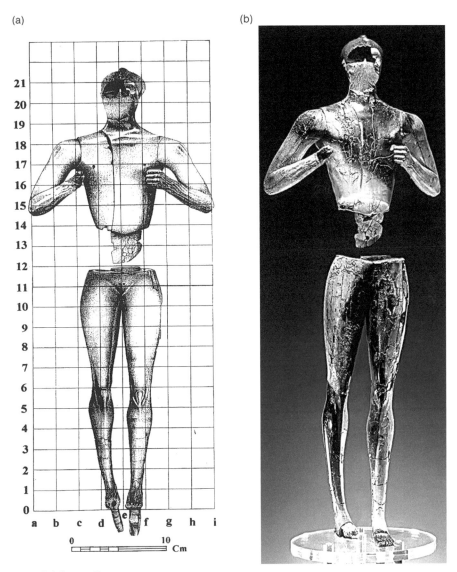

7.28 Palaikastro Kouros.
Macgillivray et al. (2000), 96, fig. 6.1. HM 8506. BSA

walls, and held a stone *baetyl* next to a stone-covered pit. The main room held
an LM I cult statuette of an ivory and stone (head) statuette 50 cm high
covered with gold foil of a young male, discussed below (Fig. 7.28). An
amphora and cup for libations were placed next to him. At the rear was a
storeroom with large jars.

At Agia Triada the LM IIIA Building H was a bench shrine that faced out on
to a courtyard. Its frescoed floor depicted a marine scene of dolphins and fish.
On the rear bench were inverted cups and miniature vases. Snake tubes and
basins were on the floor.

At LM IIIB Gournia a separate single-room shrine faced out onto a street. It had a bench on its south side. In the northeast corner of the room was an offering table with a snake tube on it and four others around it (Fig. 9.4). Next to the table was a statuette of a goddess with upraised arms and a snake wrapped around her arms and shoulder. Fragments of two similar statuettes were found: one with a snake and another possibly with a dove. One snake tube also had a snake in relief on it. At least one *pithos* sat in the shrine.[31]

HOUSEHOLD CULT

Families carried out religious rites at small shrines inside their houses and at their family tombs. Domestic shrines have been identified within a room or interior space by the presence of a small bench and/or an assemblage of religious items (female figurines and clay models of birds, beetles, and seashells) but often only an offering table, cups, or *rhyta*. Libations and the sacrifice of animals took place at these shrines. On the south coast the "villa" at Pyrgos/Myrtos possessed a second-floor shrine whose belongings included four clay tubular stands (to burn incense or hold offerings), a Marine-style jug, a bowl, two triton shells, a faience triton shell, a Linear A tablet (recording ninety units of wine), and two clay sealings.[32] Three LM IB houses, AF, BQ, and BS/BV at Pseira, produced deposits from the upper-floor shrine that included *rhyta*, cups, offering tables, and a triton shell.[33] At Kommos, House X produced an interior space with a LM IIIA domestic shrine furnished with a small stone slab table.[34] On the table were two juglets, a conical cup containing pebbles, and bivalve shells. Next to the table were a brazier and incense burner. On the floor in front of the table were stacks of vases – juglets, conical cups, bowls, and nearby a Canaanite jar. Set on the floor were two bowls filled with ash, perhaps the remains of burned incense. Next to the slab were sea pebbles and a triton shell. Other vases included braziers, and there were incense burners and a fragmentary snake tube. To whom were the offerings made in House X? Certainly to a sea goddess, but perhaps to other deities as well.

Funerary practices at family tombs become more varied after the MM I period. Burials were made in different types of graves – chamber tombs (at Poros), ossuary chambers (Myrtos/Pyrgos), *tholos* tombs (Kamilari), and in *pithoi* (Sphoungaras). Individual burials were also made in clay coffins called *larnakes* or in different types of jars. The dead received provisions for the afterlife that were quite elaborate and included new types of offerings, such as certain stone vase shapes, possibly for perfumes and cosmetics, seashells and sea pebbles, and clay models of boats. Objects in tombs of Egyptian derivation become particularly popular. Egyptianizing clay and stone vases were common. The Egyptian *sistrum* was a popular tomb gift. Clay models of a *sistrum*, a musical instrument, associated with the Egyptian goddess Hathor and

Isis, have been found in a child's tomb at Phournoi (Archanes) and the Agios Charalambos cave burial in Lasithi.[35] The *sistrum* seems to have accompanied the deceased into the Afterworld so they could enjoy its music, an Egyptian belief.

In northern Crete, wealthy families commonly used a small tomb in the shape of a miniature house. At the town of Gournia, for example, two house-shaped tombs were built at the edge of the town in MM I (1900 BC) and were used until MM III.[36] Tomb I has two rooms with many burials and a silver *kantharos* (Fig. 4.6), clay and stone vases, tweezers, two seals, a necklace of silver beads, and ivory inlays from a wooden box. Tomb II has two rooms and a door on the north. A stone platform attached to its south wall held a stone *kernos* for offerings. Burials were accompanied by clay cups, jugs, an offering table, stone vases, an animal-shaped amulet, a sealstone, and several bronze tweezers. Gournia had a second cemetery (EM II–LM III) located below the town nearer to the coast, at Sphoungaras, consisting mostly of cist and jar burials, and *larnakes*. Jars were placed upside down to cover the body. Only a few of the *pithoi* contained personal possessions, usually a hairpin, beads, a ring, or a sealstone. Offerings were often made in small vases outside the *pithoi*.

Excavated chamber tombs from Poros, the port town of Knossos, have produced many rich burials from the MM IIB–LM IB period.[37] The deceased was laid out in the tomb on a wooden bier with their possessions, for example gold, silver, and bronze jewelry (seals, earrings, and necklace beads), many cups and jugs filled with liquid, bronze weapons (mostly robbed out in antiquity), and boar's tusk helmets.

PERSONAL RELIGIOUS BELIEFS

Our best evidence for popular religion at the individual level is the imagery found on rings and seals. They often depict scenes of Minoans in the act of worshiping the gods. This worship took different forms – a procession bearing offerings to a deity (Fig. 7.12), the sacrifice of an animal, making a libation, offering a flower at an altar, dancing in front of a shrine, and figures tugging at a tree and praying at a *baetyl* (Fig. 7.13).[38] Dancing and the ecstatic poses of the figures suggest the performances may have involved considerable emotion. Dancing in cult scenes may have been a process of entering into a rhythm with a deity, as in Hindu religion with the god Shiva. Trees and *baetyls* were believed by the Minoans to have prophetic powers.[39] Hesiod (*Theogony* 35) implies such a practice, and Plato (*Phaedrus* 275b) records "The naïve ancients used to listen to trees and rocks for prophecy." In some cases, the god is shown responding to worship by making an appearance, in the form of a bird or as a young male descending from the sky (Fig. 7.15).

Seals show shapes and many motifs derived from Egypt, such as the scarab (Fig. 4.3), lion, monkey, sphinx, griffin, fly, foot, *sistrum*, scorpion, hippopotamus, crocodile, the ankh sign, and frog.[40] In Egypt, the monkey was sacred to Toth, god of writing and knowledge, and also associated with female fertility and eroticism. Images of monkeys – their hieroglyphic sign means "good" or "beautiful" – are found on objects associated with women, such as cosmetic vessels and toiletry objects. The Egyptian sphinx was a symbol of strength and royal power. The griffin was a powerful beast who protected Egyptian kings. Scorpions depicted on Egyptian seals have been interpreted as protective – against the bite of the scorpion – and may have had a similar function on Crete. Locally made Minoan seals, often in imported ivory, are made in Egyptian shapes: the *ankh*, scarab beetle, baboons, monkeys, lions, frogs, cows, ducks, and a fly.

The Minoans may have borrowed certain Egyptian motifs and shapes for their amulets in the belief that they provided strength or protection by assimilating the powers of certain animals or an associated deity. The scarab signified the regeneration of the dead via the power of the sun. The frog was the symbol of Heqet, Egyptian goddess of childbirth and newborns. Some Minoan seals depict the profile of a bee, an image that matches the Egyptian glyph (L 2), the royal title *bi'ty*, "bee-keeper," designating the king of Lower Egypt. A number of seals, from Phaistos, Knossos, and Malia, feature the bee sign in combination with a floral design, a flower, or a branch. In Egypt the royal title *nswt bi'ty*, "king of Upper and Lower Egypt," was written in the same way, next to a floral motif.[41]

MINOAN IDEAS OF THE AFTERLIFE

During the Early Minoan period (Chapter 3) Minoans made offerings at tombs indicating that they believed in a life after death. This cult practice continued into the palatial period. From the evidence, it seems that the Minoans envisioned a heaven-like Afterworld. Beginning in the fourteenth century BC the Cretans adopted an Egyptian type of coffin called a *larnax*, which they painted with a series of motifs and scenes that illustrated their beliefs about the Afterworld. The best known example, from Agia Triada (Fig. 7.29), actually shows a burial ceremony taking place. Two scenes are on the front. On the right, a procession of three men bring calves and a boat model to the deceased who stands outside his tomb. On the left a woman pours a libation into a vase set between two double axes while a woman behind her plays a lyre as part of the ceremony. On the back, a procession of women lead to the sacrifice of a bull on an altar and a libation is being made on another altar. The two short sides depict pairs of goddesses in chariots pulled by griffins and wild goats. Many of the details in the ceremony scenes are derived from Egyptian art.[42]

Like Egyptian tomb paintings, Minoan *larnakes* can show people mourning the deceased. In Egypt, it was believed that the soul of the deceased crossed the waters of the Nile to reach the Underworld. Near Eastern myth (Gilgamesh) and later Greek examples (Odysseus) describe a sea journey to the edge of the earth in order to reach the Underworld. Also in the *Odyssey* (4.563–8), Menelaus is told that upon his death the gods will carry him to the Elysian Plain at the ends of the earth where the Cretan Rhadymanthus rules and life is easy. Hesiod (*Works and Days*, 170–3) describes how a generation of heroes were settled by Zeus "in faraway lands next to deep-eddying Ocean | Blessed heroes, for whom honey-sweet crops | Blossomed three times a year, born by wheat-giving fields." Minoan *larnakes* envision the Afterworld in similar terms: lush Nilotic scenes with papyri, date palms, flowers, waterfowl, and fish. On

7.29 Funeral rites on the Agia Triada sarcophagus.
Hesperia 60 (1991), pl. 83a, c. Drawing author

Minoan *larnakes* the seaward journey of the dead are depicted – octopodes, dolphins, starfish, seashells, seaweed, and ships (Fig. 7.30). A burial jar from Pacheia Ammos (Fig. 7.31) is such an example. As in Egyptian tombs, the *larnax* scenes also illustrate how the deceased would enjoy himself in the Afterworld as he had in life, hunting deer (Fig. 7.32), goats, and bulls.

THE MINOAN PANTHEON

Who were the Minoan gods? Our evidence comes from disparate sources: Minoan shrines and art, Near Eastern texts, Linear A and B, and later Greek religion. Some popular symbols, such as the bucranium and the horns of consecration, are clearly religious but do not seem to refer to just a single deity. The Minoan horns of consecration, for example, is in origin an Egyptian and Mesopotamian symbol representing twin peaks of a mountain, the abode of the gods – hence its meaning on Crete as a sacred sign, often marking a structure as sacred. Evans believed the Minoans worshiped a single Great Mother goddess. Opinion still remains divided on this question: some believe a single dominant goddess dominated Minoan religion, while others recognize many different goddesses.[43] The first view is based on the fact that many figures of goddesses in Minoan art share an association with the natural

7.30 Ship, Gazi *larnax*. HM HMC/TAP.
Photo by the author

world – animals, plants, and fertility. The same, however, is also true for Minoan male deities. By LM III, Cretan shrines produce multiple female figures each bearing different attributes, and the Linear B tablets also mention separate deities with Cretan associations.[44] Chronologically, the earliest gods on Crete are known from Neolithic–Early Minoan figurines of animals and women. These deities, logically, seem to have been associated with the fertility and protection of human beings, flocks, and the natural world. With time, these gods would have developed and acquired distinct characteristics that become apparent in the Protopalatial and Neopalatial period. We turn to this period to try to sort out what gods the Minoans believed in.

Peak and cave sanctuaries, with their mass of votives, are informative on this question. Cave and peak shrines share many of the same types of votives. One exception is that votives associated with healing are not found in cave shrines. The sites themselves have produced no images of the gods worshiped there, although shrines at Malia and Anemospilia have produced the clay feet of wooden cult statues. The diversity of votives and cult objects at peak shrines suggest multiple Minoan deities – connected with rain/weather, healing (anatomical models), fertility in humans (women in childbirth) and the natural

world (figurines of birds and snakes), war (-
weapons), crafts (tools), and female and male
maternity. *Kernoi* received first-fruit offerings
in thanks for a successful harvest of grain, oil,
and wine. Scholars have suggested a range of
possible deities worshiped on peak sanctuaries:
a nature goddess, an Artemis-like Mistress of
the Animals, as well as a variety of gods drawn
from the Near East.[45] The best known piece
of evidence is the famous "Mountain
Mother" sealing (Fig. 7.33) from Knossos that
depicts a goddess atop a mountain represented
in Eastern fashion (with arcades, an artistic
convention of the Near East) flanked by two
lions. Lions are unknown on Crete and an
exact iconographic parallel for this divine
figure exists as Ishtar in the Near East, who
was the goddess of love, fertility, and war.

A number of votives offered at Minoan
shrines resemble symbols or attributes of certain Near Eastern gods, which may suggest
the presence of similar figures on Crete.
Beetles, for example, are the symbol of the
Egyptian god Khephri, who gives regeneration and resurrection. Doves appear as attributes of a deity on Minoan seals and hence
were also an appropriate offering to a divinity. In the Near East the dove was a symbol of
love and female fertility. Ishtar and Astarte,
goddesses of love, sex, and fertility, were
associated with doves, as was the later, similar
Greek goddess Aphrodite. Snakes appear as
divine attributes on statuettes of Minoan
goddesses, as votive figurines, and as decor-
ations on cult objects. In the Near East figures holding snakes have been identified as
the maternal goddesses Asherah. Minoan
marine votives – seashells, figurines of fish
and boats – and marine motifs on ritual vases

VASE OF TRANSITIONAL STYLE ·
M. M. III – L.M I PERIODS

7.31 Dolphins on burial jar from Pacheia
Ammos cemetery.
Seager (1916), pl. IX

7.32 Deceased hunting in the Afterworld,
larnax from Episkopi. Hesperia 60, pl. 93a.
Drawing author

point to a deity of the sea. A wall painting at Pseira shows two female figures
by the sea, probably goddesses.[46] In LM III and later that deity would be the
Greek god Poseidon, but during the Minoan period a goddess of the sea is

7.33 Goddess on a mountain flanked by lions. Evans (1964), fig. 597e

7.34 Goddess holding dolphins. Laffineur and Hagg (2001), pl. CIV. *CMS* V Supplement 1B, 116

7.35 Goddess of the sea. *CMS* II 8, 264

probable, like Asherah, whose title was "Lady Ahirat of the Sea" or the later goddess Aphrodite who was born from the sea. Minoan sealings show a goddess holding two dolphins (Fig. 7.34), fish, and ducks, riding on a ship, or surrounded by waves (Fig. 7.35). Minoan goddesses share a common concern, fertility – of animals, humans, and plants – which is why Evans believed in a single maternal goddess. Minoan seals depict many animals and plants simply because they are attributes of the deities who would protect the seal owner.

In Minoan art deities can be recognized by their relatively large size and/or their attributes. The best known image is an Artemis-like deity called the Mistress of the Animals, depicted on the well-known sealing from Knossos, discussed above. She was one of the deities worshiped on peak sanctuaries. In other scenes goddesses are flanked by or holding crocuses, lilies, poppies, and wild animals associated with the sky, land, sea, and under-world – birds, wild goats, dolphins, and snakes.[47] Another variation shows a goddess feeding the animal (Fig. 7.36) She seems protective of these animals, like the Greek Artemis. This association continues in Greek religion: Artemis (deer, wild goats), Hermes (goat), Aphrodite (dove and dolphins), Athena (birds, snakes). A male version of this Minoan figure, called today the Master of the Animals, is also found in Minoan art (Fig. 7.37). He is shown as a young male holding lions, bulls, stags, dolphins, and wild goats, one in each hand.[48] In the Near East, the Master of Animals motif is associated with heroes such as Enkidu and Gilgamesh, royalty, and with the gods. The later Greek version of this figure would be Apollo or Hermes. Deities have been identified on Aegean seals by their pose (receiving worshippers), by their attributes (staff, bow, sword, flower, sea), and by their companions (griffin, dragon, lion, wild goat, hound, bird, dolphin).[49] Like the later Greek gods, Bronze Age deities probably had more than one attribute or companion, so the total number of Minoan deities depicted on seals is uncertain.

Particularly striking is the absence in Minoan art of the popular type of violent male god in the Near East (Baal), Egypt (Seth), or Mycenaean Greece (Poseidon) shown with a weapon and/or thunderbolt. Ruler iconography is also conspicuous by its absence on Crete. The predecessor to the Greek Zeus on Crete seems to have been a young male, linked as son or spouse to a fertility goddess like Tammuz and Ishtar in the Near East, who annually brought rain and fertility to the crops, celebrated in a cycle of birth and death. Such a youthful god, called Zeus Welchanos in later writing, seems to have survived in Crete into the Greek period. At Palaikastro a hymn of c.200 BC invokes him as "the greatest kouros" (young man) who dies and reappears annually. As a dancer with his worshippers, he is invoked to "leap for full jars, and leap for fleecy flocks, and leap for fields of fruit and for hives to bring increase."[50] This Cretan Zeus, according to

7.36 Goddess feeding a wild goat. *CMS* V Supplement 1A, 175

7.37 Master of Animals holds two lions. Evans (1964), 467, fig. 391

local tradition, died and was buried on Mount Jouktas. Like Jesus, his death and rebirth was celebrated yearly. The storm gods Zeus and Poseidon seem only to have been introduced into Crete after the Mycenaeans' arrival in the LM III–Early Iron Age.

The Minoan youthful god may be depicted in a LM I statuette (Fig. 7.28), known now as the Palaikastro Kouros, carved from ivory and stone and covered with gold foil.[51] His hairlocks are those of a young male. The pose is the same as votive figurines from Petsophas and on other peak sanctuaries. Based on his Egyptian canon of proportions and Eastern ivory, the excavators have likened him with Osiris, the god of the underworld and regeneration. The Egyptians syncretized Osiris with the constellation of Orion because the rising of Orion marked the start of the sprouting of vegetation in the cycle of the new year. This yearly rise and setting of Orion in the sky could have been observed from Petsophas. In later Greek tradition (Hesiod, *Works and Days*,

7.38 Tawaret.
CMS II 5, 322

598–620), the rising of Orion marked the time to gather the wheat harvest. At Palaikastro a hymn celebrating the arrival of Diktaian Zeus at harvest time was recited. For this reason, the excavators identify the statuette as a young male god who was born and died yearly in accordance with the agricultural cycle. In Minoan art, the sacred symbol of the double ax (*labrys*) is held by a goddess. Perhaps it was her son, who in a seasonal cycle spent part of the year underground and part above, like Demeter's daughter Persephone. Such a cycle would explain why the *labrys* was dedicated at such different shrines as the peak sanctuary of Mount Jouktas and in the Dictaean Cave.

Near Eastern texts and art also provide us with information on the Minoan gods. An Egyptian medical text of the fourteenth century names two Minoan healing gods, like the later Apollo and Near Eastern Reshep, in incantations to cure illnesses – the gods are named: Razaja, the great god, and Ameja.[52] The hippopotamus goddess Taweret, called Mistress of Pure Water, was a divine nurse and protector of women and children in Egypt whose milk protects one in the afterlife. On Minoan seals this goddess, labeled a "Genius" by Evans, is recognizable as Taweret (Fig. 7.38): she holds a jug to pour a libation or hunts an animal.[53] Minoan artisans make Tawaret a lion-headed libation bearer. It is clear that the Minoans understood this aspect of Taweret because they depict her carrying and pouring from a lustral jug.

Later texts can also be helpful on the question of Minoan deities. Names of deities have been identified in Linear A: *A-sa-sa-ra* (Hittite goddess Isha-sarra), *A-ta-no* (Athena), and *No-pi-na*.[54] The LM III Linear B tablets mention Zeus, Hera, Poseidon, Hermes, Artemis, Athena Potnia (Mistress Athena), Enyalis (epithet of Ares) Paiawon (epithet of Apollo), Hephaistos, Potnia sito (Mistress of Wheat, Demeter), and Eleuthia (Eileithyia). Aside from Zeus and Poseidon, these gods probably have Minoan prototypes. Many Bronze Age shrines on Crete and elsewhere in the Aegean certainly continued into the Iron Age.

NOTES

1   S. Todaro, "Craft Production and Social Practices at Prepalatial Phaistos," in I. Schoep, P. Tomkins, and J. Driessen, eds., *Back to the Beginning,* Oxford: Oxbow Books, 2012, 195–235.

2   V. Watrous, "Cretan International Relations during the Middle Minoan IA Period and the Chronology of Seager's Finds from the Mochlos Tombs," in R. Laffineur and E. Greco, eds., *EMPORIA*, vol. 1, Aegaeum 25, Liege: University of Liege, 2005, 107–16.

3   A. Evans, *The Palace of Minos, I*, New York: Biblo and Tannen, 1964, 463–523, 556–61; A. Evans, *The Palace of Minos, II*, vol. 1, New York: Biblo and Tannen, 1964, 803–10. M. Panagiotaki, "The Central Palace Sanctuary at Knossos," *BSA* Supplement 31 (1999).

4   M. Cameron, "The Palatial Thematic System in the Knossos Murals," in R. Hagg and N. Marinatos, eds., *The Function of the Minoan Palaces*, Stockholm: Astroms Forlag, 1987, 320–8. N. Marinatos, *Minoan Religion: Ritual, Image and Symbol*, Columbia: University of South Carolina Press, 1993, 50–75.

5   R. Koehl, "A Marinescape Floor from the Palace at Knossos," *AJA* 90 (1986) 407–17.

6   L. Goodison, "From Tholos Tomb to Throne Room: Perceptions of the Sun in Minoan Ritual," in R. Laffineur and W.-D. Niemeier, eds., *POTNIA: Deities and Religion in the Aegean Bronze Age,* Aegaeum 22, Liege: University of Liege, 2001, 77–88.

7   G. Gesell, "Town, Palace and House Cult in Minoan Crete," *SIMA* 67 (1985) 90–2, 106. J.-C. Poursat, "Cult Activity at Malia in the Protopalatial Period," in A. D'Agata and A. Van de Moortel, eds., *Archaeologies of Cult*, *Hesperia* Supplement 42 (2009) 71–8.

8   N. Platon, *Zakros: The Discovery of a Lost Palace of Ancient Crete*, New York: Charles Scribner's Sons, 1971.

9   V. Watrous et al., "Excavations at Gournia, 2010–2012," *Hesperia* 84 (2015) 397–465.

10 V. Watrous, "A Peak Sanctuary for Gournia," *Soles Festschrift*, in press.

11 J. Moody, "Environmental Change and Minoan Landscapes," in D'Agata and van de Moortel, *Archaeologies of Cult*, 241–50.

12 B. Davis, "Libation and the Minoan Feast," in L. Hitchcock and R. Laffineur, eds., *DAIS: The Aegean Feast*, Aegaeum 29, Liege: University of Liege, 2008, 47–56.

13 M. Helms, *Access to Origins: Affines, Ancestors and Aristocrats*, Austin: University of Texas Press, 1998, 38–9; 77.

14 A. Peatfield, "The Topography of Minoan Peak Sanctuaries," *BSA* 78 (1983) 273–80. A. Peatfield, "Minoan Peak Sanctuaries: History and Society," *Opuscula Atheniensia* 18 (1990) 117–31. K. Nowicki, "Some Remarks on the Pre- and Protopalatial Peak Sanctuaries in Crete," *Aegean Archaeology* 1 (1994) 31–48.

15 I. Tzachili, *Βρυσινας ΙΙ. Η Κεραμεικη της Ανασκαφης 1972–1973*, Athens: Archaeological Society of Athens, 2016.

16 Kythera Peak Sanctuary: G. Sakellaraki,. *Κυθερα. Ο Αγιος Γεοργος στον Βουνο*, Athens: Ammos Publications, 2013, 3–166. Epidauros: B. Rutkowski, *The Cult Places of the Aegean*, New Haven, CT: Yale, 1986, 202–3. Rhodes: T. Marketou, "Ialysos and Its Neighboring Areas in MBA and LB I: A Chance for Peace," in C. Macdonald, E. Hallager, and W.-D. Niemeier, eds., *The Minoans in the Central, East and North Aegean – New Evidence.* Monographs of the Danish Institute at Athens 8 (2009), 73–96. Kea (Troullos): J. Caskey, "Excavations in Keos, 1964–1965," *Hesperia* 35 (1966) 375–6 and J. Caskey, "Investigations in Keos: Part 1," *Hesperia* 40 (1997) 392–5.

17 N. Marinatos, *Minoan Kingship and the Solar Goddess*, Urbana: University of Illinois Press, 2010, 91–7.

18 J. Myres, "Excavations at Palaikastro, II. The Sanctuary-Site of Petsofa," *BSA* 9 (1902–3) 356–87.

19 G. Henriksson and M. Blomberg, "Evidence for Minoan Astronomical Observations from the Peak Sanctuaries of Petsophas and Troastalos," *Opus Atheniensa* 21 (1996) 99–114. J. MacGillivray, J. Driessen, and H. Sackett, *The Palaikastro Kouros*, *BSA* Studies 6 (2000) 15–130.

20 A. Evans, *The Palace of Minos, I*, New York: Biblo and Tannen, 1964, 141, 151–62, 623–4; A. Evans, *The Palace of Minos, II*, New York: Biblo and Tannen, 1964, 66, 68, 81, 385, 439, 585, 596, 623–4, 768. A. Karetsou, "The Peak Sanctuary of Mt. Juktas," in R. Hagg and N. Marinatos, eds., *Sanctuaries and Cults in the Aegean Bronze Age*, Stockholm: Almqvist &

Wiksell, 1980, 137–53. Recent excavations, A. Karetsou and A.-M. Jasnik, "A Hieroglyphic Seal from the Juktas Peak Sanctuary," in C. Macdonald, E. Hatzaki, and S. Andreou, eds., *The Great Islands*, Athens: Kapon Editions, 2015, 94–9. Karetsou, (p. 95) writes that the altar at the top of the sanctuary "produced abundant fragmentary pottery, mainly dated MM IB–MM II." The altar at Jouktas (p. 96) "is dated to the earliest phase of the sanctuary, as around it were found Protopalatial layers of ash mixed with bones and concentrations of votive offerings displaying a wide variety of types and material." Next to the altar a chasm in the bedrock was filled with votive debris, the earliest recovered pottery from which was Protopalatial. Recent summary: M. Moss, "The Minoan Pantheon," *BAR International Series* 1343 (2005) 99–103.

21 Y. Sakellarakis and E. Sapouna-Sakellaraki, "Drama of Death in a Minoan Temple," *National Geographic* 159 (1981) 205–22; Y. Sakellarakis and E. Sapouna-Sakellaraki, *Archanes: Minoan Crete in a New Light, I*, Athens: Ammos Publications, 1997, 268–311.

22 Kato Syme: A. Lembessi, "Η σθνεχεια της κρητομυχηωαικης λατρειας: Επιβιοσσεις και αωαβισσεις," *Archaeologiko Epherimis* 120 (1981) 1–24. A. Lembessi and P. Muhly, "Aspects of Minoan Cult. Sacred Enclosures: The Evidence from the Syme Sanctuary (Crete)," *Archaeologischer Anzeiger* (1990) 315–36. English summary: Moss, "The Minoan Pantheon," 145–7.

23 Peatfield, "Minoan Peak Sanctuaries," 59–87. A. Peatfield, Divinity and Performance on Minoan Peak Sanctuaries," in Laffineur and Niemeier, *POTNIA*, 51–5. A. Peatfield, "Rural Ritual in Bronze Age Cret," *Cambridge Archaeological Journal* 2 (1992) 59–87.

24 L. Tyree, *Cretan Sacred Caves: Archaeological Evidence,* PhD thesis University of Missouri, 1974. L. Tyree, "Diachronic Changes in Minoan Cave Cult," in in Laffineur and Niemeier, *POTNIA*, 39–49.

25 V. Watrous, *The Cave Sanctuary of Zeus at Psychro*, Aegaeum 15, Liege: University of Liege, 1996.

26 S. Marinatos, "Anaskaphai en Kriti," *Praktika tis en Athnais Arxaiologikis Etaipeias* (1929), 95–109. B. Rutkowski and K. Nowicki, *The Psychro Cave and Sacred Grottoes in Crete*, Warsaw: Art and Archaeology, 1996, 21–4. Summaries in Watrous, *The Cave Sanctuary of Zeus at Psychro*, 61, Moss, "The Minoan Pantheon," BAR International Series 1343, 2005 122–3. For the LM III tablet, M. Ventris and J. Chadwick, *Documents in Mycenaean Greek*, Cambridge: Cambridge University Press, 1973, 310.

27 R. Dawkins and M. Laistner, "The Excavation of the Kamares Cave in Crete," *BSA* 19 (1912–13) 1–34. Summary: Watrous, *The Cave Sanctuary of Zeus at Psychro*, 60–1. Moss, "The Minoan Pantheon," 127–9. A. van de Moortel, "A Re-examination of the Pottery from the Kamares Cave," in M. Weiner et al., eds., *Pottery and Society: The Impact of Recent Studies of Minoan Pottery*, Boston: Archaeological Institute of America, 2006, 73–93. A. van de Moortel, "The Phaistos Palace and the Kamares Cave: A Special Relationship," in W. Gauss et al., eds., *Our Cups are Full: Pottery and Society in the Aegean Bronze Age*, BAR International Series 2227 (2011) 306–318.

28 P. Mountjoy, "Ritual Associations for LM IB Marine Style Vases," *L'Iconographie Minoenne*, BCH Supplement 11 (1985) 231–42. F. Vandenabeele, "Le monde marin dans les sanctuaires minoens," in R. Laffineur and G. Basch, eds., *Thalassa: L'Egee prehistorique et la mer*, Aegaeum 7, Liege: University of Liege, 1991, 239–52.

29 J.-C. Poursat, "Un sanctuaire de Minoen moyen II a Mallia," *BCH* 90 (1966) 514–51. Gesell, "Town, Palace and House Cult in Minoan Crete," 106–7. Poursat, "Cult Activity at Malia in the Protopalatial Period," 71–8. Poursat in A. D' Agata et al., <u>Archaeologies of Cult</u>, Hesperia Supplement 42, 2009.

30 MacGillivray et al., *The Palaikastro Kouros*. BSA Studies 6, Athens, 2000.

31 H. Boyd-Hawes et al., *Gournia, Vasiliki and Other Prehistoric Sites on the Isthmus of Hierapetra, Crete*, Philadelphia: INSTAP Academic Press, 2014 (reprint), 47–8. The material from house shrines has been meticulously collected by Geraldine Gesell in "Town, Palace, and House Cult in Minoan Crete," *SIMA* 67 (1985).

32 G. Cadogan, "A Probable Shrine in the Country House at Pyrgos," in Hagg and Marinatos, *Sanctuaries and Cults*, 169–71.

33 P. Betancourt, "The Household Shrine in the House of the Rhyta at Pseira," in *Potnia: Deities and Religion in the Aegean Bronze Age*, Aegeaum 22, Liege: University of Liege and Austin: University of Texas, 2001, 145–9.

34 J. and M. Shaw, "Excavations at Kommos (Crete) during 1986–1992," *Hesperia* 62 (1993) 131–61 and especially 149–53 and pls. 23 and 24 for House X shrine. G. Gesell, "Town, Palace and House Cult in Minoan Crete," lists over forty examples of domestic shrines in houses.

35 P. Betancourt, "Egyptian Connections at Hagios Charalambos," in R. Laffineur and E.Greco, eds., *EMPORIA, II*, Aegeaum 25, Liege: University of Liege, 2005, 449–53.

36 J. Soles, "The Prepalatial Cemeteries at Mochlos and Gournia," *Hesperia* Supplement 24 (1992) 1–40.

37 P. Muhly, Μινικος Λαξευτος Ταφος στον Πορο Ηρακλειου, Athens: Bibliothiki tis en Athhnais Arxaiolikis Etaireias, 1992, summary in English, 182–97. N. Dimopoulou, "The Neopalatial Cemetery of the Knossian Harbor Town at Poros: Mortuary Behavior and Social Ranking," in *Eliten in der Bronzezeit*, Mainz: Verlag der Romisch- Germanisches Zentralmuseums and Rudolf Habelt Verlag, 1999, 27–36.

38 P. Warren, "Of Baetyls," *Opus Atheniensia* 18 (1990) 193–206. S. Crooks, "What are Queer Stones? Baetyls: Epistemology of a Minoan Fetish," *BAR* International Series 2511 (2013). Sacred stones as the focus of worship also existed among the Hittites: bull sacrifice (e.g. *CMS* I 180); flower offering (e.g. *CMS* V, supplement vol. IB 113. I 27).

39 L. Goodison, "Why All This about Oak or Stone? Trees and Boulders in Minoan Religion," in D'Agata and Van de Moortel, *Archaeologies of Cult*, 51–7.

40 C. Andrews, *Amulets of Ancient Egypt*, London: British Museum Press, 1994. More recently, N. Marinatos, "Religious Interaction between Egypt and the Aegean in the Second Millennium BCE," in P. Creaseman and R. Wilkinson, eds., *Pharoah's Land and Beyond*, Oxford: Oxford University Press, 2017, 229–37.

41 F. Woudhuizen, "The Bee Sign (Evans No. 86): An Instance of Egyptian Influence on Cretan Hieroglyphic," *Kadmos* 36 (1997) 97–110.

42 V. Watrous, "The Origin and Iconography of the Late Minoan Painted Larnax," *Hesperia* 60 (1991) 285–307. N. Marinatos, *Minoan Kingship and the Solar Goddess*, Champaign: University of Illinois, 2010, 140–50.

43 Several deities: L. Goodison, "Beyond the 'Great Mother': The Sacred World of the Minoans," in L. Goodison, and C. Morris, eds. *Ancient Goddesses: The Myths and the Evidence*, Madison: University of Wisconsin Press, 1998, 113–32. One goddess (and child): N. Marinatos, *Minoan Kingship and the Solar Goddess*, especially 151–66. G. Rethemiotakis, "The 'Divine Couple' Ring from Poros and the Origins on the Minoan Calendar," *Athemensiche Miteillungen* 131/2 (2016/17) 1–29.

44 Cretan Linear B tablets list gods associated with Crete: Enualios (later name of Ares), Atana Potnija (Mistress Athena), Potnija Dapuritojo (Mistress of the Labyrinth), Pade, Qersija, Pipituna, Eleuthia (Eileithyia), Paiawon (later name of Apollo), and Hephaestus. R. Hagg, "Religious Syncretism at Knossos?" in J. Driessen and A. Farnoux, eds., *La Crete Mycenienne*, *BCH* Supplement 30, 1997, 163–8. Artemis and Hermes should probably added to the above list.

45 Marinatos, *Minoan Religion*, University of South Carolina Press, 1993 147–66.

46 See A. Evans, *The Palace of Minos, III*, New York: Biblo and Tannen, 1964, 28, fig. 15a. This scene resembles the frescoes from Melos that show flying fish and a seated sea goddess holding a net.

47 A. Barclay, "The Potnia Theron: Adaptation of a Near Eastern Image," in Laffineur and Niemeier, *POTNIA*, 373–86, and S. Hiller, "Potnia/Potnios Aigion: On the Religious Aspects of Goats in the Aegean Late Bronze Age," in Laffineur and Niemeier, *POTNIA*,

293–304. Lilies from frescoes at Amnissos, Agia Triada, and SE House and House of the Frescoes at Knossos. See Hood, *The Arts in Prehistoric Greece*, New Haven, CT: Yale University Press, 1978, 55. These animals are published in the *CMS* volumes: dogs (VII 118), birds (VII 134), waterfowl (IX 154), snakes, goats, and dolphins (V supl. IB 116), dogs (VII 118), and birds (VII 134).

48   Scenes appear in the *CMS* volumes: lions (IX 153), bulls (VIII 147), hounds (II.8 248), stags (V 594), dolphins (V 181), and wild goats (IX 153).

49   J. Crowley, "In Honour of the Gods – But Which Gods? Identifying Deities in Aegean Glyptic," in *DAIS: The Aegean Feast*, Aegaeum 29, Liege: University of Liege, 2008, 75–88.

50   Macgillivray et al., *The Palaikastro Kouros*.

51   A. Macgillivray, J. Driesson and H. Sackett, *The Palaikastro Kouros*, BSA Studies 6, 2000, 96, 106.

52   P. Haider, "Minoan Deities in an Egyptian Medical Text," Laffineur and Hagg, *POTNIA*, 479–82.

53   J. Weingarten, *The Transformation of Egyptian Taweret into the Minoan Genius: A Study in Cultural Transmission in the Middle Bronze Age*, SIMA 88 (1991). For Taweret, J. Weingarten, "The Transformation of Egyptian Taweret into the Minoan Genius," in A. Karetsou, ed., *ΚΡΗΤΗ-ΑΙΓΥΠΤΟΣ. Πολιτισμικοι δεσμοι τριων χιλιετιων* (Essays), *Athens: Kapon Editions*, 2000, 114–19 and J. Weingarten, "The Arrival of Egyptian Taweret and Bes(et) on Minoan Crete: Contact and Choice," in L. Bombardieri et al., eds., *Identity and Connectivity*, BAR International Series 2581 (2013) 371–78. F. Blakolmer, "Was the 'Minoan Genius' a God?" in P. Creaseman and R. Wilkinson, eds., *Ancient Mediterranean Interconnections, Journal of Ancient Egyptian Interconnections* 7 (2015) 29–40.

54   A. Furumark, "Linear A and Minoan Religion," *Opus Atheniensa* 17 (1988) 52–90.

EIGHT

MINOAN ART IN THE FIRST AND SECOND PALATIAL PERIODS

INTRODUCTION

The eminent scholar Martin Nilsson once observed that the civilization of Minoan Crete "has come down to us as a picturebook without a text."[1] For this reason it is difficult to overstate the importance of the Minoans' art for understanding their culture.

Minoan art is very different from that of other ancient Mediterranean peoples. Lacking an authoritarian political structure, the Minoans had no need for monumental art, as in Egypt or the Levant. A dominant royal iconography, so important in the Near East, is absent. References to historical events – military victories or political events – are also missing. The focus of Minoan art is primarily on the natural world: landscapes, animals, and plants.

The distinctive nature of Minoan society and its art can be seen by a few basic comparisons with Egypt, one of its main trading partners. In Egypt, houses and even palaces were for the living, perceived as temporary inhabitants, and so were constructed of mudbrick. Only funerary structures were carefully built of stone – to last for eternity. In contrast, upper-class Minoan houses and palaces show a love of color: they were built of specially selected stone, creamy white gypsum, blue-green or white limestone (even for streets), all carefully dressed. Minoan architecture is often polychrome: examples include red-paneled plaster floors (Malia and Pseira), blue-green schist slabs set as a border around a pebble floor (Knossos palace, South Propylaeum), red schist border fronting the veranda (Myrtos/Pyrgos), and veined gypsum dado panels (Knossos and Chania).

In Egypt, most carved and painted imagery is found on royal monuments and in tombs. In Crete, art comes from the contexts of daily life. It is absent from tombs (until the Mycenaean period). Egyptian art was commissioned by and for royalty and the nobility – hence clay pottery for the masses was left plain. The opposite was true in Crete: even objects of daily use found in lower-class homes were beautifully decorated. By the Neopalatial period, Cretan society seems to have developed a prosperous "middle" class based on various occupations and activities, that is, craftsmen of different sorts, potters, masons, mariners, textile weavers, producers of wine and oil, and merchants. Much of Minoan art was made to appeal to them.

Minoan art appears primarily in four media: (1) wall and floor frescoes, (2) seals, (3) clay vases, and (4) stone vases. Each artistic medium had its own function within Minoan society. We will begin by examining each type on its own before trying to use art to understand Minoan culture. LM III funerary art is considered in Chapter 7.

FRESCO PAINTING

Fresco paintings, an elite art form, are best understood in their architectural context. Cultural conclusions are presented in the final section (Observations on Minoan Art and Culture).

Palace

Palatial fresco scenes depict large group activities held at the palace (Figs. 7.2 and 7.3). These paintings show ceremonies (discussed in Chapters 5 and 7). Many frescoes only survive in fragments so their overall subject remains uncertain. More complete frescoes show processions, dancing, bull hunting, bull leaping, communal gatherings at ceremonies, and shrine settings.

Houses

We can recognize three partly overlapping themes in Neopalatial house scenes: (1) landscapes, (2) cult activity, and (3) narratives.

The Bluebird and Monkey fresco (Fig. 8.1) from the House of the Frescoes, Room Q, upper floor, at Knossos is a scene of nature. This brightly colored rocky landscape is alive with flowers – lily, rose, iris, crocus, vetch, papyrus, reeds, ivy, and myrtle – blue streams and monkeys. On the left (north) wall, blue monkeys on a red background have scattered flying doves from their nests. On the middle (south) and east walls, monkeys eat the eggs from the nests as the doves fly away in a creamy Nilotic-like background of reeds and

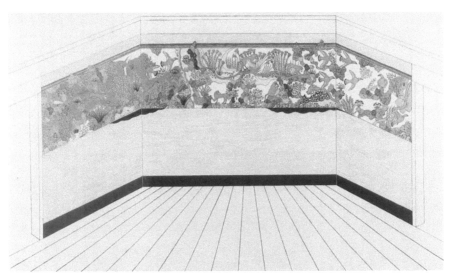

8.1 Landscape of Bluebirds and Monkeys.
Evely (1999), 247. Mark Cameron, Person Papers CAM 1

papyrus. Flowers are vividly colored: green and blue ivy stalks, pink rose, blue papyrus with orange flowers, pink and light blue iris. The scene itself is largely an artistic creation, since monkeys cannot have been a common sight in Crete. Moreover, the artist has made up colors for some plants not found in nature and combined vegetation from different environments. The intent was to celebrate nature in a striking way.

A second scene of nature is the Spring Landscape (Fig. 8.2) from Akrotiri on Thera. It is from Room D2, a bedroom that held a raised floor dais for a wooden bed. The dramatic volcanic landscape of rock outcrops has stripes of red, yellow, and blue soil with clumps of red lilies and darting swallows. White lilies (painted red) are rendered in different stages of bloom. Two swallows are excitedly interacting (Fig. 8.3). With the arrival of good weather, the two male birds are fighting over territory. This fresco presents a particularly dramatic vision of spring.

A third nature scene, the Anemones and Osiers frieze (Fig. 8.4), comes from the Unexplored Mansion, Room P, upper floor, at Knossos. The frieze shows an undulating ground line from which grow three clumps of flowers: red and white petal "anemones" with stems of blue leaves, blue- and red-frilled sprays, and "osiers" with red palm-like flowers. Rockwork and bands of friezes are along the upper border. The scene depicts plants of different seasons blooming simultaneously. This exotic paradise-like landscape finds a parallel in the *Odyssey* (VII, 114–35) in the fantasy land of Phaeacia. Odysseus sees an magical orchard there – "four spacious acres planted with trees in bloom or weighted down for picking: pear trees, pomegranates, brilliant apples, luscious figs and olives ripe and dark."

8.2 Spring Landscape, Thera.
Marinatos (1984), fig. 6.2

Cult activities, a second theme, were often depicted in homes. Our first example, from Xeste 3 at Akrotiri, Room 3a-b is a scene (Fig. 8.5, lower frieze) of girls walking to a peak sanctuary. The scene is set in the lustral basin (ground floor), north wall of Room 3a. The left girl carries a prominent necklace, probably meant as an offering. In the middle, a girl wearing a pomegranate pin around her neck and a floral spray of myrtle or olive in her hair sits on a rock. She has just cut her foot – it is bleeding – and she puts her hand up to her forehead in pain. A crocus flower that she had gathered has fallen by her foot. To the right, the third girl has unveiled her head and looks toward the sanctuary on the east wall. The sanctuary entrance is painted with lilies and stained with red crocus styles. On the west side (3b) of Room 3 (ground floor), a frieze on the north and west walls shows men climbing up a hilltop peak sanctuary and making offerings (liquid, textiles, and probably food) there. The scenes complement the daily rites that would have taken place in the lustral basin below by presenting major communal acts by men and women making their annual or semi-annual offerings at a regional peak sanctuary. The fresco scene presents an explanation of why the daily rites were carried out in the lustral basin.

A second cultic scene comes from Xeste 3 in the lustral basin (first floor) of Room 3a-b (Fig. 8.5, upper frieze). On the east wall of Room 3, three young girls gather crocuses in a rocky landscape, an entirely real event drawn from daily life. The adjoining north wall is a mixture of realism and religious belief: a

8.3 Swallows in Spring Landscape, Thera.
Detail of Fig. 8.2

fourth girl pours the crocuses she has gathered from her basket to a goddess
who sits on an elevated tripartite shrine resembling a peak sanctuary shrine.
A monkey in front of her offers the flowers to the goddess. The goddess wears
a necklace ornamented with beads, ducks, and dragonflies and is flanked by a
griffin behind her. On the west side of Room 3 (first floor) was a fowling scene
of ducks in a marshy landscape of reeds being caught in nets. Like the crocus
flowers, the ducks may have been intended as offerings to the goddess. Scenes
in houses showing people carrying out cult activities were probably understood as representing the residents there and thus showing them as pious
worshippers deserving of the gods' protection.

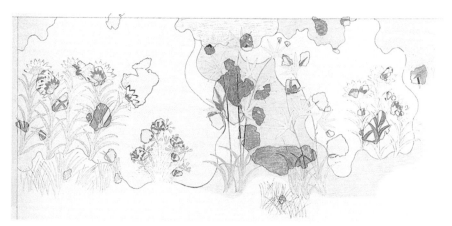

8.4 Landscape with Anemones and Osiers, Unexplored Mansion, Knossos.
Evely (1999), 209. Mark Cameron, personal papers, CAM 90

8.5 Girls walk to a peak sanctuary (lower); girls gather flowers to offer to seated goddess
(upper). Xeste 3 Thera.
Marinatos (1984), figs. 62, 64

A third scene of cult practices, from Room 14 at Agia Triada, shows a
woman gathering flowers below a goddess (Fig. 8.6), Room 14 is a narrow
rectangular bedroom with a raised dais that held a bed at its east, narrow end.
The goddess is flanked on the right by a landscape with wild animals – goats,

8.6 Goddess of Wild and Domesticated Landscapes, Agia Triada.
Evely (1999), 242. *BSA*.

cats, and birds – and mountains. On the left a kneeling woman in a tranquil
garden-like scene gathers crocuses, lilies, and violets. Above the bed, a goddess
stands in front of a shrine, her arms upraised in benedictive pose. (The bottom
part of this scene is missing – it was burned by the wooden bed when the
building was destroyed.) The goddess faces to the right, toward the rocky
landscape of jumping *agrimia*, birds, a cat stalking a bird, and flowers. In this
fresco the connection of the divine with nature is made explicit: the Artemis-
like goddess offers her protection for the woman sleeping in the room.

Within the wild landscape is a well-known detail drawn from nature of a cat
stalking a quail. I can testify to the accuracy of the scene from my own
experience. Some years ago I was walking on an archaeological survey in the
fields near Gournia. It had rained that morning and the countryside was alive
with the sounds of birds. At one point I stopped as a mother quail crossed in
front of me followed by a line her baby chicks. All of a sudden I spotted a feral
cat behind a bush who was stalking the birds. I felt I had been transported back
into the Minoan past!

Cult wall paintings in houses often depict a scene that served as a prototype
explaining the daily domestic activities carried out within the household by the
inhabitants. An example from contemporary life today might be a photograph
of the family at church for Easter Mass in a house where daily prayers were
observed. Bedroom fresco scenes could function much like Byzantine icons,
offering divine protection for the sleeping resident.

Scenes based on narrative stories also occur on house frescoes. The famous
Fleet Fresco (Fig. 8.7) from the West House, Room 5, upper floor at Akrotiri
tells a story in a clockwise fashion of a naval expedition to several places in the
Aegean and the successful return of the fleet home.[2] The owner of the house
must have been a ship's captain since an unusually large number of Minoan
vases were found in his house. The sea journey, to two towns, began on the
poorly preserved west wall. On the north wall two separate scenes are preserved. A group of reconnoitering men meet on a hill with the fleet com-
mander, identified by his elaborate cloak, to tell him what they saw in this new
land. One of them points to the right. This scene is closely paralleled in the

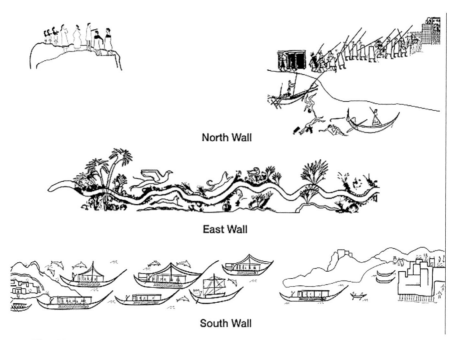

North Wall

East Wall

South Wall

8.7 Fleet Fresco.
Drawing by Arielle Channin

Odyssey (X, 80–5) when Odysseus arrives in the faraway country of Lamos. He climbs a hill and sends out a party of men to scout the territory. The second scene on the north wall shows the fleet winning a sea battle against the local natives. On the coast is a building (shipshed?), women drawing water from a well, and a group of goatherds with two herders. There the warriors of the fleet march up a hill to besiege a walled city, an event reminiscent of the Trojan War in the *Iliad*.

The east wall depicts a Nilotic river landscape populated with palm trees and papyri. A wild cat chases a duck and a griffin pursues a deer and ducks. This exotic landscape represents how the Aegeans envisioned Egypt. Aegean fleets blown off course, to exotic faraway places such as Egypt, were a popular theme in the *Odyssey*. Both Menelaos (IV, 350–480) and Odysseus (XIV, 199–264) report being diverted to the land of Egypt. Finally, on the south wall the fleet leaves a foreign town set on the coast, moves across the sea followed by jumping dolphins, and enters its home port town, probably Akrotiri. Women and men in town watch their arrival and boys run down to the wharf to greet the returning fleet.

The parallel with the *Iliad* and the *Odyssey* is obvious. Such a sea yarn must have been a popular subject for Aegean mariners meeting in Room 5 at the West House in Akrotiri to tell the inexperienced young, represented here on the corners by the two boys holding fish (an occupation that defines immature males) approaching the room.

SEALS

In Minoan society seals had two overlapping functions: (1) to identify individuals in their interactions with others, and (2) as good luck symbols that
provided a deity's protection.[3] Seals were provided with string-holes and were
worn by individual owners and as adornment. Minoan seal imagery distin-
guishes the status, profession, and identity of seal owners within society. The
result is an astonishing number and variety of scenes. Most Minoan seal
imagery differs markedly from Egyptian/Near Eastern examples in their naturalistic style and use of a single main motif. In Egypt, seals are largely amuletic,
hieroglyphic inscriptions (titles), or abstract designs.[4] In the Levant, seals of the
Akkadian–Old Babylonian periods (2500–1500 BC) largely depict cult scenes
(offerings, gods, banquets, or processions).[5] While a few Cretan seals (often
with Egyptianizing motifs, such as a scorpion or spider) appear amuletic, the
great majority depict animals and plants, religious motifs – double ax, bucania,
lily, horns of consecration, birds – cult scenes, and a few "professional"
activities, such as hunting, shepherding, weaving, battle, and seafaring.

The imagery on Minoan seals also developed over time. During the
Prepalatial period, seal designs were mostly abstract linear or geometric designs.
But with the reorganization of Minoan society (Chapter 4) in the Protopalatial
period, a new visual vocabulary was created. Seals begin to feature a wide
range of animal life – wild goats, bulls, dogs, boar, cats, stylized lions, spiders,
and bees.[6] Animals were deliberately chosen for and depicted in a way that
emphasizes their distinctive physical strength or power, for example a fierce
hound (Fig. 8.8), or agile *agrimi* (Fig. 8.9) and for their exotic or fantastic nature
(monkey and sphinx). Seals also begin to depict professions: men and women
are shown engaged in activities such weaving on a loom, holding a fish, and
hunting with a bow and arrow. Seals depicting a boat may have belonged to
seamen.

In the Neopalatial period Minoan seal scenes became even more complex,
due partly to the fact that some of the motifs and themes were derived from
larger art forms such as wall painting. Human professions become more
popular and diverse. Gestures are important: figures interact by gesture –
command, greet, beckon, point – and address one another. Neopalatial seals
often depict animals and people in landscape settings (as in wall painting) in
rocky terrain, among grass, reeds, palms, and flowers, and beside a river. Scenes
were often drawn directly from observations of daily life, for example a man
milking a cow, a goat in a tree (Fig. 8.10), and a dog scratching itself (Fig. 8.11).
These scenes instantly capture the character of their subjects. Scenes could also
carry multiple messages: a profession could also be signs of social status. For
example, an image of a ship could identify the owner as a mariner and
therefore as elite. A battle scene before a gate (Fig. 8.12) – as in *Iliad*, Book

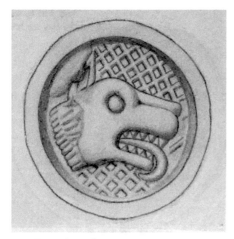

8.8 Fierce hound.
CMS II 5, 300

8.9 Wild goat (*agrimi*) in the mountains.
Poursat (2008), 238, fig. 328

22 when Hector and Achilles fight before the Skaian gate at Troy – designated the owner as a warrior and a noble. Scenes of cult and deities (Chapter 7) may have belonged to officials/priests and/or provided the protection of a deity.

Some scenes may well have been selected by the owner as a personal symbol or epithet drawn from popular sayings or narratives. Several seal scenes can be explained in this fashion, for example a lion could be understood as a symbol of an individual's strength, as "lion hearted Achilles" in the *Iliad* (V. 639, VII, 228); and a swift runner (Fig. 8.13) might be a reference to a person's reputation like "swift-footed Achilles" (*Iliad* I.58). A seaman fending off a sea monster (Fig. 8.14) could represent a mariner's exotic overseas adventures, similar to Odysseus experiences, as with Scylla (*Odyssey*, 12, 85–100). These scenes depict the *kleos* (reputation) of the owner, as dramatic scenes do in Homeric epic.

STONE AND METAL VASES

Minoan stone and metal vases were expensive objects often decorated with designs and scenes. In MM III–LM I stone vases were made for domestic use, for ritual and elite gatherings, and as objects for overseas exchange. Vases were made in many shapes, including specialized ones for cult practices, such as *rhyta* with lion and bovine heads. Used in elite social gatherings, stone vases, mostly *rhyta*, are decorated with ceremonial or ritual scenes of boxing, hunting, a sacrificial offering, peak sanctuaries, and bull leaping. Other specialized objects made in stone were offering tables, *kernoi*, and ladles.

The stone Harvester Rhyton (Fig. 8.15), from the Agia Triada, depicts a procession of twenty-seven men moving from left to right, led by a leader wearing a special cloak and holding a staff. On their way out to the fields at harvest time for olives, the men are carrying branched staffs used to beat the olives off the trees. They are singing out loud to the musical accompaniment of

(a)   (b)

8.10 Sealing of wild goat in a tree (a); photo of a wild goat in a tree in mountains above (b). Kritsa CMS III 150.
Photo by Sabine Beckmann

a singer who plays a *sistrum*. The men are clearly enjoying themselves – they are smiling and looking at one other, and in all the excitement one has actually stumbled. The scene is a reference to the oil that would have been in this ceremonial vase.

The Boxer Rhyton (Fig. 8.16), from Agia Triada, has four registers with young males taking part in violent athletic contests. The uppermost depicts standing boxers wearing helmets and gloves fighting one another in an architectural setting indicated by columns. The second frieze shows acrobats

8.11 Sealing of dog scratching itself. *CMS* II 7, 64

and bulls in a flying gallop. One leaper has been gored by a bull – the horn protrudes from his back. The third and fourth friezes of boxers repeat the first register except one of each boxing pair has been knocked to the ground.

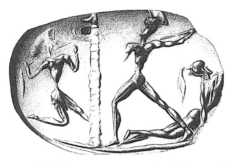

8.12 Battle between two warriors in front of a gate.
CMS II 6, 17

8.13 Seal from Kato Syme, runner.
Crowley (2013), fig. I. 40

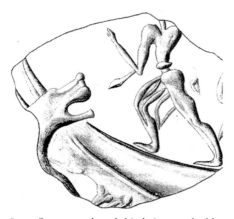

8.14 Seaman on board ship being attacked by a sea monster.
CMS 8. 2. 1

Technical details and the style of a gold cup (Fig. 8.17) from the Vapheio tomb in Sparta mark this cup as Minoan.[7] The frieze depicts three bulls and a cow in a landscape with a rough ground line, a rocky background, and two olive trees. The frieze tells a story that reads from right to left. A bull, head lowered, has smelled the scent of a cow. In the center, the bull has found the cow. She turns her head to him and her raised tail signals her sexual attraction to the bull. The bull's head snuggles her head, in an expressive frontal pose, as if they were nuzzling affectionately. But the cow was a decoy meant to distract the bull, so in the next scene to the left the hunter has snuck up on the bull and is tying his leg while the bull roars with rage!

Minoan metalworkers made many other types of vases, for example cauldrons, jugs, cups, and basins. Some vases made for wealthy patrons were embossed with decorative designs such as spirals, meanders, arcades, ivy, rosettes, and bucrania.

CLAY VASES

Minoan clay vases, regardless of their use, were almost all decorated in one way or another with painted or relief designs. Many bore details – including spirals, marine scenes, and floral motifs – derived from wall painting. They are still astonishing today for their natural beauty and movement. Minoan vases were exported to Egypt and the Near East where such painted clay vases were unknown. During the Protopalatial period, the finest Minoan pottery is called Kamares ware, from the cave where vases of this type were first found by excavators. Kamares cups often have eggshell-thin walls and angular shapes imitative of metal, such as this Kamares cup (Fig. 8.18), from the palace at Phaistos. The cup is decorated with white bands on the lip and rim and with pendant arcades holding orange flowers on the body. Kamares ware vases are painted with exquisite floral, curvilinear, and geometric designs in

(a)

(b)

8.15 A row of harvesters.
Marinatos (1993), 138, fig. 108

8.16 Young men boxing and bull leaping.
Koehl (2006), 164–6, fig. 29

8.17 Gold cup; bull caught through the use of a cow as a decoy.
Evans (1964), 179, fig. 123 B

8.18 Kamares ware cup. HM 10570. HMC/TAP. SAA.
Photo by the author

8.19 Bowl painted with floral sprays. HM 3856. HMC/TAP. *BSA.*

8.20 Marine-style vases. HM 3383, 393, 3396. HMC/TAP. *BSA.*

white, red, and orange against a dark background. Later, in the Neopalatial period,
vases were decorated with dark on light
motifs imitative of stone as well as religious
motifs, and a wide variety of details from the
natural world, such as plants (Fig. 8.19) and
marine creatures (Fig. 8.20). Marine creatures – fish, dolphins, Argonauts, tritons,
etc. – become especially popular after the
disastrous Theran eruption as appropriate
imagery for vases intended for use to pour
libations to a powerful sea deity.[8]

8.21 Bees on a honeycomb. HM 559. HMC/
TAP.
Photo by Mark Williams

JEWELRY

In Minoan society jewelry was worn by both
sexes.[9] Beginning in the Early Minoan
period (Chapter 3) gold leaf was used to make diadems, hair pins, bracelets,
hair sprays, chain pendants of leaves and sprays, necklaces beads in simple
shapes, and clothing ornaments in the shape of disks, stars, and strips. By the

Protopalatial period, some jewelry becomes more substantial and elaborate. Jewelry shapes include bracelets, hoop earrings, and finger rings with bezels. Pendants use globular beads of amethyst, crystal, and faience. Colorful stone beads were made of amethyst, cornelian, agate, jasper, lapis lazuli, chalcedony, rock crystal, and simple steatite. A gold pendant (Fig. 8.21) from the Chrysolakkos tomb at Malia features two filigreed bees placed heraldically above a honeycomb. The bees are storing a drop of honey in the comb. Above is a small cage with a gold bead. Three granulated disks hang from the bees.

8.22 Hound stalking a wild goat. *CMS* VI, 180

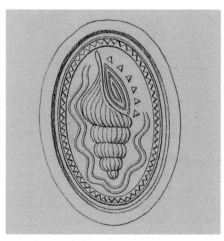

8.23 Triton shell. SM. HMC/TAP. Photo by the author

In the Neopalatial period, pendant beads assumed many diverse shapes drawn from nature: grains of wheat, drums, almonds, melons, lotus, papyrus-lily, ivy, shell, flower, pomegranate, and palm leaves.[10] Single pendants are made with spirals or in the shape of animals, for example a lion, goat, fish, and bull. Crocus blossoms and the iris appear as gold hair pins. Small signet rings, meant to be suspended from a necklace or bracelet, feature gold or rock crystal bezels.

OBSERVATIONS ON MINOAN ART AND CULTURE

Based on our descriptions above, what can we say generally about Minoan art? Three distinctive aspects of Minoan art stand out. First, Minoan art was created to have an immediate effect on the viewer. Minoan landscapes seem to depict the world naturalistically, often in a striking fashion. This can be achieved by boldly inventive and impressionistic color and detail in a way that is intended to delight the viewer. Scenes reveal the artist's joy with nature and storytelling. Figures can be dramatic, even violent. Hunters aim their weapon, duel with an animal, or may be trampled by a bull or boar. Scenes of war (Fig. 8.12) and bull leaping (cover and Fig. 7.3) are depicted at a climactic moment. Hunt scenes include wild animals being stalked by a dog (Fig 8.22), chased, wounded, and howling in pain.

Second, Minoan art was produced and made for a wide segment of society, both elite and commoner. Cretan society possessed a large and prosperous middle class (Chapters 4 and 5) that enjoyed substantial socioeconomic power. The tastes of common people were appealed to. Personal possessions such as jewelry and seals depicted a wide range of interesting shapes and scenes. Even the clay vases from village houses were beautifully painted, showing an unpretentious enjoyment of nature.

Third, most Minoan art focuses on the world of nature. The Minoans seem to have had an intimate relationship with their surrounding landscape. In present-day Greece, the visitor is struck by how the rural landscape – mountaintops, caves, springs, gorges, rivers – are marked by an Orthodox chapel. Many of these sites also bear archaeological traces of being an earlier shrine in Minoan–Roman antiquity. This religious connection – a perception that the features of the natural world are associated with divinities – are likely the result of the Orthodox Church's appropriation of an ancient religious idea to further its own acceptance by the people. This could not be more different than the situation in Egypt and the Near East where cities were surrounded by desert wastelands regarded as hostile and chaotic. As described in Chapter 1, Minoan closeness with nature was probably a result of the islanders' economic dependency on a diverse vertical (sea, plains, mountains) environment. The number and variety of Minoan representations of nature are astonishing. Scenes are drawn from *all* the environmental zones of Crete: the sea, shoreline, land, rivers, mountains, and sky.[11] From the sea come octopus (Fig. 8.20), dolphins (Fig. 7.31), flying fish, mackerel, nautilus, tunny fish, sea bream, sword fish, eel, cuttlefish, argonauts, triton (Fig. 8.23),

8.24 Narcissus in blossom, offering table, Palaikastro. HM 3692. Photo by Janet Spiller

8.25 A bank of reeds.
CMS II 6, 124

cockle shell, and sea urchin. From the beach and shoreline come Pancratium lilies, crab, and date palms. The triton shell, an object found in shrines, suggest

8.26 Waterbirds.
CMS II 6, 124

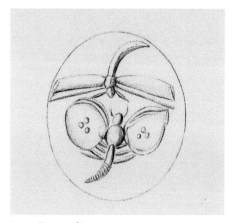

8.27 Dragonflies.
CMS VII, 68

8.28 Flying birds.
CMS II 8, 289

these animals may have been understood as attributes for a deity. Plant and animal motifs from the plains and hills are many: flowers, blossoming narcissus (Fig. 8.24), saffron crocus, grass, ivy, olives, sheep, and bulls. River courses are marked by reeds (Fig. 8.25), papyrus, egrets, water birds (Fig. 8.26), and dragonflies (Fig. 8.27). Mountain scenes include cypress, wild goats (Figs. 8.9 and 8.10), and stag. The sky produces flying birds (Fig. 8.28) such as the eagle, dove, owl, hoopoe, and bluebird, as well as bees and butterflies. Significantly, scenes of nature often record its fertility. Goats copulate (Fig. 8.29). Mother dogs and goats are shown with their puppies (Fig. 8.30) or kid (Fig. 8.31). A fleet stag and his deer frolic together, shown with their heads nuzzling (Fig. 8.32). Many Minoan scenes of nature display love or affection. Minoan art depicts nature as vividly alive, active, and abundantly fertile.

Minoan art suggests that the natural world was understood as being a divine manifestation. Nature is depicted as imbued with a divine presence. In later periods this concept is called pantheism. This is done in several ways. Easiest to understand are scenes showing mortals and deities together in the same landscape. In the Xeste 3 fresco (Fig. 8.5) mortal girls gather saffron and offer it to a goddess. In the Agia Triada fresco (Fig. 8.6) a woman picks flowers in the presence of a protective goddess who controls wild animals. Nature often appears with attributes symbolic of specific deities. In religious shrines and sanctuaries, the Minoan gods (Chapter 7) appear with specific animals and plants – birds, poppies, crocuses, lilies, birds, snakes, wild goats, dogs, ducks, fish, seashells, and dolphins, to name a few. Deities are often depicted in scenes interacting with – controlling or nourishing – plants and animals. Several flowers appear in religious contexts:

painted on offering tables (crocus, narcissus, Fig. 8.23), altars (lily), and votives at sanctuaries (beetles and fish). Many other images – bees, cicadas, beetles, narcissus, ivy, dittany – were also religious emblems.[12] Hence, when these plants and animals appear in landscapes, their divine connection is understood. For this reason, the numerous animals in Minoan art, especially on scals, may be understood as religious symbols meant to provide the owner with the relevant deity's protection. The triton shell (Fig. 8.23) for example, is often found in Minoan shrines. The dragonfly (Fig. 8.27) is worn as jewelry by the goddess in the Xesti 3 fresco (Fig. 8.5). The same may be true for plants in Minoan art. This Minoan tradition continues into the later Greek period. In Homer's *Iliad* (3, 371–3), Athena appears as a bird. In Greek art, the gods also had animals and plants as attributes: Zeus is associated with the eagle, Athena the owl, Aphrodite the dolphin and dove, Poseidon fish and dolphins, Artemis deer, and Demeter wheat and the poppy.

This divine aspect of nature is sometimes made explicit when the Minoan artist deliberately mixes plants and animals of different seasons of the year and from different environments in a single scene. Crocuses, an autumn flower, appear together with spring-time lilies in scenes found on jewelry and ritual vessels suggesting a fertile cycle of regeneration. In the Xeste 3 fresco a landscape of flowers of different environments are depicted side by side: rocky (crocus, lily) and marsh (reeds, papyrus). The landscape (Fig. 8.1) from the House of the Frescoes at Knossos deliberately mixes animals from different environmental zones – monkeys and rock doves – to create an imaginative natural event. The artist creates hybrid versions of plants. They are given unrealistic colors and

8.29 Wild goats copulating.
CMS II 3, 339

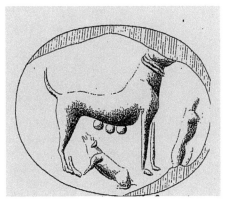

8.30 Mother dog and pups.
CMS II 6, 70

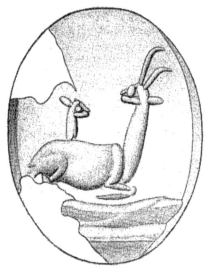

8.31 Mother goat and kid.
CMS II 3, 339

different shaped leaves or numbers of petals from the original species. This mixture transcends reality: it expresses a super abundance, a rich profusion of animals and plants, regeneration and renewal in nature. The underlying message is that the fruitfulness and abundance depicted in these landscape scenes has a divine origin. Growth of nature to fruition and fertility is a power caused by the gods.

8.32 Stag and his deer.
CMS 6, 70

In the contemporary West we are accustomed to carefully distinguishing between what is secular and what is religious in the world around us. This modern perspective did not exist in Minoan prehistory. Minoan culture viewed the natural world pantheistically. One of the reasons for the attractiveness of Minoan art today is the nostalgic pang we feel when we look at the Minoan world of natural beauty, just like ours, but filled with a caring divine presence.

NOTES

1   M. Nilsson, *The Minoan-Mycenaean Religion and Its Survival into Greek Religion*, Lund: CWK Gleerup, 1950, 7.

2   V. Watrous, "The Fleet Fresco, The Odyssey and Greek Epic Narrative," S. Morris and R. Laffineur, eds., *EPOS: Reconsidering Greek Epic and Aegean Bronze Age Archaeology*, Aegaeum 28, Liege: University of Liege, 2007, 97–105. Motifs: lions, star(fish), butterfly (psyche, soul), flower, dolphins, doves, crocus blossom; all motifs found on Minoan seals and used as divine attributes. Herodotus (1.171) records that islanders manned the ships of King Minos. The fresco may therefore depict a Theran-Cretan expedition.

3   D. Collon makes the same observation for Near Eastern seals in *First Impressions: Cylinder Seals in the Ancient Near East*, London: British Museum Press, 2005, 113. J. Crowley, "Prestige Clothing in the Bronze Age Aegean," in M.-L. Nosch and R. Laffineur, eds., *Kosmos: Jewellery, Adornment and Textiles in the Aegean Bronze Age*, Aegaeum 33, Liege: Peeters, 2012, 231–9 documents the connection between identity/social status and clothing as they appear on seal scenes. Also, O. Krzyszkowska, "Worn to Impress? Symbol and Status in Aegean Glyptic," in Nosch and Laffineur, *Kosmos*, 739–48. The following description is based on seals found on Crete, that is, *CMS* vols. II 2, 5, 6, 7, and 8 (1 and 2), III 1, and IV.

4   E. A. Wallis Budge, *Amulets and Superstitions*, New York: Dover, 1978. P. Germond, *The Symbolic World of Egyptian Amulets*, Milan: 5 Continents Edition, 2005.

5   D. Collon, *First Impressions: Cylinder Seals in the Ancient Near East*, Chicago: University of Chicago Press, 1987. D. Collon, *Near Eastern Seals*, Oakland: University of California Press, 1990. J. Black and A. Green, *Gods, Demons and Symbols of Ancient Mesopotamia*, Austin: University of Texas at Austin, 1992. B. Tessier, *Ancient Near Eastern Cylinder Seals from the Marcopoli Collection*, Berkeley: University of California Press, 1984. I owe the second reference to Marta d' Andrea.

6   Minoan seals are published in the magisterial set of over thirty-five volumes in the *Corpus der Minoischen und Mykenischen Siegel* (*CMS*), Berlin. J. Crowley, *The Iconography of Aegean Seals*, Aegaeum 34, Liege: University of Liege, 2013 is a useful assemblage. For

Protopalatial seals, see O. Krzyszkowska's excellent study, *Aegean Seals: An Introduction*, *BICS* Supplement 85, London, 2005, 79–118.

7   E. Davis, "The Vapheio Cups: One Minoan and One Mycenaean?" *Art Bulletin* 56 (1974) 472–87.

8   P. Mountjoy, "Ritual Associations for LM IB Marine Atyle Vases," in *L'Iconographie Minoenne*, *BCH* supplement 11 (1985) 231–42.

9   See the articles in M.-L. Nosch and R. Laffineur, eds., *Kosmos: Jewellery, Adornment and textiles in the Aegean Bronze Age*, Aegeaum 33, Liege: Peeters, 2012.

10   Minoan jewelry: M. Effinger, "Minoischer Schmuck," *BAR* International Series 646 (1996). J. Younger and P. Rehak, "Neopalatial, Final Palatial and Postpalatial Crete," in T. Cullen, ed., *Aegean Prehistory: A Review*, *AJA* Supplement 1 (2001) 403–19.

11   See A. Evans, *The Palace of Minos, I*, London: MacMillan, 1925, 536–51; A. Evans, *The Palace of Minos, II*, vol. 2, London: MacMillan, 1927, 468–512. N. Marinatos, *Minoan Religion: Ritual, Image and Symbol*, Columbia: University of South Carolina Press, 1993, 193–6. M. Gill, "Some Observations on Representations of Marine Animals in Minoan Art, and their Identification," *BCH* Supplement 11 (1985) 63–81, identifies some seventeen different sea creatures: dolphin fish, mackerel, pilot fish, sea bream, nautilus, dolphin, flying fish, squid, tunny fish, crab, eel, swordfish, cuttlefish, mollusks (triton, cockle, etc.), starfish, and sea urchin. A. Chapin, "Power, Privilege and Landscape in Minoan art," *Hesperia* Supplement 33 (2004) 47–64, is a good introduction to Minoan frescoes.

12   Evans, *The Palace of Minos, II*, vol. 2, 450–99. P. Warren, "The Fresco of the Garlands from Knossos," *L'Iconographie Minoenne*, *BCH* Supplement 11 (1985) 186–207. N. Marinatos, *Minoan Religion: Ritual, Image, and Symbol*, Columbia: University of South Carolina Press, 1993, 193–200.

NINE

CRETE AT THE TIME OF THE FINAL PALACES (LM IIIA) AND THE POSTPALATIAL PERIOD, 1400–1050 BC

THE EASTERN MEDITERRANEAN – EGYPT, THE LEVANT, AND THE Aegean – became a closely interconnected region during the Late Bronze III period. After the island-wide horizon of destructions by the mainland Greeks in LM IB, Crete experienced three phases of broad cultural change. During the first phase (LM II–III A1, 1425–1360 BC) the population on the island was much reduced, due to the LM IB site destructions. The Mycenaean rulers took control of the palace at Knossos and from it administered a large kingdom that included over half of the island. The second phase (LM IIIA2–IIIB, 1360–1200 BC) began with a destruction of the Knossos palace toward the end of LM IIIA. During this period the island recovered, the island's population grew, settlements were rebuilt, and the island enjoyed wide international trade relations. Finally, in the third period (LM IIIC, 1200–1070 BC) the entire eastern Mediterranean world entered an era of violent turmoil. Many sites in southern Anatolia and Syria-Palestine were destroyed. The population on Crete dropped sharply, numerous settlements were abandoned, and groups of settlers retreated to defensive refuge settlements in the mountains.

CRETE IN LM II–IIIA1/2, 1425–1360 BC

Many Cretan settlements, for example Malia, Gournia, Vasiliki, Pseira, Palaikastro, Mochlos, Myrtos/Pyrgos, and Zakros, suffered violent destructions by fire in LM IB (Fig. 4.1).[1] At Mochlos, the excavator found skeletons in the destroyed houses. Final LM IB levels at Zakros, Petras, and Epano Zakros have also produced human bones. The island's population dropped sharply. In the area of Gournia, for example, a regional survey has shown that the number of LM I sites dropped from seventy-two down to ten in LM IIIA.[2] LM IB hidden caches of bronze objects have been found in Crete and they suggest that people knew of an impending invasion. In the succeeding LM II–IIIA1 period the Mycenaean Greek invaders were in control of the island. A new writing script, called Linear B, based on Minoan Linear A, was introduced. The language of Linear B is Greek. Deciphered by 1953 by Michael Ventris, Linear B can be read today. This script, made up of syllabic and pictographic signs, was restricted mainly to the palaces where it was used for the purpose of record keeping (described below). The Mycenaean rulers also took over and expanded the island's international trade relations. Trade with Cyprus, for its copper, boomed. Foreign imports arrive on Crete, for example a cartouche of Amenhotep III from a Knossian tomb,[3] a sealing of a Cypriote cylinder seal from the palace at Knossos,[4] and a scarab of Queen Tiye from Agia Triada.[5] A column in the temple of Amenhotep III (1391–1353 BC) at Luxor in Egypt lists countries known to the Egyptians – Keftiu (Crete), Mitanni, and Hittites. Another list from a statue base at Thebes lists Keftiu (Cretan) cities, Amnissos, Phaistos, Kydonia, and Lyktos.[6] A massive shipshed of this period for seagoing ships has been discovered at the port of Knossos at Katsambas in Heraklion. Seals become less numerous and are limited to rich burials. Their imagery becomes formal and less diverse: human figures, cult scenes, hunts, and combat are rare. Marine life and birds disappear in LM III.

Cretan towns suffered major changes during this period. Knossos, for example, was extensively rebuilt. Some ruined houses (South House, House of the Chancel Screen, House of the Frescoes, and House of the High Priest) remained unused. Other houses were rebuilt or reoccupied (Unexplored Mansion, Royal Villa, South-East House). The Little Palace was repaired and remodeled: scribes on the upper floor wrote Linear B tablets and many commodities (recorded by attaching over a hundred sealings) were stored there.

While the Mycenaean palace at Knossos retained its basic Minoan functions in LM II–IIIA1, many rough walls were inserted in the corridors to allow more centralized control of stored produce. Mycenaean Greek was introduced as the administrative language of the palace. Based on Minoan prototypes, the LM II–IIIA Grand Procession fresco on the west entrance corridor shows men bearing vases approaching a goddess. In the Throne Room the last phase of frescoes of the crouching griffins flanking the throne date to LM II/IIIA but also have parallels in earlier Minoan art.[7] At the beginning of LM IIIA2 the palace was destroyed. It was reused later (see below) but its days as an administrative center were over.

During LM II–IIIA1 the palace at Knossos became the administrative center of a kingdom controlling much of Crete.[8] Our evidence comes from the Linear B tablets found in the palace that mention place names – a total of some one hundred citations occur in the archives – that we can recognize. The tablets list second-order sites: settlements and sanctuary sites, for example *ku-do-ni-ja* (Chania), tu-ri-so (Tylissos), *pa-i-to* (Phaistos), *da-wo* (Agia Triada?), *se-to-i-ja* (perhaps Malia?), *da-*22-to* (near Rethymnon?), and *a-mi-ni-so* (Amnissos). These names suggest that the Knossos kingdom included 50–70 percent of Crete. Certainly, much of the pottery found on sites across Crete at this time imitates the central Knossian style.

The Knossian tablets mention different types of transactions carried out by the palace. Wool (for export of textiles), cereals, and olives were important. The palace supervised the production and shipment of commodities (barley, flax, livestock, perfumed oil, and bronze). Goods were brought to the palace center as taxes, gifts, or items for trade. Some tablets (Mc series) list tax assessments in the form of commodities that the areas within the kingdom were expected to pay. The palace also monitored holdings, such as flocks of sheep, in areas away from Knossos but under its control. Resources stored in the palace were used to feed or pay officials and workers, and for offerings to the shrines of the gods. Tablets (Da–Dg) list totals of about 100,000 sheep, belonging to shepherds at thirty different places, including Phaistos, Kydonia, Aptara, and Tylissos, with a local official's name supplied. In the areas beyond direct palatial control, Knossos kept track of responsible individuals called "collectors" who managed flocks and textile production. Some twenty-five of these collectors are known from the Knossos tablets. Tablets also record the collection of aromatic herbs, coriander, cypress, and a "Phoenician spice." An individual named Kyprios was responsible for perfumed oil at Knossos. Tablet K 700 lists an impressive total of 1,800 stirrup jars used to store perfumed oil. Chariots at Knossos and elsewhere in the kingdom were kept track of on lists. Other tablets (Dk, Dl) list sheep and set targets for wool production. Wool was collected and then assigned to textile workers who were paid rations by the palace. As many as 1,000 women were employed in this fashion. Other tablets record the delivery of the wool cloth to the palace, and sometimes for whom (i.e. for officials) or for export. Villages were also taxed (N series) amounts of linen or flax.

The sociopolitical hierarchy of the Knossian kingdom can be reconstructed from officials mentioned in tablets. In order of importance, they are: *wanax* (king), *lawagetas* (military leader?), *te-re-ta* (fief-holders), *e-qe-ta* (military officials), *qa-si-re-u* (feudal lord), and *ko-re-te* (local mayor). The king is associated with the preparation of banquets held at the palace. The tablets name occupations: shepherds, goatherds, huntsmen, wood-cutters, masons, carpenters, shipwrights, bronze smiths, bow-makers, potters, cloth producers (carders, spinners, and weavers), tailors, and bakers. Lookalike metal rings, already known in the Protopalatial period, are associated with an official (*qa-si-re-u*) who dealt with metal and was responsible for the palaces' metal stores.[9] One tablet (Am 826) lists more than forty-five fief-holders and five carpenters at the west Cretan site of Aptara. Rations take the form of wheat, barley, oil, and figs paid to workers. Some names on the tablets, located at Knossos and elsewhere, are Greek and others are non-Greek.

During this period we can, for the first time, identify by name some of the gods worshiped on Crete. The Linear B tablets from Knossos mention Zeus, Hera, Diwa, Poseidon, Potnia, Athena, Hephaistos, Hermes, Ares, wind goddesses, Paiaion (Apollo), and Eileithyia. Since of these gods only Zeus (and probably Poseidon) has an obvious Greek name, the others may have been Minoan deities. Local cults on LM II–IIIA1 Crete continued, though at small urban and rural shrines, such as at Gournia, Psychro Cave, Kamares, and Kato Syme. The Knossian palace also kept calendars (Fp) that listed offerings of oil to be made by the month to the gods, for example, "In the month of Deukios, 12 liters of oil to Diktaian Zeus" (Gg 705). "One jar of honey to Eleuthia" probably refers to the Cave of Eileithyia at Amnissos mentioned in the *Odyssey* XIX, 18. Tablet V 52 records offerings to Mistress Athena, to Enyalios (an epithet of Ares), to Paian (healer god, later identified with Apollo), and to Poseidon.

The presence of a new Mycenaean warrior class at Knossos is also apparent in rich new burials, the so-called "warrior graves," or "burials with bronzes" (Fig. 9.1).[10] This funerary practice is clearly a Mycenaean custom, known from the earlier shaft graves at Mycenae. These graves, in the form of shafts or chamber tombs, have been found near the Knossos palace at Zapher Papoura, Sellopoulo, and Isopata. They are filled with weapons (swords, daggers, and spears), bronze vessels, gold, silver, and faience jewelry. Another impressive tomb at Isopata contained swords, stone vases, and lamps (including alabaster Egyptian imports), large painted jars, a bronze mirror, two silver *kylikes*, a gold hairpin, a necklace of imported lapis lazuli beads, pendants, a crystal pommel of a knife, and sealings (for wooden boxes?). At nearby Archanes, at the Phournoi cemetery, Tholos A produced another wealthy burial: a woman was buried in a *larnax* with a set of bronze vessels, four gold signet rings (one a Neopalatial heirloom), a necklace of blue glass beads, an ivory footstool, and a horse sacrificed outside the entrance of the tomb. The same cemetery also held a small Mycenaean-type grave circle with tombstones and graves enclosed with a wall, as at Mycenae.

The Knossian rulers also seized control in the Mesara Plain in LM II–IIIA1. The LM IB destructions there had taken a disastrous toll: the local population had plummeted. At Phaistos the palace ceased to have an administrative function. The town was greatly reduced, consisting only of a scatter of small

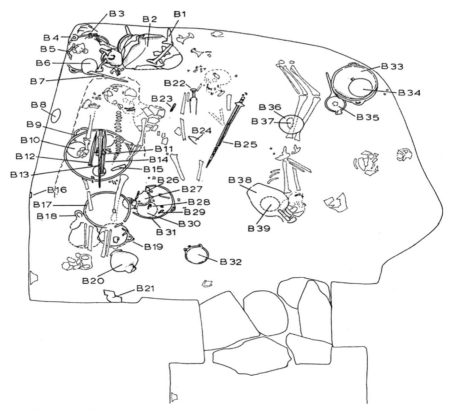

9.1 "Burial with bronzes" warrior grave, Knossos.
Popham and Catling (1974), 226, fig. 15

houses around the palace. A Mycenaean presence, however, is signaled by the
rich Mycenaean burials at nearby Kalivia, in the LM IIIA1 Tombe dei Nobilii
(especially Tomb 8) and perhaps in an elite building at Chalara with LM IIIA1
Knossian-style pottery. In contrast, the local tombs at Liliana ("Tomba della
Plebe") were quite poor.[11]

Agia Triada replaced Phaistos as the administrative center of the region.
Both Agia Triada and Kommos not only grew in size in LM IIIA, but were
transformed by monumental building programs. At Agia Triada the Villa
Royale opened on to an upper court. Next to it were built the large
Mycenaean-looking market ("Megaron") and stoa (Fig. 9.2). The types of
masons' marks on the building blocks hint that the architects were Knossian.
At the east edge of the court was a LM IIIA bench shrine (Building H) with a
floor fresco painted with dolphins and fish. Conical cups and miniature vases
were placed on the bench; floor accumulation produced seven snake tubes and
a lamp. A tomb in the cemetery to the northeast produced the famous Agia
Triada painted stone sarcophagus (Chapter 7). The town was certainly a
prosperous center.[12]

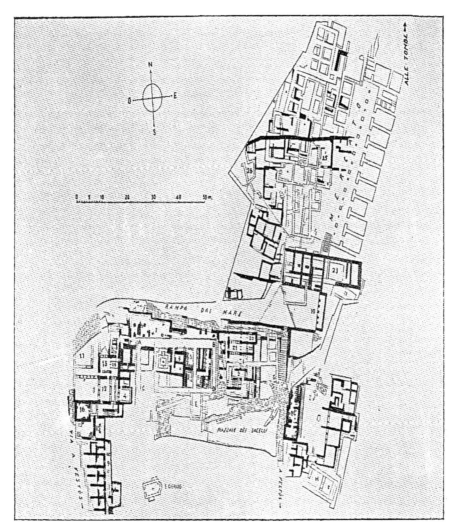

9.2 Plan of Agia Triada. LM III walls appear in relief.
Myers and Myers (1992), fig. 7.1

Kommos served as the port for LM III Agia Triada. The Neopalatial stoa
(Building T) was converted for a short time into a collection of small spaces
with hearths. In LM IIIA2 the monumental shipshed (Building P) with six
large galleries was built, and the port regained its status as an international
harbor with connections to Cyprus, Sardinia, Egypt, and the Levant.[13] In the
town, houses were not rebuilt, but rather subdivided; the community seems
transformed from a prosperous agricultural and commercial community to an
industrial depot manned by dependent laborers.[14]

In east Crete, sites such as Malia, Gournia, Mochlos, Palaikastro, and Zakros
shared a similar experience: destruction in LM IB and reduced reoccupation.
Malia seems to have only been sporadically inhabited. Knossian pottery is

common on the site. An excavated complex (Nu) there possessed a mainland Megaron-type plan and fixed hearth and stirrup jars inscribed in Linear B. The town of Gournia was not widely reoccupied after LM IB. On the other hand, a Mycenaean-type Corridor House (He) was erected on the south edge of the central court in LM IIIA1. The building produced a horns of consecration and Knossian-style pottery, and probably housed a Mycenaean official. Other such houses known at Chania, Agia Triada, and Plati in the Lasithi Plain may have had a similar function. Further east, Palaikastro recovered quickly after the LM IB destruction and was extensively rebuilt along former lines. Zakros had a limited LM III reoccupation; in LM IIIB the town was almost completely deserted.

In west Crete, the town of Chania was extensively rebuilt following its LM IB destruction. The LM III settlement was located on the hill of Kastelli and its south slope.[15] With its close connections to the Mycenaean Peloponnese, the city became wealthy through international trade. An LM IIIA1 warrior burial produced bronze weapons, a bowl, and a seal stone. Cypriote pottery and a scarab with the cartouche of Amenhotep III reaffirm Chania's international status.[16]

CRETE IN LM IIIA2–IIIB, 1360–1200 BC

During this second phase, the island's population partly recovered.[17] International trade expanded: Cretan transport jars traded across the Aegean at this time point to a wide trade in oil.[18] A scarab bearing the name of the wife of King Tutankhamen has been found at Poros, the harbor of Knossos.[19] A mid-thirteenth-century BC tablet from Ugarit mentions that the King of Ugarit is exempting the merchant Sinaranu from taxes on grain, oil, and beer when his ship returns from Crete.[20] Large merchant ships were part of this trade as evidenced by massive Near Eastern-type stone anchors found on Crete, at Kommos and Chania. At this time pottery from the Cyclades, mainland Greece, Cyprus, and the Levant is common on most Cretan sites. The port at Kommos received Egyptian, Syrian, Anatolian, and Sardinian pottery.[21] Numerous Minoan vases found on Cyprus point to the close relations between the two islands. The presence of Greek mainlanders can be recognized at some Cretan sites. At Archanes, for example, a grave circle of seven shaft graves may have belonged to mainlanders. After another destruction of the Knossos palace in early LM IIIB, regional styles of Cretan pottery reappear, signaling economic independence across the island.

After the LM IIIA destruction of the Knossos palace, parts of the town were abandoned. Some earlier houses, for example the Royal Villa, Unexplored Mansion, and Southeast House, were partly reoccupied. Tombs around Knossos decrease in number and wealth. The palace was reoccupied but it

9.3 Shrine of the Double Axes, palace at Knossos.
Evans (1927), 337, fig. 189

appears to have ceased as an administrative center. A small room, the Shrine of
the Double Axes, was built in LM IIIB at the outer southeast edge of the palace
during its last phase (Fig. 9.3). The shrine possessed a back bench and a floor
laid with sea pebbles. On the bench Evans found three statuettes, a male votary
offering a dove, two female votaries with their hands on their breasts, a goddess
figure with upraised arms with a dove on her head, two plaster horns of
consecration, a miniature steatite double ax, and a "primitive" half-seated
female figurine. On the pebble dais in front of the bench were an offering
table, two champagne goblets, a bowl, and three juglets. On the earth floor
near the entrance there were two small jars, a cook pot, two amphoras, and
two stirrup jars. Similar shrines are known from elsewhere on Crete. The
building's final destruction appears to have been late in LM IIIB.[22]

In the LM III period, Chania was partly settled by Mycenaean Greeks, and
prospered from international trade: imported vases testify to relations with
Greece, Cyprus, the Levant, Egypt, and Italy. LM III pottery from Chania and
Central Crete have been identified on Sardinia.[23] The local "Kydonia
Workshop" exported vases to all parts of Crete, and to Cyprus and Sardinia.
Some of the stirrup jars from this workshop are inscribed with the Linear
B adjective for king, *wa-na-ka-te-ro*, on their shoulder. Linear B tablets dis-
covered in LM IIIB Chania also imply the existence of a literate palace there in
this period. Chania's eastern cemetery has yielded many (over 170) rich graves.

One pit grave had a warrior burial with an ivory comb, a bronze mirror, a necklace with glass beads, three sealstones, a long sword, knives, and many arrowheads. Others, also filled with weapons, bronzes, and jewelry, are clearly burials of Mycenaean warriors.

In the Mesara, at Agia Triada, the earlier Megaron and stoa continued in this period, probably as administrative structures. In the lower town, a larger stoa was erected to face on to an open space (Agora), bounded on the south by a massive storage facility (Bastione) and on the northwest by a large Mycenaean-type Corridor House (NW Building and Building P). The town enjoyed prosperous commercial contacts throughout LM IIIA. At Kommos the shipshed (Building P) also continued to function: vases arrived there from Chania, Knossos, and the Cyclades (Naxos).[24]

In eastern Crete Malia was only inhabited by a few resettled houses. One complex has been excavated, Quartier Nu. In LM IIIA2–B this Megaron complex possessed a room with a pebble mosaic and three stirrup jars inscribed in Linear B. Malia was destroyed again in mid-LM IIIB and abandoned in IIIC. Mochlos was partly reoccupied by a series of small houses reusing earlier walls. One large house (Alpha) may have housed the local Mycenaean official. Some local LM IIIA pottery is imitative of the Knossian ceramic style. Imported vases there from Chania, Palaikastro, Knossos, the Greek mainland, and Syria point to wide commercial relations. One tomb (15), because of its large group of drinking vessels, has been identified as that of a Mycenaean. Weapon-filled warrior tombs have also been recognized at other sites, at Palaikastro and Myrsini.

At Gournia only a few houses (E, Eh, Ei, Ej, He, and Hf) yielded signs of occupation. In LM IIIB the inhabitants of the site worshiped at a small one-room shrine on the hilltop, whose contents include statuettes of goddesses with birds and with snakes and stands decorated with snakes (Fig. 9.4). Pottery from Gournia and Mochlos shows continuing commercial relations with Chania, Knossos, Palaikastro, and the Greek mainland. Both sites were

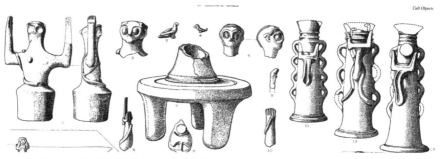

9.4 Finds from the LM III shrine at Gournia.
Boyd-Hawes et al. (2014), pl. XI

abandoned in LM IIIB. In the far east of Crete, Palaikastro suffered another destruction by fire in LM IIIA2, and was rebuilt again. After an earthquake *c.*1250 BC the town was finally abandoned except for a small LM IIIC refuge settlement on the nearby hilltop of Kastri. The town of Zakros was reoccupied in LM IIIA2, but mostly deserted by LM IIIB.

CRETE IN LM IIIC, 1200–1070 BC

During this period, many sites in the Aegean and Near East suffered destruction by seaborne invaders ("Sea Peoples"), an instability probably spurred by drought-like climatic conditions.[25] Many sites on Crete – Gournia, Malia, Palaikastro, and Zakros – were abandoned, especially those along the coast.[26] A few larger sites, such as Knossos, Chania (Kastelli), and Phaistos (Acropolis mediana), continued on a smaller scale. Most of Knossos, for instance, was abandoned early in LM IIIC, and what appears to be a small new settlement was established on the west slope of the town.[27] The mountaintop shrine at Mount Jouktas was converted into a (walled) settlement. At Chania the LM IIIC settlement seems to have been concentrated on the hill of Kastelli. Phaistos experienced a growth after the abandonment of Agia Triada and Kommos in LM IIIC. Agia Triada was transformed into an open-air sanctuary (Piazzale dei Sacelli) that attracted hundreds of votive offerings – figurines of bulls, horns of consecration, monsters (sphinxes?), horses, and male figures.[28]

Much of the population of Crete retreated from coastal areas and low-lying valleys to smaller refuge sites inland on the island.[29] These sites, at Karphi, Vrokastro, Kavousi Kastro, and Katalimata are situated on defensible mountainous locations and fortified with massive walls. Karphi and Vrokastro possess a steep defensible north slope or cliff – indicating the threat was seen as coming from the sea. A generation or two after these first refuge sites were founded (*c.*1200) some new sites, such as Vronda, Chalasmenos, and Papoura, were established nearby, somewhat lower and nearer to good land. Most LM IIIC settlements had a public shrine building that contained one or more clay statuettes of a goddess with upraised arms adorned with Minoan symbols, such as birds, snakes, horns of consecration, and flowers, suggesting a cultural connection or continuity with the Minoan past. In fact, most LM III burial customs on Crete resemble those of the Minoan period.

The best known LM IIIC settlement on Crete is Karphi in the central part of the island.[30] At 1,147 meters above sea level, the site sits on a rocky summit (Fig. 9.5) of a mountain range that defines the northern edge of the upland Lasithi Plain. Water is available from a nearby spring. Visible today on site are about 25–30 excavated houses. Karphi may have possessed as many as 125–50 houses, with a population of *c.*1,500 people. The settlement consisted of cobbled lanes and public squares as well as small blocks of houses, each usually

9.5 Reconstruction of LM III site at Karphi.
Nowicki (2000), 162, fig. 93

of 2–3 rooms, constructed of local limestone rubble. One house, the so-called
"Great House," stands out for its unusual size, impressive threshold, anteroom,
and an unusually large amount of vases for drinking, suggesting its owner may
have been a community leader. The inhabitants lived from agriculture and
shepherding. On its north edge, on the highest spot of the site, was a public
shrine with two small storage spaces and a main room provided with a bench
for clay statuettes of a goddess with upraised arms that faced on to an open
square. A few vases from Karphi show possible contacts with elsewhere on
Crete, the islands, the mainland, and Cyprus. A cemetery of small *tholos* tombs
was located on a slope south of the site. Karphi seems to have been abandoned
at the end of LM IIIC for the large Early Iron Age site of Papoura below it.

In east Crete, the site at Katalimata is a particularly dramatic example of a
LM IIIC refuge settlement (Fig. 9.6).[31] The high cliff-side western face of the
Thryphti mountain range is broken by a deep ravine (Cha Gorge) from which
mountain water flows into the lowlands of the Isthmus. High above the floor

9.6 View of Katalimata in Cha Gorge, Isthmus of Ierapetra.
Photo by the author

of the Isthmus, some ten small houses were built on separate terraces (A–K) on the precipitous north face of the ravine (Fig. 9.7). Access is gained along a precarious narrow cliff-side ledge from the north. A small fortified construction guarded access. The inhabitants of Katalimata would have farmed the fields below and grazed their sheep above in the mountains.

On the slope below Katalimata, a small group of 5–6 houses were settled at Chalasmenos somewhat later in mid-LM IIIC.[32] Five Megaron plan houses were set around an open space. One house (A–B) because of its large size, storage facilities, and many cups may have belonged to the community leader who hosted communal feasts. A public shrine at the east edge of the hamlet produced nine female statuettes with upraised arms, snake tubes, bowls, and three *pithoi*. The west sector (B) was used by the community for food preparation, cooking, and storage. The site was abandoned before the end of the LM IIIC period.

Cretan society in LM IIIC consisted for the most part of such small village communities, under 500 people, scattered across the island. The social

9.7 LM IIIC Houses (A, B, C, D) on cliff of Katalimata Gorge.
Nowicki (2000), 93, fig 41

hierarchy of earlier Minoan culture, expressed in monumental *tholos* tombs and
rich contents and simple pot burials, had almost disappeared. LM IIIC cemeteries consist for the most part of small family tombs, although a few cemeteries
still display some signs of wealth distinction.[33]

Continued connections with the Minoan past can be seen in LM IIIC urban shrines (e.g. the Spring Chamber at Knossos, Temple A at Kommos) that yield Minoan-type votives, such as goddess statuettes with Minoan attributes.[34] The shrine ("Piazzale dei Sacelli") at Agia Triada also produced traditional human and animal figurines, double axes, a boat model, and horns of consecration. Similar forms of worship and votive offerings also continued at Minoan sacred caves, such as Psychro, Tsoutsouros, Skoteino, Mount Ida, and Amnissos. Some mountaintop shrines, for example Kato Syme, Mount Jouktas, and Ephendi Christos at Phaistos, also still functioned at this time and into the Early Iron Age. Worshippers there must have been descendants of the Minoan population. Reuse of Minoan tombs, known at Knossos, also points to a continuing Minoan identity by the local population.

LM III Cretan society absorbed certain Mycenaean features. Obvious examples include the Greek language, certain forms of architecture (i.e. Megaron and Corridor Houses), pottery shapes (the deep bowl and *krater*), shaft graves and burials with bronzes/weapons, and some religious beliefs (e.g. *larnakes* depicting the concept of the deceased riding a chariot to the Underworld). The archaeological evidence on LM III Crete for these two traditions suggests there were two cultural groups living side by side, or mixed at times within a single settlement. Minoan palatial culture had effectively come to an end by this time (1200 BC).

EPILOGUE: THE MINOAN HERITAGE

Minoan culture had a substantial influence on the later Greeks, especially in the field of religion.[35] Like the Minoan deities, the Greek gods lived on a mountain (Mount Olympus). Diodorus Siculus (*History*, V. 64.1 and 77.3) reports many people of his time (first century BC) believed that the main Greek gods came from Crete. The Minoan origin of several later Greek deities, such as Artemis the *Potnia theron*, was discussed in Chapter 7. Eileithyia, the Greek goddess of childbirth, can also be traced back to Minoan Crete where she was worshiped in her shrine at Amnissos. According to the *Homeric Hymn to Demeter* (122–5), Demeter and her Mysteries at Eleusis were introduced from Crete. The name Eleusis is derived from the Minoan name Eileithyia. The Minoan goddess shown with poppies may be the prototype for the later Demeter whose symbol was a poppy. Clay votives of branches and pigs have been found on rural Minoan sanctuaries; this ritual closely resembles the *Thesmophoria*, a popular Greek agricultural festival of Demeter held at the month of sowing (October; Pyanopsion) where women ascended (*anodos*) a hill outside the city to make sacrifices that included pigs and branches. The Classical Greek tradition of rural nymphs who inhabit the mountains, sea, rivers, and forests may well go back to Minoan beliefs.

Minoan votives and scenes point to a god of healing, prophecy, and initiation into adulthood; in Classical Greece this was Apollo. Both the mountain location and prophetic function of the Delphic oracular sanctuary derive from Minoan Crete. According to the *Homeric Hymn to Pythian Apollo* (390–545), the priesthood of the famous prophetic sanctuary of Apollo at Delphi were originally Minoans from Knossos. Aside from Poseidon, the Classical deity of the sea was Aphrodite; Greeks prayed to Aphrodite Euploeia for a safe sea journey. Such a sea goddess probably existed in Minoan times (Chapter 7). Minoan metal workshops were often provided with an attached shrine, as for example in the House with the Snake Tube at Kommos.[36] This god later became Hephaistos, the patron deity of bronze workers.

Turning to political matters, it is worth remembering that Herodotus (1.65) records that the Spartans believed that their constitution had been brought from Crete by Lykourgos. It is tempting to see the Spartan *gerousia*, the council of elders (that passed on all matters brought before the assembly and had the power to try all Spartans including Spartan kings), as being derived from the small elite groups that were hosted at the Minoan palaces.

NOTES

1   See J. Driessen and C. Macdonald, *The Troubled Island*, Aegaeum 17, Liege: University of Liege, 1997, 35–118.

2   V. Watrous, D. Haggis, K. Nowicki, N. Vogeikoff-Brogan, and M. Schultz, *An Archaeological Survey of the Gournia Landscape*, Philadelphia: Instap Academic Press, 2012, 65–67.

3   J. Aruz, *Marks of Distinction: Seals and Cultural Exchange between the Aegean and the Orient ca 2600–1360 BC. CMS* Beiheft 7, Mainz: Verlag von Zabern, 2008, fig. 363, catalogue number 29.

4   Aruz, *Marks of Distinction*, fig. 392, catalogue number 224.

5   Aruz, *Marks of Distinction*, fig. 365, catalogue number 30.

6   Aruz, *Marks of Distinction*, 188. For LM III trade, see H. Haskell, "Region to Region Export of Transport Stirrup Jars from LM III A2B Crete," in A. D'Agata and J. Moody, eds., *Ariadne's Threads: Connections between Crete and the Greek Mainland in Late Minoan III*, Athens: Scuola Archeologica Italiana di Atene, 2005, 205–42.

7   S. Immerwahr, *Aegean Painting in the Bronze Age*, University Park: Pennsylvania State University Press, 1990, 84–98. Smaller frescoes, such as the Taureador scene, the Palanquin chariot scene, the Campstool fresco and La Parisienne, dated to the LM IIIA period, depict Minoan ceremonies. See also J. Shaw, "The Middle Minoan Slipway for Ships at the Kommos Harbour and Harbour Development in Prehistoric Crete," in Q. Letesson and C. Knappett, eds., *Minoan Architecture and Urbanism*, Oxford: Oxford University Press, 2017, 228–58.

8   J. Bennet, "The Structure of the Linear B Administration at Knossos," *AJA* 89 (1985) 231–49.

9   J. Weingarten, "The Sealing Bureaucracy of Mycenaean Knossos," in J. Driessen and A. Farnoux, eds., *Crete Mycenienne*, *BCH* Supplement 30 (1997) 517–35. A. D'Agata and J. Moody, eds., *Ariadne's Threads: Connections between Crete and the Greek Mainland in Late Minoan III*, Athens: Scuola Archeologica Italiana di Atene, 2005.

10   M. Popham, E. Catling, and H. Catling, "Sellopolo Tombs 3 and 4, Two Late Minoan
     Graves near Knossos," *BSA* 69 (1974) 195–258. One pre-Mycenaean "burial with bronzes"
     is known from Crete, at Poros, the harbor of Knossos.

11   For LM III Phaistos, see A. Kanta, "The Late Minoan III Period in Crete: A Survey of Sites,
     Pottery, and their Distribution," *SIMA* 58 (1980) 96–100.

12   V. LaRosa, "Hagia Triada A L'Epoque Mycenienne: L'Utopie d'un Ville Capitale," in
     Driessen and Farnoux, *Crete Mycenienne*, 249–66.

13   P. Day et al., "A World of Goods: Transport Jars and Commodity Exchange at the Late
     Bronze Age Harbor of Kommos, Crete," *Hesperia* 80 (2011) 511–58.

14   J. and M. Shaw, "'Mycenaean' Kommos," in Driessen and Farnoux, *Crete Mycenienne*,
     BCH Supplement 30, 1997 423–34.

15   M. Andreadaki-Vlazaki, "La necropole du minoen recent III de la ville de la Canee," in
     Driessen and Farnoux, *Crete Mycenienne*, 487–509. M. Andreadaki-Vlazaki, "Khania
     (Kydonia)," in E. Cline, ed., *The Oxford Handbook of the Bronze Age Aegean*, Oxford:
     Oxford University Press, 2010, 518–28.

16   Aruz, *Marks of Distinction*, 186–7 and fig. 366.

17   A. Kanta (supra n 11) lists the sites. Her conclusions about LM III Crete appear on pages
     318–326.

18   H. Haskell, "Region to Region Export of Transport Stirrup Jars from LM IIIA2/B Crete,"
     and A. Kanta, "Response to Halford Haskell," in D'Agata and Moody, *Ariadne's Threads*,
     205–242. Eight LM IIIB stirrup jars from central Crete were found in the Cape Iria
     shipwreck.

19   Kanta, "The Late Minoan III Period in Crete," BCH Supplement 30, 1997 315.

20   E. Cline, *Sailing the Wine-Dark Sea: International Trade and the Late Bronze Age Aegean*, BAR
     International Series 591 (1994) 120.

21   J. Rutter, "Cretan External Relations during LM IIIA2–B (1370–1200 BC): A View from
     the Mesara," in W. Phelps, et al., *The Point Iria Wreck: Interconnections in the Mediterranean ca
     1200 BC*, Athens: Hellenic Institute of Marine Archaeology, 1999, 139–86.

22   E. Hallager, *The Mycenaean Palace at Knossos: Evidence for the Final Destruction in the LM IIIB
     Period*, Medelhausmuseet Memoire 1 (1977).

23   R. Jones and L. Vagnetti, "Traders and Craftsmen in the Central Mediterranean:
     Archaeological Evidence and Archaeometric Research," in N. Gale, ed., *Bronze Age
     Trade in the Mediterranean*, SIMA 90 (1991) 133.

24   V. Watrous, *Kommos III: The Late Bronze Pottery*, Princeton: Princeton University Press,
     1992, 138–54.

25   J. Moody, "Unravelling the Threads: Climate Changes in the Late Bronze III Aegean," in
     D'Agata and Moody, *Ariadne's Threads*, 443–74.

26   For LM III society and changes, see S. Wallace, *Ancient Crete: From Successful Collapse to
     Democracy's Alternatives, Twelfth to Fifth Centuries BC*, Cambridge: Cambridge University
     Press, 2010, 30–194. W. Coulson et al., "Excavations on the Kastro at Kavousi: An
     Architectural Overview," *Hesperia* 66 (1997) 315–90. L. Day, "The Late Minoan IIIC
     Period at Vronda, Kavousi," in J. Driessen and A. Farnoux, eds., *Crete Mycenienne*, BCH
     Supplement 30 (1997) 391–406.

27   E. Hatzaki, "Postpalatial Knossos: Towns and Cemeteries from LM IIIA2 to LM IIIC," in
     D'Agata and Moody, *Ariadne's Threads*, SAA, 2005 65–105.

28   A. D'Agata, "The Shrines on the Piazzale dei Sacelli at Ayia Triada," in Driessen, and
     Farnoux, *Crete Mycenienne*, 85–100.

29   See the discussion in J. McEnroe, *Architecture of Minoan Crete*, Austin: University of Texas
     Press, 2010, 146–59.

30   L. Day, *The Pottery from Karphi: A Re-examination*, BSA Studies 19 (2011) and Wallace,
     Ancient Crete, with earlier bibliography.

31   K. Nowicki, *Monastiraki Katalimata: Excavation of a Cretan Refuge Site, 1993–2000*,
     Philadelphia: Instap Academic Press, 2008.

32   M. Tsipopolou, "Mycenaeans" at the Isthmus of Ierapetra: Some Preliminary Thoughts on the Foundation of the (Eteo)Cretan Cultural Identity," in D'Agata and Moody, *Ariadne's Threads*, 302–52.

33   Wallace, *Ancient Crete*, Cambridge University Press, 2010 150–63.

34   Wallace, *Ancient Crete*, Cambridge University Press, 2010 328.

35   The best discussion of this subject remains M. Nilsson, *The Minoan-Mycenaean Religion and Its Survival in Greek Religion*, 2nd edition, New York: Biblo and Tannen, 1971, 485–583. N. Momigliano and A. Farnoux, eds. *Cretomania: Modern Desires for the Minoan Past*, Abingdon: Routledge, 2017, collects instances of the influence of Minoan studies on modern artists, writers, and cultural trends.

36   J. and M. Shaw, eds., *Kommos I, Part 2*, Princeton: Princeton University Press, 1996, 219, 227.

LIST OF ILLUSTRATIONS/CREDITS

This list was compiled with the help of the copyright editor Angela Drakakis-Smith. We are particularly grateful to the Greek Ministry of Culture, the archaeological museums of Herakleion, Agios Nikolaos, and Siteia and their ephorias, the foreign schools at Athens, and scholarly presses for permission to reproduce the images cited below. Our special thanks go to the following scholars who have also granted us permission: Ingo Pini, Phil Betancourt, Manfret Biatak, Keith Branigan, Matthew Buell, Gerald Cadogan, C. Davaras, J. Driessen, Robert Koehl, Olga Krzyszkowska, Robert Laffineur, C. Macdonald, Sandy Macgillivray, Nanno Marinatos, John McEnroe, Christof Nowicki, Clairy Palyvou, J.-C. Poursat, Georgos Rethemiotakis, Jeffery Soles, Metaxia Tsipopoulou, Joseph and Maria Shaw, Ian Swindale, Antonis Vasilikis, and Peter Warren,

The following abbreviations appear below:

AN — Agios Nikolaos Museum
BSA — *Annual of the British School at Athens*
CMS — *Corpus der minoischen und mykenischen Siegel*
EFA — Ecole Francaise d' Athenes
HM — Herakleion Museum
HMC — Hellenic Ministry of Culture
MMA — Metropolitan Museum of Art
SAA — Scuola archeologica di Atene e delle Missioni italiane in Oriente
SM — Siteia Museum
TAP — Archaeological Receipts Fund

CHAPTER 1

CHAPTER 8

GLOSSARY

agora – an open public area in ancient Greek architecture.

agrimi – the Cretan wild goat.

anathemata – small metal plaques given as votives in chapels as a thank offering or request for help from the local saint. The depict anatomical parts of the human body, children, men, women, etc.

ankh – an Egyptian religious symbol in the shape of a stemmed loop symbolizing eternal life.

ashlar – square cut stone blocks.

ashlar orthostate – a type of wall construction using tall rectangular cut blocks resting on a leveling course of narrow cut stones.

baetyl – an uncarved sacred standing stone. In the Near East they represent a divinity.

bamah – in the Near East, altars located on high places.

Barbotine – a type of ceramic decoration consisting of small points set in relief on the surface of a ceramic vase.

Chamaizi vase – a special type of miniature ceremonial inscribed juglet made at Malia.

Corridor House – a mainland type of house with small rooms set along a side corridor.

cretulae – a generic term for Minoan stamped clay administrative objects.

cyclopean masonry – a Bronze Age architectural style that uses immense boulders as its building blocks. Called *cyclopean* by the amazed classical Greeks because the blocks were so large they believed that only Cyclopes could have built them.

erontas – modern Greek for erotic love

ex oriente lux – Latin: "light from the East", the idea that the highly developed civilizations of the Near East had a formative influence on simpler Western cultures.

hectare – metric measure of land, equivalent to 2.5 acres.

horns of consecration – a term invented by Evans to describe a clay or stone Minoan cult symbol in the shape of a bull's horns set on a stand, used to identify the religious nature of a room or building.

horta – leafy green vegetables in modern Greek.

kalimari – squid.

kaloures – a modern (Greek) term for large circular pits found in the west courts of Minoan palaces.

kapheion – a traditional Greek cafe.

kernos, -oi – a flat stone that has small depressions pecked out on its upper surface. Depending on its context, it is interpreted as used for sacrificial offerings or as a game board.

kleos – in Homer, the reputation earned by a heroic figure.

lapis lazuli – a precious blue glass-like stone imported to Crete from the East.

larnax, -akes – Minoan rectangular clay coffins whose shape imitates wooden Egyptian examples.

light well – a ground floor space within a house left open to the sky so as to bring light into the adjacent rooms.

lustral basin – a term adapted for a type of sunken, elaborately plastered room reached by a staircase found in Minoan architecture. Cult equipment, *rhyta*, an offering table, horns of consecration and miniature unguent vases suggest purifying rites of anointing and lustration, similar perhaps to the Jewish *mikveh*, a sunken room with water used for ritual immersion and cleanliness.

lyra – a Cretan stringed instrument similar to a mandolin.

mantinada – fifteen-syllable rhyming couplets in traditional Cretan dialect and song.

> "Vre kaimeni amigdala pou antheseis
>   to januari,
> Perimene kai anthesisome amadi."

The olive that blossoms in the Spring tree calls to the almond tree:

> "Poor almond tree who blossoms in
>   January,
> Wait, and we'll blossom together!"

Marine style – a form of decoration on vases that depicts sea creatures.

masons' mark – engraved signs marking stone blocks produced by a single gang of workers within a quarry, used in Egypt to keep track of the gangs' productivity.

Megaron – a mainland house form with a large hall, central entrance, and porch.

meltemia – strong northern winds, especially common during the winter.

Minoan hall – a large set of central rooms that include a forehall, light well, and pier and door partition.

Mirabello ware – medium-sized practical vases (jugs, amphoras, jars) made at Gournia and exported over much of MM I - LM I Crete.

mitato – stone huts lived in by shepherds in the mountains.

nodules – stamped clay knobs used as receipts, at times fastened to a container.

orthstate – a long rectangular stone slab set upright on its small base.

pier and door partition (polythyron) – a partition consisting of a set of 2–3 small doors at one end of the Minoan hall that could be closed or left open.

pillar crypt – a large ground floor room with 1–2 central pillars used for storage.

pithos, -oi (modern Greek pithari) – a large Minoan storage jar.

Potnia theron – Mistress of wild animals, the Homeric epithet fro the goddess Artemis.

pyxis (plural pyxides) – a small circular container for valuables such as jewelry or scented cosmetics.

raki – a clear highly alcoholic drink, distilled from grape must, similar to grappa.

roundel – stamped clay discs often with an inscription recording a commodity, used as a receipt of a transaction.

rython – a ceremonial vase provided whose base or wall held a small punctured hole for pouring a liquid.

sistrum (plural sistra) – a handheld rattle-like musical instrument, native to Egypt.

snake tube – tubular clay stands, often decorated with snakes in relief, found in Minoan shrines. These were surmounted by a cup for offering incense.

steatite – a soft gray stone found on Crete.

stoa – in Greek architecture, a columned veranda or porch.

tholos – a beehive-shaped Minoan stone-built tomb.

BIBLIOGRAPHY

Alexiou, S. 1951. "Πρωτομινωικαι παρα το Κανλι Καστελλι Ηερακειο." *Κρητικα Χρονικα* 5: 275–294.

Allbaugh, L. 1953. *Crete: A Case Study of an Underdeveloped Area.* Princeton: Princeton University Press.

Allsebrook, M. 1992. *Born to Rebel: The Life of Harriet Boyd Hawes.* London: Short Run Press.

Andreadaki-Vlazaki, M. 2010. "Khania (Kydonia)." In *The Oxford Handbook of the Bronze Age Aegean*, edited by E. Cline, 518–28. Oxford: Oxford University Press.

Andreadaki-Vlazaki, M. 1997. "La necropole du minoen recent III de la ville de la Canee." In *Crete Mycenienne*, edited by J. Driessen and A. Farnoux. *BCH* Supplement 30: 487–509.

Andreadaki-Vlazaki, M. 2008. "Resources for Life: From Food to Aromatics." In *From the Land of the Labyrinth, II*, edited by M. Andreadaki-Vlazaki, G. Rethemiotakis, and N. Dimopoulou-Rethemiotaki, 110–17. New York: Onassis Foundation.

Andrews, C. 1994. *Amulets of Ancient Egypt.* London: British Museum Press.

Aruz, J. 2008. *Marks of Distinction: Seals and Cultural Exchange between the Aegean and the Orient ca 2600–1360 BC.* CMS Beiheft 7:40, 57–61, 76–82, 160–1, 186–7. Mainz: Verlag von Zabern.

Aruz, J. 1984. "The Silver Cylinder Seal from Mochlos." *Kadmos* 23: 186–7.

Aruz, J. 1995. "Syrian Seals and the Evidence of Cultural Interaction." In *Corpus der Minoischen und Mykenischen Siegel, Sceaux Minoens at Myceniens, Beiheft V*, edited by I. Pini and J.-C. Poursat, 1–22. Berlin: Gebr. Mann Verlag.

Aruz, J. et al., eds. 2013. *Cultures in Contact: From Mesopotamia to the Mediterranean in the Second Millennium B.C.* New York: Metropolitan Museum of Art.

Barber, E. 1991. *Prehistoric Textiles.* Princeton: Princeton University Press.

Barber, E. 1994. *Womens' Work: The First 20,000 Years.* New York: Norton.

Barber, R. 1987. *The Cyclades in the Bronze Age.* London: Duckworth.

Barclay, A. 2001. "The Potnia Theron: Adaptation of a Near Eastern Image." In *POTNIA: Deities and Religion in the Aegean Bronze Age*, edited by R. Laffineur and W. D. Niemeier. Aegaeum 22: 373–86. Liege: University of Liege.

Beckmann, S. 2014. "An 'Agricultural Calendar' from the Bronze Age?" In *Exploring and Explaining Agricultural Diversity*, edited by A. van Gijn, J. Whittaker, and P. Anderson, 319–37. Oxford: Oxbow Books.

Beckmann, S. 2012. *Domesticating Mountains in Middle Bronze Age Crete: Minoan Agricultural Landscaping in the Agios Nikolaos Region, Volumes I–II.* PhD thesis. Rethymnon: University of Crete.

Bennet, J. 1985. "The Structure of the Linear B Administration at Knossos." *AJA* 89: 231–49.

Betancourt, P. 2013. *Aphrodite's Kephali: An Early Minoan I Defensive Site in Eastern Crete.* Philadelphia: Instap Academic Press.

Betancourt, P., ed. 2006. *The Chrysokamino Metallurgy Workshop and Its Territory.* Hesperia Supplement 36. Princeton: Princeton University Press.

Betancourt, P. 2005. "Egyptian Connections at Hagios Charalambos." In *EMPORIA II, Aegeans in the Central and Eastern Mediterranean*, edited by R. Laffineur and E. Greco. Aegaeum 25: 449–54. Liege: University of Liege.

Betancourt, P. 2014. *Hagios Charalambos: A Minoan Burial Cave in Crete.* Philadelphia: Instap Academic Press.

Betancourt, P. 2001. "The Household Shrine in the House of the Rhyta at Pseira." In *Potnia: Deities and Religion in the Aegean Bronze Age,* 145–9. Aegeaum 22. Liege: University of Liege and Austin: University of Texas.

Betancourt, P. 2007. "Lasithi and the Malia-Lasithi State." In *Krinoi kai Limenes: Studies in Honor of Joseph and Maria Shaw,* edited by P. Betancourt, M. Nelson, and H. Williams, 209–20. Philadelphia: INSTAP Academic Press.

Betancourt, P. 1998. "Middle Minoan Objects in the Near East." In *The Aegean and the Orient in the Second Millennium,* edited by E. Cline and D. Harris-Cline. Aegaeum 18: 5–11. Liege: University of Liege.

Betancourt, P., C. Davaras, and R. Hope Simpson, eds. 2005. *The Archaeological Survey of Pseira Island, II.* Philadelphia: INSTAP Academic Press.

Bietak, M. 2005. "The Setting of the Minoan Wall Paintings at Avaris." In *Aegean Wall Painting: A Tribute to Mark Cameron,* edited by L. Morgan. *BSA* Studies 13: 83–90.

Bietak, M. 1995. "Connections between Egypt and the Minoan World: New Results from Tell el-Dab'a." In *Egypt, the Aegean and the Levant,* edited by W. Davies and L. Schofield, 19–28. London: British Museum Press.

Bittel, K. 1976. *Die Hethiter.* Munich: Beck.

Black, J. and A. Green 1992. *Gods, Demons and Symbols of Ancient Mesopotamia.* Austin: University of Texas at Austin.

Blakolmer, F. 2015. "Was the 'Minoan Genius' a God?" In *Ancient Mediterranean Interconnections,* edited by P. Creaseman and R. Wilkinson. *Journal of Ancient Egyptian Interconnections* 7: 29–40.

Blitzer, H. 2004. "Agriculture and Subsistence in the Late Ottoman and Post-Ottoman Mesara." In *The Plain of Phaistos,* by V. Watrous, D. Hadzi-Vallianou, and H. Blitzer. *Monumenta Archaeologica* 23: 111–217. Los Angeles: Cotsen Institute of Archaeology, University of California Press.

Blong, R. 1980. "The Possible Effects of Santorini Tephra Fall on Minoan Crete." In *Thera and the Aegean World, II,* edited by C. Doumas, 217–26. Athens: The Thera Foundation.

Boschloos, V. 2017. "Traded, Copied and Kept: The Ubiquitous Appeal of Scarabs." In *Pharaoh's Land Beyond,* edited by P. Creaseman and R. Wilkinson, 149–66. Oxford: Oxford University Press.

Boulotis, C. 2008. "From Mythical Minos to the Search for Cretan Kingship." In *From the Land of the Labyrinth, II,* edited by M. Andreadaki-Vlazaki, G. Rethemiotakis, and N. Dimopoulou-Rethemiotakis, 44–55. New York: Onassis Foundation.

Boyd-Hawes, H. et al., eds. 2014 (reprint). *Gournia, Vasiliki and Other Prehistoric Sites on the Isthmus of Hierapetra, Crete.* Philadelphia: Instap Academic Press.

Branigan, K. 1974. *Aegean Metalwork of the Early and Middle Bronze Age.* Oxford: Oxford University Press.Branigan, K. 1968. "Copper and Bronze Working in Early Bronze Age Crete." *SIMA* 19.

Branigan, K. 1971. "Cycladic Figurines and Their Derivatives in Crete." *BSA* 66: 57–78.

Branigan, K. 1981. "Minoan Colonialism." *BSA* 76: 23–33.

Broodbank, C. 2000. *An Island Archaeology of the Early Cyclades.* Cambridge: Cambridge University Press.

Broodbank, C. 2004. "Minoanization." *Proceedings of the Prehistoric Society* 50: 46–91.

Broodbank, C. and E. Kiriatzi 2007. "The First Minoans of Kythera Revisited: Technology, Demography, and Landscape in the Prepalatial Aegean." *AJA* 111: 241–74.

Broodbank, C. and T. Strasser 1991. "Migrant Farmers and the Neolithic Colonization of Crete." *Antiquity* 65: 233–45.

Brown, A. 1983. *Arthur Evans and the Palace of Minos.* Oxford: Ashmolean Museum.

Buell, M. and J. McEnroe 2017. "Community Building/Building Community at Gournia." In *Minoan Architecture and Urbanism,* edited by Q. Letesson and C. Knappett, 204–27. Oxford: Oxford University Press.

Burke, A. 2014. "Introduction to the Levant during the Middle Bronze Age." In *The Oxford Handbook to the Archaeology of the Levant*, edited by M. Steiner and A. Killebrew, 403–13. Oxford: Oxford University Press.

Burke, B. 2012. "Textiles." In *The Oxford Handbook of the Bronze Age Aegean*, edited by E. Cline, 430–5. Oxford: Oxford University Press.

Cadogan, G. 1992. "Myrtos-Pyrgos." In *The Aerial Atlas of Ancient Crete*, edited by J. Myers, E. Myers, and G. Cadogan, 282–5. Berkeley: University of California Press.

Cadogan, G. 1980. "A Probable Shrine in the Country House at Pyrgos." In *Sanctuaries and Cults in the Aegean Bronze Age*, edited by R. Hagg and N. Marinatos, 169–71. Stockholm: Almqvist & Wiksell.

Cadogan, G. 1977–8. "Pyrgos, Crete, 1970–1977." *Archaeological Reports* 24: 70–84.

Cameron, M. 1987. "The Palatial Thematic System in the Knossos Murals." In *The Function of the Minoan Palaces*, edited by R. Hagg and N. Marinatos, 320–8. Stockholm: Astroms Forlag.

Caskey, J. 1966. "Excavations at Keos: 1964–1965." *Hesperia* 35. 375–6.

Caskey, J. 1971. "Investigations in Keos: Part 1." *Hesperia* 40: 392–5.

Chapin, A. 2004. "Power, Privilege and Landscape in Minoan Art." *Hesperia* Supplement 33: 47–64.

Cherry, J. 1983. "Evolution, Revolution and the Origins of Complex Society in Minoan Crete." In *Minoan Society*, edited by O. Krzyszkowska and L. Nixon, 33–45. Bristol: Bristol Classical Press.

Chryssoulaki, S. 1999. "Minoan Roads and Guard Houses – War Regained." In *Polemos: Le Contexte Guerrier en Egee a l'age du Bronze*, edited by R. Laffineur. Aegaeum 19: 75–85. Liege: University of Liege.

Cline, E., ed. 2010. *The Oxford Handbook of the Aegean Bronze Age*. Oxford: Oxford University Press.

Cline, E. 1994. *Sailing the Wine-Dark Sea: International Trade and the Late Bronze Age Aegean. BAR* International Series 591: 120–268.

Colburn, C. 2008. "Eastern Imports in Prepalatial Crete." *AJA* 112: 203–24.

Coldstream, N. and G. Huxley, eds. 1973. *Kythera*. Park Ridge, NJ: Noyes Press.

Collon, D. 1987. *First Impressions: Cylinder Seals in the Ancient Near East*. Chicago: University of Chicago Press.

Collon, D. 2005. *First Impressions: Cylinder Seals in the Ancient Near East*. London: British Museum Press.

Collon, D. 1990. *Near Eastern Seals*. Oakland: University of California Press.

Coulson, W. et al. 1997. "Excavations on the Kastro at Kavousi: An Architectural Overview." *Hesperia* 66: 315–90.

Crooks, S. 2013. "What Are Queer Stones? Baetyls: Epistemology of a Minoan Fetish." *BAR* International Series 2511.

Crowley, J. 2013. *The Iconography of Aegean Seals*. Aegaeum 34. Liege: University of Liege.

Crowley, J. 2008. "In Honour of the Gods – But Which Gods? Identifying Dieties in Aegean Glyptic." In *DAIS: The Aegean Feast*. Aegaeum 29: 75–88. Liege: University of Liege.

Crowley, J. 2012. "Prestige Clothing in the Bronze Age Aegean." In *Kosmos: Jewellery, Adornment and Textiles in the Aegean Bronze Age*, edited by M.-L. Nosch and R. Laffineur, 231–9. Aegaeum 33. Liege: Peeters.

D'Agata, A. 1997. "The Shrines on the Piazzale dei Sacelli at Ayia Triada." In *Crete Mycenienne*, edited by J. Driessen and A. Farnoux. BCH Supplement 30: 85–100.

D'Agata, A. and J. Moody, eds. 2005. *Ariadne's Threads: Connections between Crete and the Greek Mainland in Late Minoan III*. Athens: Scuola Archeologica Italiana di Atene.

Davaras, C. 1979. "Chronika." *Αρχαιολογικον Δελτιον* 34 B2.

Davaras, C. 1972. "The Oval House at Chamaizi Reconsidered." *AAA* 5: 283–8.

Davaras, C. and P. Betancourt 2004–12. *The Hagia Photia Cemetery, I–II*. Philadelphia: Instap Academic Press.

Davis, B. 2008. "Libation and the Minoan Feast." In *DAIS: The Aegean Feast*, edited by L. Hitchcock and R. Laffineur. Aegaeum 29: 47–56. Liege: University of Liege.

Davis, E. 1974. "The Vapheio Cups: One Minoan and One Mycenaean?" *Art Bulletin* 56: 472–87.

Davis, J. 1984. "Cultural Innovation and the Minoan Thalassocracy at Ayia Irini." In *The Minoan Thalassocracy*, edited by R. Hagg and N. Marinatos. Aegaeum 32: 159–66. Liege: The University of Liege.

Davis, J. 1986. *Keos V, Ayia Irini: Period V.* Mainz: Philipp von Zabern.

Dawkins, R. 1904–5. "Excavations at Palaikastro. IV." *BSA* 11: 260–1.

Dawkins, R. and M. Laistner 1912–13. "The Excavation of the Kamares Cave in Crete." *BSA* 19: 1–34.

Day, L. 1997. "The Late Minoan IIIC Period at Vronda, Kavousi." In *Crete Mycenienne*, edited by J. Driessen and A. Farnoux. *BCH* Supplement 30: 391–406.

Day, L. 2011. *The Pottery from Karphi: A Re-examination. BSA* Studies 19.

Day, P. et al. 2011. "A World of Goods: Transport Jars and Commodity Exchange at the Late Bronze Age Harbor of Kommos, Crete." *Hesperia* 80: 511–58.

Dickinson, O. 1994. *The Aegean Bronze Age.* Cambridge: Cambridge University Press.

Dimopoulou, N. 1999. "The Neopalatial Cemetery of the Knossian Harbor Town at Poros: Mortuary Behavior and Social Ranking." In *Eliten in der Bronzezeit*, 27–36. Mainz: Verlag der Romisch-Germanisches Zentral Museums and Rudolf Halbet Verlag.

Dimopoulou-Rethemiotakis, N., D. Wilson, and P. Day 2007. "The Earlier Prepalatial Settlement of Poros-Katsambas: Craft Production and Exchange at the Harbor Town of Knossos." In *Metallurgy in the Early Bronze Age Aegean*, edited by P. Day and C. Doonan. Sheffield Studies in Aegean Archaeology 7: 84–97. Oxford: Oxbow Books.

Driessen, J. 2010. "Malia." In *The Oxford Handbook of the Aegean Bronze Age*, edited by E. Cline, 556–70. Oxford: Oxford University Press.

Driessen, J. 2014. "Recent Developments in the Archaeology of Minoan Crete." *Pharos* 20: 75–115.

Driessen, J. and C. Macdonald 1997. *The Troubled Island.* Aegaeum 17. Liege: University of Liege.

Driessen, J. and I. Sakellarakis 1997. "The Vathypetro Complex: Some Observations on Its Architectural History and Function." In *The Function of the Minoan Villa*, edited by R. Hagg, 63–78. Stockholm: Astroms Forlag.

Driessen, J., A. MacGillivray, and H. Sackett, eds. 2002. "Excavations at Palaikastro in East Crete 1902–2002: A Centenary Exhibit." *BSA* 5–6.

Duhoux, Y. 2003. *Des Minoens en Egypte?* Louvain: University of Louvain Press.

Effinger, M. 1996. "Minoischer Schmuck." *BAR* International Series 646.

Emory, W. 1961. *Archaic Egypt.* Baltimore: Penguin.

Evans, A. 1897. "Further Discoveries of Cretan and Aegean Script, with Libyan and Proto-Egyptian Comparisons." *Journal of Hellenic Studies* 17: 327–95.

Evans, J. 1971. "Neolithic Knossos: The Growth of a Settlement." *PPS* 37: 95–117.

Evans, A. 1925. *The Palace of Minos, I.* London: Macmillan.

Evans, A. 1964. *The Palace of Minos, I.* New York: Biblo and Tannen.

Evans, A. 1927. *The Palace of Minos, II.* London: Macmillan.

Evans, A. 1964. *The Palace of Minos II*, vol. 1. New York: Biblo and Tannen.

Evans, A. 1964. *The Palace of Minos, III.* New York: Biblo and Tannen.

Evans, A. 1964. *The Palace of Minos, IV.* New York: Biblo and Tannen.Evans, J. 1943. *Time and Chance: The Story of Arthur Evans and His Forebears.* London: Longmans and Green.

Evely, D. 1999. *Fresco: Passport into the Past – Minoan Crete through the Eyes of Mark Cameron.* Athens: British School at Athens.

Evely, D., H. Hughes-Brock, and N. Momigliano, eds. 1994. "Knossos: A Labyrinth of History." Papers presented to Sinclair Hood, British School at Athens.

Fiandra, E. 1975. "Ancora a propsito delle cretule di Festos." *Bollettino del arte* 60: 1–25.

Fiandra, E. 1968. "A che cosa serviano le cretule di Festos." In *Pepragmena tou B'Diethnous*

Kritologikou Synedriou, 383–97. Athens: Italian School of Archaeology at Athens.

Finkelberg, M. 2001. "The Language of Linear A: Greek, Semitic, or Anatolian?" In *Greater Anatolia and the Ind-Hittite Language Family*, edited by R. Drews, *Journal of Indo-European Studies*, Monograph 38.

Fitton, L. 1996. *The Discovery of the Greek Bronze Age*. Cambridge: Harvard University Press.

Foster, K. 2018. "Mari and the Minoans." *Groniek* 217: 343–62.

Furumark, A. 1988. "Linear A and Minoan Religion." *Opuscula Atheniensia* 17: 52–90.

Galanakis, Y., ed. 2013. *The Aegean World: A Guide to the Minoan and Mycenaean Antiquities in the Ashmolean Museum*. Athens: Kapon Editions.

Gale, N., ed. 1991. "Bronze Age Trade in the Mediterranean." *SIMA* 90: 327–34.

Gale, N. 1990. "The Provenance of Metals for Early Bronze Age Crete – Local or Cycladic?" *Πεπραγμένα του ΣΤ' Διεθνοθος Κρητολογικου Συνεδριου I*: 299–316. Chania.

Gere, C. 2009. *Knossos and the Prophets of Modernism*. Chicago: University of Chicago Press.

Germond, P. 2005. *The Symbolic World of Egyptian Amulets*. Milan: 5 Continents Edition.

Gesell, G. 1985. "Town, Palace, and House Cult in Minoan Crete." *SIMA* 67: 74–176.

Gill, M. 1985. "Some Observations on Representations of Marine Animals in Minoan Art, and their Identification." *BCH* Supplement 11: 63–81.

Godart, L. and J.-P. Olivier 1976–85. *Recueil des inscriptions en Lineaire*, vols. 1–5. *Etudes Cretoises* 21. Paris: Librairie Orientaliste Paul Geuthner.

Goodison, L. 2001. "From Tholos Tomb to Throne Room: Perceptions of the Sun in Minoan Ritual." In *POTNIA: Deities and Religion in the Aegean Bronze Age*, edited by R. Laffineur and W.-D. Niemeier. Aegaeum 22: 77–88. Liege: University of Liege.

Goodison, L. 1998. "Beyond the 'Great Mother': The Sacred World of the Minoans." In *Ancient Goddesses: The Myths and the Evidence*, edited by L. Goodison and C. Morris, 113–32. Madison: University of Wisconsin Press.

Goodison, L. 1990/2. *Moving Heaven and Earth: Sexuality, Spirituality and Social Change*. London: Women's Press.

Goodison, L. 2009. "Why All This about Oak or Stone? Trees and Boulders in Minoan Religion." In *Archaeologies of Cult*, edited by A. D'Agata and A. Van de Moortel. *Hesperia* Supplement 42: 51–7.

Graham, W. 1962. *The Palaces of Crete*. Princeton: Princeton University Press.

Guarducci, M. 1935–50. *Inscriptiones Creticae*. Rome: Libreria dello Stato.

Hadjidaki, E. 2019. *The Minoan Shipwreck at Pseira, Crete*, Philadelphia: INSTAP Press.

Hadzidaki, E. and P. Betancourt 2005–6. "A Minoan Shipwreck off Pseira Island, East Crete: Preliminary Report." *Eulimine* 4: 79–96.

Hagg, R., ed. 1997. *The Function of the Minoan Villa*. Stockholm: Astroms Forlag.

Hagg, R. 1997. "Religious Syncretism at Knossos?" In *La Crete Mycenienne*, edited by J. Driessen and A. Farnoux. *BCH* Supplement 30: 163–8.

Hagg, R. and N. Marinatos, eds. 1984. *The Minoan Thalassocracy*. Aegaeum 32: 205–15. Stockholm: Astroms Forlag.

Hagg, R. and N. Marinatos, eds. 1980. *Sanctuaries and Cults in the Aegean Bronze Age*. Stockholm: Almqvist & Wiksell.

Haggis, D. 2012. "The Lakkos Pottery and Middle Minoan IB Petras." In *Petras, Siteia – 25 Years of Excavation and Studies*, edited by M. Tsipopoulou. Monographs of the Danish Institute of Athens, vol. 16: 191–201. Athens: Danish Institute at Athens.

Haggis, D. 1997. "The Typology of the Early Minoan I Chalice and the Cultural Implications of Form and Style in Early Bronze Age Ceramics." In *TEXNH*, edited by R. Laffineur and P. Betancourt. Aegaeum 16: 296–9. Liege: University of Liege.

Haider, P. 2001. "Minoan Deities in an Egyptian Medical Text." In *POTNIA: Deities and Religion in the Aegean Bronze Age*, edited by

R. Laffineur and W.-D. Niemeier. Aegaeum 22: 479–82. Liege: University of Liege.

Halbherr, F. 1893. "Amnissos." *The Antiquary* 27: 112.

Halbherr, F. 1888. "The Idaean Cave." *Monumenti Antichi* 2: 690ff.

Halbherr, F. 1888. "Scoperte nell'antro di Psychro." *Museo Italiano de antichita Classica* 2: 905–12.

Hallager, B. P. 1985. "Crete and Italy in the Late Bronze III Period." *AJA* 89: 293.

Hallager, E. 1985. "The Master Impression: A Clay Sealing from the Greek-Swedish Excavations at Kastelli, Khania." *SIMA* 69.

Hallager, E. 1996. "The Minoan Roundel and Other Sealed Documents in the Neopalatial Linear A Administration, I-II." Aegaeum 14: 39–77. Liege: University of Liege.

Hallager, E. 1977. "The Mycenaean Palace at Knossos: Evidence for the Final Destruction in the LM IIIB Period." *Medelhausmuseet Memoire* 1.

Hamilakis, Y., ed. 2002. *Labyrinth Revisited: Rethinking Minoan Archaeology.* Oxford: Oxbow Books.

Hansen, J. 1988. "Agriculture in the Prehistoric Aegean." *AJA* 92: 39–52.

Haskell, H. 2005. "Region to Region Export of Transport Stirrup Jars from LM III A2B Crete." In *Ariadne's Threads: Connections between Crete and the Greek Mainland in Late Minoan III*, edited by A. D'Agata and J. Moody, 205–42. Athens: Scuola Archeologica Italiana di Atene.

Hatzaki, E. 2005. "Postpalatial Knossos: Towns and Cemeteries from LM IIIA2 to LM IIIC." In *Ariadne's Threads: Connections between Crete and the Greek Mainland in Late Minoan III*, edited by A. D'Agata and J. Moody, 65–105. Athens: Scuola Archeologica Italiana di Atene.

Hazzidakis, J. 1886. "Amnissos." *Parnassos* 10: 339–42.

Hazzidakis, J. 1912–13. "An Early Minoan Sacred Cave at Arkalochori." *BSA* 19: 35–47.

Helms, M. 1998. *Access to Origins: Affines, Ancestors and Aristocrats.* Austin: University of Texas Press.

Helms, M. 1988. *Ulysses' Sail: An Ethnographic Odyssey of Power, Knowledge, and Geographic Distance.* Princeton: Princeton University Press.

Henriksson, G. and M. Blomberg 1996. "Evidence for Minoan Astronomical Observations from the Peak Sanctuaries of Petsophas and Troastalos." *Opus Atheniensa* 21: 99–114.

Herzfeld, M. 1982. *Ours Once More: Folklore, Ideology, and the Making of Modern Greece.* Austin: University of Texas Press.

Hiller, S. 1984. "Pax Minoica versus Minoan Thalassocracy: Military Aspects of Minoan Culture." In *The Minoan Thalassocracy*, edited by R. Hagg and N. Marinatos. Aegaeum 32: 27–31. Liege: University of Liege.

Hiller, S. 2001. "Potnia/Potnios Aigion: On the Religious Aspects of Goats in the Aegean Late Bronze Age." In *POTNIA: Deities and Religion in the Aegean Bronze Age*, edited by R. Laffineur and W.-D. Niemeier. Aegaeum 22: 293–304. Liege: University of Liege.

Hoflmayer, F., ed. 2017. *The Late Third Millennium in the Ancient Near East.* Chicago: University of Chicago Press.

Hood, S. 1978. *The Arts in Prehistoric Greece.* New Haven, CT: Yale University Press.

Hood, S. 1984. "A Minoan Empire in the Aegean in the 16th and 15th Centuries BC?" In *The Minoan Thalassocracy*, edited by R. Hagg and N. Marinatos. Aegaeum 32: 33–8. Liege: University of Liege.

Immerwahr, S. 1990. *Aegean Painting in the Bronze Age.* University Park: Pennsylvania State University Press.

Isaakidou, V. 2014. "The Fauna and Economy of Neolithic Knossos Revisited." In *Escaping the Labyrinth: The Cretan Neolithic in Context*, edited by V. Isaakidou and P. Tomkins. Sheffield Studies in Aegean Archaeology 8: 90–114. Oxford: Oxbow Books.

Jones, B. R. 2015. *Ariadne's Threads: The Construction and Significance of Clothes in the Aegean Bronze Age*, Aegaeum 38, Liege: Peeters.

Jones, R. and L. Vagnetti 1991. "Traders and Craftsmen in the Central Mediterranean:

Archaeological Evidence and Archaeometric Research." In *Bronze Age Trade in the Mediterranean*, edited by N. Gale. *SIMA* 90: 133.

Kanta, A. 1980. "The Late Minoan III Period in Crete: A Survey of Sites, Pottery and Their Distribution." *SIMA* 58: 96–326.

Kanta, A. and A. Tzigounaki 1999. "The Protopalatial Multiple Sealing System: New Evidence from Monasteraki." In *Administrative Documents in the Aegean and Their Near Eastern Counterparts,* edited by M. Perna, 193–210. Torino: Paravia Scriptorium.

Karageorghis, V. 1982. *Cyprus*. London: Thames and Hudson.

Karageorghis, V., A. Kanta, N. Stampolidis, and Y. Sakellarakis, eds. 2014. *Kypriaka in Crete*. Philadelphia: Instap Academic Press.

Karetsou, A., ed. 2000. *Crete–Egypt: Political Connections over Three Millennia*. Athens: Kapon Editions.

Karetsou, A., ed. 2000. *KPHTH-AIΓΥΠΤΟΣ. Πολιτισμικοι δεσμοι τριων χιλιετιων* (essays). Athens: Kapon Editions.

Karetsou, A. 1980. "The Peak Sanctuary of Mt. Juktas." In *Sanctuaries and Cults in the Aegean Bronze Age*, edited by R. Hagg and N. Marinatos, 137–53. Stockholm: Almqvist & Wiksell.

Karetsou, A., M. Andreadaki-Vlazaki, and N. Papadakis, eds. 2000. *Κρητη-Αιγυπτος* (catalog). Herakleion: Archaeological Museum of Herakleion.

Karetsou, A., M. Andreadaki-Vlazaki, and N. Papadakis, eds. 2001. *Crete-Egypt: Three Thousand Years of Cultural Links* (catalog translation). Herakleion and Cairo: Hellenic Ministry of Culture: Ephorates 23–5.

Karetsou, A. and A.-M. Jasnik 2015. "A Hieroglyphic Seal from the Juktas Peak Sanctuary." In *The Great Islands*, edited by C. Macdonald, E. Hatzaki, and S. Andreou, 94–9. Athens: Kapon Editions.

Kazantzakis, N. 1965. *Report to Greco*. New York: Simon and Schuster.

Kemp, B. and R. Merrillees 1980. *Minoan Pottery in Second Millennium Egypt*. Mainz: Verlag Philipp von Zabern.

Koehl, R. 2006. *Aegean Bronze Age Rhyta*. Philadelphia: Instap Academic Press.

Koehl, R. 1986. "A Marinescape Floor from the Palace at Knossos." *AJA* 90: 407–17.

Krzyszkowska, O. 2005. *Aegean Seals: An Introduction*. British Institute of Classical Studies Supplement 85: 57–192. London: University of London.

Krzyszkowska, O. ed. 2010. *Cretan Offerings*. Studies in Honour of Peter Warren, *BSA* Studies 18.

Krzyszkowska, O. 1983. "Wealth and Prosperity in Prepalatial Crete: The Case of Ivory." In *Minoan Society*, edited by O. Krzyskowska and L. Nixon, 166. Bristol: Bristol Classical Press.

Krzyszkowska, O. 2012. "Worn to Impress? Symbol and Status in Aegean Glyptic." In *Kosmos: Jewellery, Adornment and Textiles in the Aegean Bronze Age*, edited by M.-L. Nosch and R. Laffineur, 739–48. Aegeaum 33. Liege: Peeters.

La Marle, H. 2002. *Introduction au linéaire A*. Paris: Geuthner.

La Marle, H. 2002. *L'aventure de l'alphabet: les écritures cursives et linéaires du Proche-Orient et de l'Europe du sud-est à l'Âge du Bronze*. Paris: Geuthner.

La Marle, H. 2007. *Les racines du crétois ancien et leur morphologie: communication à l'Académie des Inscriptions et Belles Lettres*. Paris: Geuthner.

La Marle, H. 1997–9, 2006. *Linéaire A, la première écriture syllabique de Crète*, 4 vols. Paris: Geuthner.

Laffineur, R. 1998. "From West to East: The Aegean and Egypt in the Early Late Bronze Age." In *The Aegean and the Orient in the Second Millennium*, edited by E. Cline and D. Harris-Cline. Aegaeum 18: 58–68. Liege: University of Liege.

Laffineur, R. and R. Hagg 2001. *Potnia, Deities and Religion in the Aegean Bronze Age*, Aegaeum 22.

Laneri, N. and M. Schwartz 2011. "Southeastern Eastern Anatolia in the Middle Bronze Age." In *The Oxford Handbook of Ancient Anatolia*, edited by S. Steadman and G. McMahon, 337–60. Oxford: Oxford University Press.

LaRosa, V. 1997. "Hagia Triada A L'Epoque Mycenienne: L'Utopie d'un Ville Capitale." In *Crete Mycenienne*, edited by J. Driessen and A. Farnoux. *BCH* Supplement 30: 249–66.

LaRosa, V. 1997. "La Villa Royale de Haghia Triada." In *The Function of the Minoan Villa*, edited by R. Hagg, 79–89. Stockholm: Astroms Forlag.

Lawson, J. 1910. *Modern Greek Folklore and Ancient Greek Religion. A Study in Survivals*, Cambridge: Cambridge University Press.

Legakis, A. and Z. Kypriotakis 1994. "A Biogeographical Analysis of the Island of Crete." *Journal of Biogeography* 21: 441–5.

Lembessi, A. 1981. "Η σθνεχεια της κρητομυχηωαικης λατρειας: Επιβιοσσεις και αωαβισσεις." *Archaeologiko Epherimis* 120: 1–24.

Lembessi, A. and P. Muhly 1990. "Aspects of Minoan Cult Sacred Enclosures: The Evidence from the Syme Sanctuary (Crete)." *Archaeologischer Anzeiger.* 315–36.

Levi, D. 1976/88. *Festos e la civilta minoica, I-II.* Incunabula 9. Rome: Edizioni dell' Ateneo.

Levi, D. 1961. *The Recent Excavations at Phaistos.* SIMA 11.

Levi, D. 1961-2. "La Tomba a Tholos de Kamilari presso a Festos." *Annuario della Scuola Archeologica de Atene* 23–4: 7–148.

Macdonald, C., E. Hallager, and W.-D. Niemeier, eds. 2009. *The Minoans in the Central, Eastern and Northern Aegean – New Evidence*, vol. 8. Athens: Monographs of the Danish Institute at Athens.

MacGillivray, J. 2000. *Minotaur: Sir Arthur Evans and the Archaeology of the Minoan Myth.* New York: Farrar, Straus and Giroux.

MacGillivray, J., J. Driessen, and H. Sackett 2000. *The Palaikastro Kouros. BSA* Studies 6.

Manning, S. 2017. "Comments on Climate, Intra-regional Variations, Chronology, the 2200 B.C. Horizon of Change in the Eastern Mediterranean Region and Then Socio-political Change in Crete." In *The Late Third Millennium in the Ancient Near East,* edited by F. Hoflmayer, 451–80. Chicago: University of Chicago.

Marangou, L., ed. 1992. *Minoan and Greek Civilization from the Mitsotakis Collection.* Athens: C. Adam and N.P. Goulandris Foundation – Museum of Cycladic Art.

Marinatos, N. 1984. *Art and Religion in Thera.* Athens: I. Mathioulakis and Company.

Marinatos, N. 2005. "The Ideals of Manhood in Minoan Crete." In *Aegean Wall Painting,* edited by L. Morgan. *BSA* Studies 13: 149–58.

Marinatos, N. 2010. *Minoan Kingship and the Solar Goddess.* Champaign: University of Illinois Press.

Marinatos, N. 1993. *Minoan Religion: Ritual, Image and Symbol.* Columbia: University of South Carolina Press.

Marinatos, N. 2017. "Religious Interaction between Egypt and the Aegean in the Second Millennium BCE." In *Pharoah's Land and Beyond,* edited by P. Creaseman and R. Wilkinson, 229–37. Oxford: Oxford University Press.

Marinatos, S. 1929. "Anaskaphai en Kretes." *Praktika tis en Athnais Arxaiologikis Etaipeias*: 95–109.

Marinatos, S. 1968–72. *Excavations at Thera, I–V.* Athens: The Archaeological Society at Athens.

Marinatos, S. 1939. "The Volcanic Destruction of Minoan Crete." *Antiquity* 13: 425–39.

Marketou, T. 2009. "Ialysos and Its Neighboring Areas in MBA and LBI: A Chance for Peace." In *The Minoans in the Central, Eastern and Northern Aegean – New Evidence,* edited by C. Macdonald, E. Hallager, and W.-D. Niemeier. Athens: Monographs of the Danish Institute at Athens 8: 73–97.

Martinez, L. et al. 2008. "Middle Eastern and European DNAS Lineages Characterize Populations from Eastern Crete." *American Journal of Physical Anthropology* 137: 213–23.

Matsas, D. 1995. "Minoan Long-Distance Trade: A View from the Northern Aegean." In *Politeia I: Society and State in the Aegean Bronze Age,* edited by R. Laffineur and W. D. Niemeier. Aegaeum 12: 235–48. Liege: University of Liege.

McEnroe, J. 2010. *Architecture of Minoan Crete.* Austin: University of Texas Press.

McEnroe, J. 2001. *Pseira V: The Architecture of Pseira*. Philadelphia: Instap Academic Press.

McEnroe, J. 1995. "Sir Arthur Evans and Edwardian Archaeology." *Classical Bulletin* 71: 3–18.

McEnroe, J. 1982. "A Typology of Minoan Neopalatial Houses." *AJA* 86: 3–116.

McGeorge, P. 1988. "Health and Diet in Minoan Times." In *New Aspects of Archaeological Science in Greece*, edited by R. Jones and H. Catling. *BSA* Occasional Paper 3: 47–54.

McGeorge, P. 2008. "Morbidity and Medical Practice in Minoan Crete." In *From the Land of the Labyrinth, II*, edited by M. Andreadaki-Vlazaki, G. Rethemiotakis, and N. Dimopoulou-Rethemiotaki, 118–27. New York: Onassis Foundation.

Megas, G. 1963. *Greek Calendar Customs*. Athens: Rhodis.

Militello, P. 2012. "Emerging Authority: A Functional Analysis." In *Back to the Beginning: Reassessing Social and Political Complexity on Crete during the Early and Middle Bronze Age*, edited by I. Schoep, P. Tomkins and J. Driessen, 236–72. Oxford: Oxbow Books.

Miller, H. 1941. *The Colossus of Maroussi*. New York: New Directions.

Momigliano, N. and A. Farnoux, eds. 2017. *Cretomania: Modern Desires for the Minoan Past*. Abingdon: Routledge.

Moody, J. 2009. "Environmental Change and Minoan Landscapes." In *Archaeologies of Cult*, edited by A. D'Agata and A. Van de Moortel. *Hesperia* Supplement 42: 241–50.

Moody, J. 2005. "Unraveling the Threads: Climate Changes in the Late Bronze III Aegean." In *Ariadne's Threads: Connections between Crete and the Greek Mainland in Late Minoan III*, edited by A. D'Agata and J. Moody, 443–74. Athens: Scuola Archeologica Italiana di Atene.

Moss, M. 2005. "The Minoan Pantheon." *BAR* International Series 1343: 99–147.

Mountjoy, P. 1985. "Ritual Associations for LM IB Marine Style Vases." *L'Iconographie Minoenne*, *BCH* Supplement 11: 231–42.

Muhly, J. 1973. "Copper and Tin: The Distribution of Mineral Resources and the Nature of the Metals Trade in the Bronze Age." *Transactions of the Connecticut Academy of Art and Sciences* 43: 293–4.

Muhly, P. 1992. *Μινωος Λαξευτος Ταφος στον Πορο Ηρακλειου–*. Athens: Bibliothiki tis en Athnais Arxaiolikis Etaireias.

Myers, J. 1902–3. "Excavations at Palaikastro, II. The Sanctuary-Site of Petsofa." *BSA* 9: 356–87.

Myers, J., E. Myers, and G. Cadogan, eds. 1992. *The Aerial Atlas of Ancient Crete*. Berkeley: University of California Press.

Nagy, G. 1965. "Observations on the Sign-Grouping and Vocabulary of Linear A." *AJA* 69: 295–330.

Niemeier, W.-D. 1984. "The End of the Minoan Thalassocracy." In *The Minoan Thalassocracy*, edited by R. Hagg and N. Marinatos. Aegaeum 32: 205–15. Liege: University of Liege.

Niemeier, W.-D. 1991. "Minoan Artisans Traveling Overseas: The Alalakh Frescoes and the Painted Plaster Floor at Tel Kabri." In *Thalassa: L'Egee Prehistorique et la Mer*, edited by R. Laffineur and L. Basch. Aegaeum 7: 189–202. Liege: University of Liege.

Niemeier, W.-D. and B. 1997. "Minoan Frescoes in the Eastern Mediterranean." In *The Aegean and the Orient in the Second Millennium*, edited by E. Cline and D. Harris-Cline. Aegaeum 18: 69–98. Liege: University of Liege.

Niemeier, W.-D. 2009. "Minoanisation versus Minoan Thalassocracy – An Introduction." In *The Minoans in the Central, Eastern and Northern Aegean – New Evidence*, edited by C. Macdonald, E. Hallager and W.-D. Niemeier, vol. 8, 11–30. Athens: Monographs of the Danish Institute at Athens.

Nikolapoulou, I. 2009. "'Beware Cretans Bearing Gifts': Tracing the Origins of Minoan Influence at Akrotiri, Thera." In *The Minoans in the Central, Eastern and Northern Aegean – New Evidence*, edited by C. Macdonald, E. Hallager, and W.-D. Niemeier, vol. 8, 31–40. Athens: Monographs of the Danish Institute at Athens.

Nilsson, M. 1950. *The Minoan-Mycenaean Religion and Its Survival in Greek Religion.* Lund: CWK Gleerup.

Nilsson, M. 1971. *The Minoan-Mycenaean Religion and Its Survival in Greek Religion.* 2nd edition. New York: Biblo and Tannen.

Nosch, M.-L. and R. Laffineur, eds. 2012. *Kosmos: Jewellery, Adornment and Textiles in the Aegean Bronze Age.* Aegeaum 33. Liege: Peeters.

Nowicki, K. 2000. *Defensible Sites in Crete.* Aegaeum 21. Philadelphia: Instap Academic Press.

Nowicki, K. 2014. *Final Neolithic Crete and the Southeast Aegean.* Berlin: De Gruyter.

Nowicki, K. 2008. *Monastiraki Katalimata: Excavation of a Cretan Refuge Site, 1993–2000.* Philadelphia: Instap Academic Press.

Nowicki, K. 2010. "Myrtos Fournou Korifi: Before and After." In *Cretan Offerings: Studies in Honour of Peter Warren,* edited by O. Krzyszkowska. *BSA* Studies 18: 223–38. London: Short Run Press.

Nowicki, K. 1994. "Some Remarks on the Pre- and Protopalatial Peak Sanctuaries in Crete." *Aegean Archaeology* 1: 31–48.

Owens, G. 1999. "The Structure of the Minoan Language." *Journal of Indo-European Studies* 27: 15–56.

Palmer, R. 1995. "Linear A Commodities: A Comparison of Resources." In *Politeia: Society and State in the Aegean Bronze Age,* edited by R. Laffineur and W.-D. Niemeier. Aegeaum 12: 133–56. Liege: University of Liege.

Palyvou, C. 2018. *Daidalos at Work.* Philadelphia: INSTAP Academic Press.

Panagiotaki, M. 1999. "The Central Palace Sanctuary at Knossos." *BSA* Supplement 31.

Peatfield, A. 2001. "Divinity and Performance on Minoan Peak Sanctuaries." In *POTNIA: Deities and Religion in the Aegean Bronze Age,* edited by R. Laffineur and W.-D. Niemeier. Aegeaum 22: 51–5. Liege: University of Liege.

Peatfield, A. 1990. "Minoan Peak Sanctuaries: History and Society." *Opuscula Atheniensia* 18: 117–31.

Peatfield, A. 1992. "Rural Ritual in Bronze Age Crete." *Cambridge Archaeological Journal* 2: 59–87.

Peatfield, A. 1983. "The Topography of Minoan Peak Sanctuaries." *BSA* 78: 273–80.

Pelon, O. 1966. "Maison D'Hagia Varvara et Architecture Domestique a Mallia." *BCH* 90: 552–85.

Peltenburg, E. 1989. *Early Society in Cyprus.* Edinburgh: Edinburgh University Press.

Pendlebury, J. and H. M. Money-Coutts 1935–6. "Excavations in the Plain of Lasithi, I." *BSA* 36: 9–13.

Pendlebury, J. and H. M. Money-Coutts 1937–8. "Excavations in the Plain of Lasithi, III Karphi." *BSA* 38: 57–148.

Pernier, L. 1935. *Il Palazzo Minoico di Festos, I.* Rome: La Libreria dello Stato.

Phillips, J. 2008. *Aegyptiaka on the Island of Crete in Their Chronological Context: A Critical Review,* vols. 1–2. Vienna: Austrian Academy of Science 18.

Pini, I. 1990. "Eine fruhkretissche Siegelwerkstatt?" *Pepragmena tou ST' Diethnous Kritologikou Synedriou* 6 (A2): 115–27.

Platon, L. 2010. "Kato Zakros." In *The Oxford Handbook of the Bronze Age Aegean,* edited by E. Cline, 509–17. Oxford: Oxford University Press.

Platon, N. 1971. *Zakros: The Discovery of a Lost Palace of Ancient Crete.* New York: Charles Scribner's Sons.

Pope, K. 1993. "Geology and Soils." *Hesperia* 62: 202–24.

Popham, M., E. Catling, and H. Catling 1974. "Sellopolo Tombs 3 and 4, Two Late Minoan Graves near Knossos." *BSA* 69: 195–258.

Poursat, J.-C. 2008. *L'Art Egeen, I.* Paris: Picard.

Poursat, J.-C. 2009. "Cult Activity at Malia in the Protopalatial Period." In *Archaeologies of Cult,* edited by A. D'Agata and A. Van de Moortel. *Hesperia* Supplement 42: 71–8.

Poursat, J.-C. 2012. "The Emergence of Elite Groups at Protopalatial Malia: A Biography of Quartier Mu." In *Back to the Beginning: Reassessing Social and Political Complexity on Crete during the Early and Middle Bronze Age,* edited by I. Schoep, P. Tomkins, and J. Driessen, 177–83. Oxford: Oxbow Books.

Poursat, J.-C. 1978–2005. *Fouilles executees a Malia: Le Quartier Mu, I–IV (Etudes Cretoises 22, 26, 32–4)*. Paris: De Boccard.

Poursat, J.-C. 1992. *Guide de Malia, Le Quartier Mu*. Paris: De Boccard.

Poursat, J.-C. 2010. "Malia: Palace, State, City." In *Cretan Offerings: Studies in Honour of Peter Warren*, edited by O. Krzyszkowska. *BSA* Studies 18: 259–68.

Poursat, J.-C. 1966. "Un sanctuaire de Minoen moyen II a Mallia." *BCH* 90: 514–51.

Poursat, J.-C. and M. Loubet 2005. "Metalurgie et contacts exterieurs a Malia (Crete) au Minoen Moyen II: Remargues sur une serie d'analyses isotopiques du plomb." In *EMPORIA I*, edited by R. Laffineur and E. Greco. Aegaeum 25: 117–21. Liege: University of Liege.

Prevelakis, P. 1991. *The Cretan*. Athens: Nostots.

Preziosi, D. and L. Hitchcock 1999. *Aegean Art and Architecture*. Oxford: Oxford University Press.

Rackham, O. and J. Moody 1996. *The Making of the Cretan Landscape*. Manchester: University of Manchester Press.

Rehak, P. 1998. "Aegean Natives in the Theban Tomb Paintings: The Keftiu Revisited." In *The Aegean and the Orient in the Second Millennium*, edited by E. Cline and D. Harris-Cline. Aegaeum 18: 39–52. Liege: University of Liege.

Relaki, M. 2012. "The Social Arenas of Tradition: Investigating Collective and Individual Social Strategies in the Prepalatial and Protopalatial Mesara." In *Back to the Beginning: Reassessing Social and Political Complexity on Crete during the Early and Middle Bronze Age*, edited by I. Schoep, P. Tomkins, and J. Driessen, 290–324. Oxford: Oxbow Books.

Rethemiotakis, G. 2016/17. "The 'Divine Couple' Ring from Poros and the Origins on the Minoan Calendar." *Atheniensiche Miteillungen* 131/2: 1–29.

Rutkowski, B. 1986. *The Cult Places of the Aegean*. New Haven, CT: Yale University Press.

Rutkowski, B. and K. Nowicki 1996. *The Psychro Cave and Sacred Grottoes in Crete*. Warsaw: Art and Archaeology.

Rutter, J. 1999. "Cretan External Relations during LM IIIA2–B (1370–1200 BC): A View from the Mesara." In *The Point Iria Wreck: Interconnections in the Mediterranean ca 1200 BC*, edited by W. Phelps et al., 139–86. Athens: Hellenic Institute of Marine Archaeology.

Rutter, J. 2017. *House X at Kommos, II, The Pottery*. Philadelphia: Instap Academic Press.

Sakellarakis, Y. 2013. *Κυθερα: Ο Αγιος Γεοργιος στον Βουνο*. Athens: Ammos Publications.

Sakellarakis, Y. 1996. "Minoan Religious Influence in the Aegean: The Case of Kythera." *BSA* 91: 81–99.

Sakellarakis, Y. and E. Sapouna-Sakellarakis 1997. *Archanes: Minoan Crete in a New Light, I–II*. Athens: Ammos Publications.

Sakellarakis, Y. and E. Sapouna-Sakellarakis 1981. "Drama of Death in a Minoan Temple." *National Geographic* 159: 205–22.

Σακελλαράκης, Γ. 2013. "Βιβλιοθήκη της εν Αθήναις Αρχαιολογικής Εταιρείας αρ. 287." In *Κύθηρα Ο Άγιος Γεώργιος στο Βουνό Μινωική Λατρεία-Νεότεροι Χρόνοι*. Αθήνα: Η εν Αθήναις Αρχαιολογική Εταιρεία.

Sarpaki, A. 2013. "The Economy of Neolithic Knossos." In *The Neolithic Settlement of Knossos in Crete*, edited by N. Efstratiou, A. Karetsou, and M. Ntinou, 63–94. Philadelphia: Instap Academic Press.

Schoep, I. 2002. "The Administration of Neopalatial Crete." *Minos* Supplement 17: 175–99.

Schoep, I. 1995. "Context and Chronology of Linear A Administrative Documents." *Aegean Archaeology* 2: 29–64.

Schoep, I. 2006. "Looking beyond the Palaces." *AJA* 110: 37–64.

Seager, R. 1912. *Excavations on the Island of Mochlos*. Boston: American School of Classical Studies at Athens.

Seager, R. 1916. *The Cemetery of Pachyammos, Crete*. Philadelphia: University of Pennsylvania Anthropological Publications.

Shaw, J. 2017. "The Middle Minoan Slipway for Ships at the Kommos Harbour and Harbour

Development in Prehistoric Crete." In *Minoan Architecture and Urbanism*, edited by Q. Letesson and C. Knappett, 228–58. Oxford: Oxford University Press.

Shaw, J. and M. Shaw 1993. "Excavations at Kommos (Crete) during 1986–1992." *Hesperia* 62: 131–61.

Shaw, J. and M. Shaw eds. 1996. *Kommos I, Part 2*. Princeton: Princeton University Press.

Shaw, J. and M. Shaw eds. 2006. *Kommos V: The Monumental Minoan Buildings at Kommos*. Princeton: Princeton University Press.

Shaw, J. and M. Shaw 1997. "'Mycenaean' Kommos." In *Crete Mycenienne*, edited by J. Driessen and A. Farnoux. *BCH* Supplement 30: 423–34.

Shaw, M. 1970. "Ceiling Patterns from the Tomb of Hepzefa." *AJA* 74: 25–30.

Shaw, M. 2005. "The Painted Pavilion of the 'Caravanserai' at Knossos." In *Aegean Wall Painting: A Tribute to Mark Cameron*, edited by L. Morgan. *BSA Studies* 13: 91–112.

Shelmerdine, C., ed. 2008. *The Aegean Bronze Age*, Cambridge: Cambridge University Press.

Sherratt, A. 1997. *Economy and Society in Prehistoric Europe: Changing Perspectives*. Edinburgh: Edinburgh University Press.

Sherratt, A. and S. Sherratt 1991. "From Luxuries to Commodities: The Nature of Mediterranean Bronze Age Trading Systems." In *Bronze Age Trade in the Mediterranean*, edited by N. Gale, *SIMA* 90: 351–86.

Smith, W. S. 1966. *Interconnections in the Ancient Near East*. New Haven, CT: Yale University Press.

Soles, J. 2013. *Mochlos IA, Period III. Neopalatial Settlement on the Coast: The Artisans' Quarter and the Farmhouse at Chalinomouri*. Philadelphia: Instap Academic Press.

Soles, J. 1992. "The Prepalatial Cemeteries at Mochlos and Gournia and the House Tombs of Bronze Age Crete." *Hesperia* Supplement 24: 1–171.

Soles, J. 1988. "Social Ranking in Prepalatial Cemeteries." In *Problems in Greek Prehistory*, edited by E. French and K. Wardle, 49–62. Bristol: Bristol Classical Press.

Steiner, M. and A. Killebrew, eds. 2014. *The Oxford Handbook to the Archaeology of the Levant*. Oxford: Oxford University Press.

Strasser, T. 2010. "Stone Age Seafaring in the Mediterranean." *Hesperia* 79: 145–90.

Strasser, T. et al. 2018. "Palaeolithic Cave Art from Crete, Greece." *Journal of Archaeological Science: Reports* 18: 100–8.

Svoronos, J. 1972. *Numismatique de la Crete Ancienne*. Bonn: Rudolf Habelt.

Talbert, R., ed. 2000. *The Barrington Atlas of the Greek and Roman World*. Princeton: Princeton University Press.

Taramelli, A. 1897. "The Prehistoric Grotto at Miamu." *AJA* 1: 287–312.

Taramelli, A. 1901. "A Visit to the Grotto of Camares on Mount Ida." *AJA* 5: 437–51.

Tessier, B. 1984. *Ancient Near Eastern Cylinder Seals from the Marcopoli Collection*. Berkeley: University of California at Berkeley.

Thomas, H. 2012. "Cretan Hieroglyphic and Linear A." In *The Oxford Handbook of the Bronze Age Aegean*, edited by E. Cline, 340–55. Oxford: Oxford University Press.

Todaro, S. 2012. "Craft Production and Social Practices at Prepalatial Phaistos." In *Back to the Beginning: Reassessing Social and Political Complexity on Crete during the Early and Middle Bronze Age*, edited by I. Schoep, P. Tomkins, and J. Driessen, 195–235. Oxford: Oxbow Books.

Todaro, S. 2013. "The Phaistos Hills before the Palace: A Contextual Reappraisal." *Praehistorica Mediterranean 5*. Monza, Italy: Polimetrica.

Todaro, S. and S. DiTonto 2014. "The Neolithic Settlement of Phaistos Revisited." In *Escaping the Labyrinth: The Cretan Neolithic in Context*, edited by V. Isaakidou and P. Tomkins. Sheffield Studies in Aegean Archaeology 8: 177–90. Oxford: Oxbow Books.

Tsipopoulou, M. 1999. "Before, During, After: The Architectural Phases of the Palatial Building at Petras, Siteia." In *Meletemata Studies in Aegean Archaeology Presented to Malcolm H. Wiener as He Enters his 65th Year*, edited by P. Betancourt et al. Aegaeum 20, III: 848–56. Liege: University of Liege.

Tsipopoulou, M. 2007. "The Central Court of the Palace of Petras." In *Krinoi kai Limenes: Studies in Honor of Joseph and Maria Shaw*, edited by P. Betancourt, M. Nelson, and H. Williams, 749–60. Philadelphia: Instap Academic Press.

Tsipopoulou, M. 2005. "Mycenaeans at the Isthmus of Ierapetra: Some Preliminary Thoughts on the Foundation of the (Eteo) Cretan Cultural Identity." In *Ariadne's Threads: Connections between Crete and the Greek Mainland in Late Minoan III.* edited by A. D'Agata and J. Moody, 302–52. Athens: Scuola Archeologica Italiana di Atene.

Tsipopoulou, M. 2012. *Petras, Siteia – 25 Years of Excavation and Studies.* Monographs of the Danish Institute at Athens, vol. 16. Athens: Danish Institute at Athens.

Tsipopoulou, M. and E. Hallager 2010. *The Hieroglyphic Archive at Petras, Siteia.* Danish Institute at Athens Monograph 9. Aarhaus: Narayana Press.

Tyree, L. 1974. *Cretan Sacred Caves: Archaeological Evidence.* PhD thesis. Columbia: University of Missouri.

Tyree, L. 2001. "Diachronic Changes in Minoan Cave Cult." In *POTNIA: Deities and Religion in the Aegean Bronze Age*, edited by R. Laffineur and W.-D. Niemeier. Aegaeum 22: 39–49. Liege: University of Liege.

Tzachili, I. 2016. *Βρυσινας II: Η Κεραμεικη της Ανασκαφης 1972–1973.* Athens: Archaeological Society of Athens.

Ucko, P. 1968. *Anthropomorphic Figurines of Predynastic Egypt and Neolithic Crete.* London: A. Szmidla.

Vagnetti, L. 1975. "L'Insediamento Neolithico di Festos." *Asatene* 50/51: 7–138.

Van de Moortel, A. 2007. "Kommos and Its East Mediterranean Connections in the Protopalatial Period." In *Krinoi kai Limenes: Studies in Honor of Joseph and Maria Shaw*, edited by P. Betancourt, M. Nelson, and H. Williams, 177–84. Philadelphia: Instap Academic Press.

Van de Moortel, A. 2011. "The Phaistos Palace and the Kamares Cave: A Special Relationship." In *Our Cups are Full: Pottery and Society in the Aegean Bronze Age*, edited by W. Gauss et al. *BAR* International Series 2227: 306–18.

Van de Moortel, A. 2006. "A Re-examination of the Pottery from the Kamares Cave." in *Pottery and Society: The Impact of Recent Studies of Minoan Pottery*, edited by M. Weiner et al., 73–93. Boston: Archaeological Institute of America.

Van Effenterre, H. 1980. *Le palais de Malia et la cite Minoenne, I–II.* Incunabula Graeca 76. Rome: Edizioni dell'Ateneo.

Van Effenterre, H. and M. Van Effenterre 1969. "Fouilles executes a Mallia: Le Centre Politique." *Etudes Cretoises* 17: 18–24. Paris: Geuthner.

Van Soesbergen, P. 2016. *Minoan Linear A. Volume I, Hurrians and Hurrian in Minoan Crete. Part 1, Text.* Amsterdam: Brave New Books.

Vandenabeele, F. 1991. "Le monde marin dans les sanctuaires minoens." In *Thalassa. L'Egee Prehistorique et la Mer*, edited by R. Laffineur and L. Basch. Aegaeum 7: 239–52. Liege: University of Liege.

Vasilakis, A. 1989. "Ο Πρωτομινωικος Οικισμος της Τρυπυτης." *Αρχαιολογια* 30: 52–6.

Vasilakis, A. and K. Branigan 2010. *Moni Odigitria: A Prepalatial Cemetery and Its Environs in the Asterousia, Southern Crete.* Philadelphia: Instap Academic Press.

Ventris, M. and J. Chadwick 1956/73. *Documents in Mycenaean Greek.* Cambridge: Cambridge University Press.

Vercoutter, J. 1956. *L'Egypte et le monde egeen prehellenique.* Cairo: L'insitut francais de archaeologie orientale.

Wallace, S. 2010. *Ancient Crete: From Successful Collapse to Democracy's Alternatives, Twelfth to Fifth Centuries BC.* Cambridge: Cambridge University Press.

Wallis Budge, E. A. 1978. *Amulets and Superstitions.* New York: Dover.

Warren, P. 2000. "Crete and Egypt: The Transmission of Relationships." In *Κρητη-Αιγυπτος, Πολιτισμικοι δεσμοι τριων χιλιετιων* (essays) edited by A. Karetsou, 24–8. Athens: Kapon Editions.

Warren, P. 2009. "Final Summing Up." In *The Minoans in the Central, Eastern and Northern Aegean – New Evidence*, edited by C. Macdonald, E. Hallager, and W.-D. Niemeier, vol. 8, 263–5. Athens: Monographs of the Danish Institute at Athens.

Warren, P. 1985. "The Fresco of the Garlands from Knossos." *L'Iconographie Minoenne. BCH* Supplement 11: 186–207.

Warren, P. 1995. "Minoan Crete and Pharaonic Egypt." In *Egypt, the Aegean and the Levant*, edited by W. Davies and L. Schofield, 1–18. London: British Museum Press.

Warren, P. 1972. *Myrtos: An Early Bronze Age Settlement in Crete. BSA* Supplement 7. Oxford: Thames and Hudson.

Warren, P. 1990. "Of Baetyls." *Opuscula Atheniensia* 18: 193–206.

Warren, P. 2007. "The Roofing of Early Minoan Round Tombs: The Evidence of Lebena Tomb II (Gerokampos) and of Cretan Mitata." In *Krinoi kai Limenes: Studies in Honor of Joseph and Maria Shaw*, edited by P. Betancourt, M. Nelson, and H. Williams, 9–16. Philadelphia: Instap Academic Press.

Warren P. and V. Hankey 1985. *Aegean Bronze Chronology*. Bristol: Bristol Classical Press.

Warren, P., J. Tzedakis, and J. Greig 1974. "Debla: An Early Minoan Settlement in Western Crete." *BSA* 69: 293–342.

Watrous, V. 1984. "Ayia Triada: A New Perspective on the Minoan Villa." *AJA* 88: 123–35.

Watrous, V. 1996. *The Cave Sanctuary of Zeus at Psychro*. Aegaeum 15. Liege: University of Liege.

Watrous, V. 2005. "Cretan International Relations during the Middle Minoan IA Period and the Chronology of Seager's Finds from the Mochlos Tombs." In *EMPORIA*, vol. 1, edited by R. Laffineur and E. Greco, 107–16. Aegaeum 25. Liege: University of Liege..

Watrous, V. 2001. "Crete through the Protopalatial Period." *Aegean Prehistory: A Revue, American Journal of Archaeology* Supplement 1: 169–71.

Watrous, V. 2007. "The Fleet Fresco, The Odyssey and Greek Epic Narrative." In *EPOS: Reconsidering Greek Epic and Aegean Bronze Age Archaeology*, edited by S. Morris and R. Laffineur. Aegaeum 28: 97–105. Liege: University of Liege.

Watrous, V. 2012. "The Harbor Complex at Gournia." *AJA* 116: 521–42.

Watrous, V. 1992. *Kommos III: The Late Bronze Age Pottery*. Princeton: Princeton University Press.

Watrous, V. 1985. "Late Bronze Age Kommos: Imported Pottery as Evidence of Foreign Contacts." *Scripta Mediterraneana* 6: 12, 201–3.

Watrous, V. 1991. "The Origin and Iconography of the Late Minoan Painted Larnax." *Hesperia* 60: 285–307.

Watrous, V. (In press.) "A Peak Sanctuary for Gournia." *Soles Festschrift*.

Watrous, V. 2001. "Review of Aegean Prehistory III: Crete from the Earliest Prehistory through the Protopalatial Period." In *Aegean Prehistory: A Review*, edited by T. Cullen. *AJA* Supplement I: 169–98.

Watrous, V. 1987. "The Role of the Near East in the Rise of the Cretan Palaces." In *The Function of the Minoan Palaces*, edited by R. Hagg and N. Marinatos, 65–70. Stockholm: Astroms Forlag.

Watrous, V. et al. 2015. "Excavations at Gournia, 2010–2012." *Hesperia* 84: 397–465.

Watrous, V. and A. Heimroth 2011. "Household Industries of Late Minoan IB Gournia and the Socioeconomic Status of the Town." In *ΣΤΕΓΑ: The Archaeology of Houses and Households in Ancient Crete. Hesperia* Supplement 44: 199–212.

Watrous, V., D. Hadzi-Vallianou, and H. Blitzer, eds. 2004. *The Plain of Phaistos*. Monumenta Archaeologica 23. Los Angeles: Cotsen Institute of Archaeology, University of California Press.

Watrous, V., D. Haggis, K. Nowicki, N. Vogeikoff-Brogan, and M. Schultz 2012. *An Archaeological Survey of the Gournia Landscape*. Philadelphia: Instap Academic Press.

Watrous, V. et al. 2017. *The Galatas Survey*. Philadelphia: Instap Academic Press.

Wedde, M. 1991. "Aegean Bronze Age Ship Imagery." In *Thalassa: L'Egee Prehistorique et la Mer*, edited by R. Laffineur and L. Basch. Aegaeum 7: 73–94. Liege: University of Liege.

Weinberg, S. 1951. "Neolithic Figurines and Aegean Interrelations." *AJA* 55: 121–33.

Weingarten, J. 2013. "The Arrival of Egyptian Taweret and Bes(et) on Minoan Crete: Contact and Choice." In *Identity and Connectivity*, edited by L. Bombardieri et al. *BAR* International Series 2581: 371–8.

Weingarten, J. 1991. "Late Bronze Age Trade within Crete." In *Bronze Age Trade in The Mediterranean*, edited by N. Gale. *SIMA* 40: 303–24.

Weingarten, J. 2012. "Minoan Seals and Sealings." In *The Oxford Handbook of the Bronze Age Aegean*, edited by E. Cline, 317–39. Oxford: Oxford University Press.

Weingarten, J. 1997. "The Sealing Bureaucracy of Mycenaean Knossos." In *Crete Mycenienne*, edited by J. Driessen and A. Farnoux. *BCH* Supplement 30: 517–35.

Weingarten, J. 1986. "The Sealing Structures of Minoan Crete: MM II Phaistos to the Destruction of the Palace of Knossos." *Oxford Journal of Archaeology* 5: 1–25.

Weingarten, J. 2016. "The Silver Kantharos from Gournia Reconsidered." In *Studies in Aegean Art and Culture*, edited by R. Koehl, 1–10. Philadelphia: Instap Academic Press.

Weingarten, J. 1990. "Three Upheavals in Minoan Sealing Administration: Evidence for Radical Change." In *Aegean Seals, Sealings and Administration*, edited by T. Palaima. Aegaeum 5: 105–20. Liege: University of Liege.

Weingarten, J. 1991. *The Transformation of Egyptian Taweret into the Minoan Genius: A Study in Cultural Transmission in the Middle Bronze Age*. SIMA 88.

Weingarten, J. 2000. "The Transformation of Egyptian Taweret into the Minoan Genius: A Study in Cultural Transmission in the Middle Bronze Age." In *ΚΡΗΤΗ-ΑΙΓΥΠΤΟΣ: Πολιτισμικοι δεσμοι τριων χιλιετιων* (essays), edited by A. Karetsou, 114–19. Athens: Kapon Editions.

Weingarten, J. 1994. "Two Sealing Studies in the Middle Bronze Age. I: Karahoyuk, I:

Phaistos." In *Archives before Writing*, edited by P. Feroli et al., 261–95. Turin: Ministero per I Beni Culturali e Ambientali.

Weiss, H. 2014. "Altered Trajectories: The Intermediate Bronze Age in Syria and Lebanon 2200–1900 BCE." In *Oxford Handbook of the Archaeology of the Levant*, edited by A. Killebrew and M. Steiner, 367–87. Oxford: Oxford University Press.

Whitelaw, T. 2007. "House, Households and Community in Early Minoan Fournou Korifi: Methods and Models for Interpretation." In *Building Communities*, edited by R. Westgate, N. Fisher, and J. Whitley, 65–76. British School at Athens Study 15. London: Short Run Press.

Whitelaw, T. 2018. "Recognizing Polities in Prehistoric Crete." In *From the Foundations to the Legacy of Minoan Archaeology*, edited by M. Relaki and Y. Papadatos, 210–55. Sheffield Studies in Aegean Archaeology. Oxford: Oxbow Books.

Whitelaw, T. 2012. "The Urbanization of Prehistoric Crete: Settlement Perspectives and Minoan State Formation." In *Back to the Beginning: Reassessing Social and Political Complexity on Crete during the Early and Middle Bronze Age*, edited by I. Schoep, P. Tomkins, and J. Driessen, 114–76. Oxford: Oxbow Books.

Wiener, M. 2016. "Aegean Warfare at the Beginning of the Late Bronze Age in Image and Reality." In *Metaphysis: Ritual, Myth and Symbolism in the Aegean Bronze Age*, edited by E. Aram-Stern et al., 139–48. Aegaeum 39, Liege: Peeters.

Wiener, M. 2013. "Contacts: Crete, Egypt and the Near East, circa 2000 B.C." In *Cultures in Contact: From Mesopotamia to the Mediterranean in the Second Millennium B.C.*, edited by J. Aruz et al., 34–46. New York: Metropolitan Museum of Art.

Wiener, M. 1990. "The Isles of Crete? The Minoan Thalassocracy Revisited." In *Thera and the Aegean World, III*, edited by D. Hardy et al., 128–61. London: The Thera Foundation.

Wiener, M. 1991. "The Nature and Control of Minoan Foreign Trade." In *Bronze Age Trade in the Mediterranean*, edited by N. Gale, 325–50. *SIMA* 40. Jonsered: Paul Astrom.

Wilson, D. 2008. "Early Prepalatial Crete." In *The Aegean Bronze Age*, edited by C. Shelmerdine, 77–104. Cambridge: Cambridge University Press.

Wilson, D. and P. Day 2000. "Ceramic Regionalism in Prepalatial Central Crete: The Mesara Imports from EM IB to EM IIA Knossos." *BSA* 89: 21–63.

Woudhuizen, F. 1997. "The Bee Sign (Evans No. 86): An Instance of Egyptian Influence on Cretan Hieroglyphic." *Kadmos* 36: 97–110.

Wright, J. 2008. "Early Mycenean Greece." In *The Aegean Bronze Age*, edited by C. Shelmerdine, 230–57. Cambridge: Cambridge University Press.

Xanthoudides, S. 1918. "Μεγας πρωτομινοικος ταφος Πυργου." *Αρχαιολογικον Δελτιον* 4: 136–70.

Xanthoudides, S. 1922–3. "Μινωικν μεγαρον Νιρου." *Archaiologiki Ephemeris*: 1–25.

Xanthoudides, S. 1924. *The Vaulted Tombs of the Mesara*. Liverpool: University of Liverpool.

Younger, J. 1998. *Music in the Aegean Bronze Age*. Jonsered: Astroms Forlag.

Younger, J. and P. Rehak 2008. "Minoan Culture: Religion, Burial Customs and Administration." In *The Aegean Bronze Age*, edited by C. Shelmerdine, 165–85. Cambridge: Cambridge University Press.

Younger, J. and P. Rehak 2001. "Neopalatial, Final Palatial and Postpalatial Crete." In *Aegean Prehistory: A Review*, edited by T. Cullen. *AJA* Supplement 1: 403–19.

Younger, J. and P. Rehak 2001. "Review of Aegean Prehistory VII: Neopalatial, Final Palatial and Postpalatial Crete." In *Aegean Prehistory: A Review*, edited by T. Cullen. *AJA* Supplement 1: 403–19.

Yule, P. 1981. *Early Cretan Seals: A Study of Chronology*. Mainz: Verlag Philipp von Zabern.

Yule, P. 1987. "Early and Middle Minoan Foreign Relations: The Evidence from Seals." *SIMA* 25: 161–75.

Ziolkowski, T. 2008. *Minos and the Moderns: Cretan Myth in Twentieth-Century Literature and Art*. Oxford: Oxford University Press.

Zois, A. 1976. *Vasiliki I*. Athens: The Archaeological Society at Athens.

INDEX